Digital Work and the Platform Economy

"Uberization," "digitalization," "platform economy," "gig economy," and "sharing economy" are some of the buzzwords that characterize the current intense discussions about the development of the economy and work around the world, among both experts and laypersons. Immense changes in the ways goods are manufactured, business is done, work tasks are performed, education is accomplished, and so on, are clearly underway. This also means that demand for careful, first-rate social scientific analyses of the phenomena in question is rapidly growing.

This edited volume gathers distinguished researchers from economics, business studies, organization studies, medicine, social psychology, occupational health, pedagogics, and sociology to put particular work in both public and private sectors and education in both academic and vocational settings at the focus of the emerging digitalized platform economy. The authors anchor their analyses and conceptual and theoretical work in distinctive empirical developments that are taking place in one of the leading countries of digitalization processes: Finland. Finnish case studies reflect general global developments and show their particular, context-related actualization in multiple ways. This double exposure enables the authors of this multi- and interdisciplinary volume to advance conceptualization and theorization of the key phenomena in digitalizing platform societies in novel, creative, and groundbreaking directions. This book will without doubt be of great value to academic researchers and students in the fields of economics, business studies, work studies, social sciences, education, technology, digitalization, platforms, occupational health, entrepreneurship, and professions.

Seppo Poutanen is Senior Research Fellow and Docent of Sociology at the University of Turku's School of Economics, Finland.

Anne Kovalainen is Professor at the University of Turku's School of Economics, Finland.

Petri Rouvinen is Senior Economist at Avance Attorneys Ltd.

Routledge Studies in Innovation, Organizations and Technology

Strategic Renewal
Core Concepts, Antecedents, and Micro Foundations
Edited by Aybars Tuncdogan, Adam Lindgreen, Henk Volberda, and Frans van den Bosch

Service Innovation
Esam Mustafa

Innovation Finance and Technology Transfer
Funding Proof of Concept
Andrea Alunni

Finance, Innovation and Geography
Harnessing Knowledge Dynamics in German Biotechnology
Felix C. Müller

Business and Development Studies
Issues and Perspectives
Edited by Peter Lund-Thomsen, Michael Wendelboe Hansen and Adam Lindgreen

Frugal Innovation
A Global Research Companion
Edited by Adela J. McMurray and Gerrit A. de Waal

Digital Work and the Platform Economy
Understanding Tasks, Skills and Capabilities in the New Era
Edited by Seppo Poutanen, Anne Kovalainen, and Petri Rouvinen

Digital Work and the Platform Economy

Understanding Tasks, Skills and Capabilities in the New Era

Edited by Seppo Poutanen, Anne Kovalainen, and Petri Rouvinen

Routledge
Taylor & Francis Group

NEW YORK AND LONDON

First published 2020
by Routledge
52 Vanderbilt Avenue, New York, NY 10017

and by Routledge
2 Park Square, Milton Park, Abingdon, Oxon, OX14 4RN

Routledge is an imprint of the Taylor & Francis Group, an informa business

First issued in paperback 2021

Library of Congress Cataloging-in-Publication Data
A catalog record for this book has been requested

ISBN: 978-1-138-60584-8 (hbk)
ISBN: 978-1-03-208272-1 (pbk)
ISBN: 978-0-429-46792-9 (ebk)

Typeset in Sabon
by Apex CoVantage, LLC

Contents

PART III
Challenges to Skills and Capabilities in the Digital Platform Economy

PART IV
Theoretical Opportunities for Understanding New Emergent Phenomena in the Digital Platform Economy

Figures

Tables

Boxes

Acknowledgements

This edited volume is one of the key outputs of the international, multi-disciplinary and interdisciplinary research project "Smart Work in Platform Economy" (SWiPE, www.smartworkresearch.fi). The project was funded by the Strategic Research Council of the Academy of Finland for the period 2016–19 (grant 303667). The authors wish to express their gratitude for the competitive funding. In addition, the authors Martin Kenney and John Zysman were funded in part by the Ewing Marion Kauffman Foundation. Kenney and Zysman express their gratitude for this funding and emphasize that the contents of their chapter in this book are solely the responsibility of the authors. Anne Kovalainen and Seppo Poutanen also want to thank the Foundation for Economic Education for funding.

There are simply too many colleagues, entrepreneurs, freelancers, professionals, civil servants, companies and organizations to be listed here in details for thanks. We owe you all a debt of gratitude; without your invaluable contribution and cooperation, our research would not have been possible. Special thanks go to several anonymous reviewers, who altruistically gave their time and expertise in reading and commenting on the chapters. They have helped to significantly improve this book, but the responsibility for any errors and shortcomings naturally belongs to the authors. We express our thanks to Routledge's expert editors, and especially to editor Mary Del Plato, for making this a smooth publication process.

Contributors' Biographies

Satu Aaltonen is a researcher at the Department of Management and Entrepreneurship at the University of Turku. Her main topics of interest lie in migrant entrepreneurship, entrepreneurship policy and employee-driven innovations. She has studied, for example, how the service needs of migrant entrepreneurs correspond to public service provision, how to boost employees' innovative behavior and what role IT could play, and how to implement information systems in a user-driven manner. She has published in *Entrepreneurship and Innovation, International Journal of E-Services and Mobile Applications* and *International Small Business Journal* as well as in several edited books. Her background is in social sciences.

Jari J. Hakanen is currently Research Professor at the Finnish Institute of Occupational Health and a docent in social psychology at the University of Helsinki. He is particularly interested in the question of how it is possible to stay engaged and find meaningfulness at work and not burnout or boreout in different types of jobs in the middle of work-life turbulence. More generally, his areas of expertise include positive work and organizational psychology with special interests in the job demands-resources model, work engagement, burnout, servant leadership, proactive and adaptive behaviors, and the work-family interface. In addition, he has developed and implemented several research-based positive interventions to enhance work engagement and flourishing workplaces. Together with his collaborators, he has received the best article awards from *Journal of Occupational Health Psychology* in 2011–12 and from *Journal of Organizational Behavior* in 2014. He has also received several national awards, e.g. Finnish Work-Life Researcher of the Year award in 2012 and Spokesman of the Good Working-Life in Finland in 2009.

Mervi Hasu works as Associate Professor of Workplace Learning at the University of Oslo, Department of Education. She specializes in research on adult and workplace learning, workplace innovation, and organizational ethnography especially in the public sector, with a focus on work transformations, digitalized work, employee agency, user participation and collaborative action. She has published research in international journals such as *Journal of Workplace Learning, Mind, Culture, and Activity—An International Journal, Computer Supported Collaborative Work, Technology Analysis and Strategic Management, International Journal of Human Computer Studies,* and in edited volumes.

Kaisa Hytönen has a PhD in Education. She defended her dissertation in 2016. In her dissertation, she examined efforts to bridge academic and working life expertise in continuing professional education. Currently, she works as a Postdoctoral Researcher at the University of Turku's School of Economics in Finland. She works as a researcher and scientific coordinator in the SWiPE research consortium. Her research interests relate to the interfaces between education and working life, professional education, networked expertise, and social networks as well as professional learning and development.

Martin Kenney is a Distinguished Professor of Human and Community Development at the University of California, Davis, and a co-director of the Berkeley Roundtable on the International Economy (BRIE). He has published or edited six books and over 170 scholarly articles. He is a receiving editor at *Research Policy* and edits a Stanford University Press book series on innovation and globalization.

Annu Kotiranta works as a researcher at Etla, the Research Institute of Finnish Economy. Recently she has focused on innovation policy and innovation research, using econometric tools and micro-level data. She has also studied the factors behind firms' profitability, including the composition and gender of firms' leadership, firms' societal motives, and inclusion in governmental innovation programs. She is a member of The Expert Panel on Science, Technology and Innovation Policy, the Confab Club.

Anne Kovalainen is Professor at the University of Turku's School of Economics in Finland. She is leader of the three-year national research consortium, Smart Work in Platform Economy, with the Academy of Finland Strategic Research Council. An economic sociologist by training, Dr. Kovalainen works as Professor of Entrepreneurship, with a special interest in multidisciplinary analyses of society and economic life. She has worked as an academy professor and as an invited faculty fellow at the Stanford University School of Sciences and Humanities, at Harvard University, at the London School of Economics and Political Science and the University of Technology Sydney. Her research covers topics of platformization of society and economy, digital futures, gender and economy, welfare society, entrepreneurship, public sector, and qualitative research methods and innovations. She is member of the

Finnish Academy of Science and Letters. Her latest co-authored books are published by Palgrave Macmillan (2017), Sage (2016, 2008) and a co-edited book by Emerald (2019).

Martti Kulvik is Chief Research Scientist at The Research Institute of Finnish Economy. He has also held an MD clinical and research position at the Department of Neurology at Helsinki University Central Hospital since 1994. He has participated in several interdisciplinary research projects, ranging from biotechnology as a competitive edge for the Finnish forest industry to the application of boron neutron capture therapy and gene therapy in patient treatments. In 2013–14 he was a Visiting Professor at Scuola Superiore Sant'Anna, Pisa, Italy, and in 2012 he held the position of Invited Researcher at the Kellogg School of Management, Northwestern University, USA. He is an author in economic and medical publications, and he has co-written eight books on the interface of economics, biotechnology, and healthcare.

Tero Kuusi works as a chief research scientist at the Research Institute of the Finnish Economy. His research interests span different fields of public finance, macroeconomics and productivity analysis. He has initiated and participated in several productivity measurement projects in the public sector, which have created a demand for further productivity studies. The recent European Horizon 2020 project Firstrun (www.firstrun.eu) is one of Kuusi's latest international public finance research projects, with a focus on the governance of public policy in the EU's fiscal framework. He received his PhD (economics) with honors from the Aalto University School of Economics in 2013.

Sari Käpykangas is Master of Social Sciences, Social Psychologist and Researcher at FIOH. Her specialties include research on digitalization, employees agency and customer involvement in the social and healthcare sector. She is an expert in developmental evaluation and qualitative research methods. Recently, she worked as a project manager in the *At the Source of Change—Bridges to New Work* project and as a researcher in the *Smart Work in Platform Economy* project, studying service advising and implementation of digitalization in social and healthcare.

Maarit Laiho (D.Sc. Econ. & Bus. Adm.) holds a doctoral degree in management and organization. She works as a Senior Researcher at the University of Turku's School of Economics in the Department of Management and Entrepreneurship; she has been a faculty member since 2000. Laiho's current research interests include a wide range of topical working life issues, such as active colleagueship, human aspects of work automatization, HRM and organizational climate, servant leadership, formal mentoring and work counseling. Her research has been published in journals such as *Career Development International*,

Leadership and Organization Development Journal and *Social Responsibility Journal*. She received the Outstanding Paper Award at the Emerald Literati Network Awards for Excellence in 2012.

Aija Leiponen is Professor in the Dyson School of Applied Economics and Management at Cornell University (US) and is also affiliated with Aalto University and the Research Institute of the Finnish Economy. Her research focuses on the role of organizational arrangements in innovation, particularly cooperative arrangements between organizations. She studies the organization of innovation at the level of inter-organizational contracts, organizational patterns at the firm level, and at the level of inter-organizational networks of repeated collaborative innovation, particularly in the digital industries. Her recent work has examined the interaction between conflict and cooperation in wireless telecommunication standard development, and the nature and implications of markets for (big) data. Prof. Leiponen's research has been published in leading management and applied economics journals such as *Management Science, Strategic Management Journal, Research Policy, and International Journal for Industrial Organization*. She is currently finishing her leadership roles in the Technology and Innovation Management division of the Academy of Management and as co-editor of media innovations at the Strategic Management Society.

Seppo Poutanen is Senior Research Fellow and Docent of Sociology at the University of Turku's School of Economics in Finland. He is trained in both philosophy and sociology, and his areas of expertise include meta-ethics, social epistemology, social theory, sociology of science and technology, gender studies, methodology of social sciences and economic sociology. Dr Poutanen has been a Visiting Professor and Visiting Scholar at several universities (e.g. Harvard University, Stanford University, London School of Economics, University of Essex, UTS Business School Sydney). His current research projects, associated mainly with the international research project SWiPE (see www.smartworkresearch.fi), focus on the rise of entrepreneurial university, professionalism and entrepreneurship, and work and education in the new platform economy. He has published his research in *Social Epistemology, Critical Public Health, Journal of Critical Realism, Sociological Research Online, International Journal of Gender and Entrepreneurship* and in several edited volumes. Dr Poutanen's latest publications include *Gender and Innovation in the New Economy—Women, Identity, and Creative Work*, with Anne Kovalainen (New York: Palgrave Macmillan, 2017).

Annina Ropponen is a senior researcher at the Finnish Institute of Occupational Health, a research coordinator at Karolinska Institute, Sweden, and Adjunct Professor of Public Health at the University of Helsinki,

Finland. She has a PhD in exercise medicine from the University of Jyväskylä, Finland. Her primary research interest focuses on working careers and working hours with an epidemiologic perspective, and she has been the principal investigator in three large-scale longitudinal studies utilizing register data. Her publication record includes 70 international, peer-reviewed publications that have been published in *International Journal of Epidemiology* and *Pain and Occupational and Environmental Medicine*, among others (H index: 15).

Petri Rouvinen is Senior Economist at Avance Attorneys Ltd. Until January 2019, he was a research director at ETLA, the Research Institute of the Finnish Economy. He has published or edited over 10 books and dozens of scholarly articles in peer-reviewed journals. He has served as an expert for European Union projects, the Organization for Economic Cooperation and Development, United Nations University/World Institute for Development Economics Research, and the World Bank.

Eveliina Saari (PhD, adult education) is Chief Scientist at FIOH and is a docent in adult education, specializing in developmental evaluation and organizational learning at the University of Jyväskylä. She has conducted research on employee-driven innovation, digitalization of services and change of professional roles in public social and healthcare. She has developed a human-centered co-evaluation method to evaluate digital service innovations, and has several ongoing development projects, which implement the method for practitioners. Recently, she has worked as a project manager of the Revolution of the Service Economy–Human Beings at the Core of Digitalization project and worked as a researcher in the SWiPE project. She has also worked as a part-time program manager for two strategic research programs funded by the Academy of Finland called Skilled Employees— Successful Labour Markets and Health, Wellbeing and Lifestyles.

Laura Seppänen, DSc (Agr. & For.), Chief Scientist at FIOH, and Adjunct Professor at the University of Helsinki, has done qualitative research on participatory development of work and workplace learning in multiple domains including social and healthcare, agri-food systems, rail traffic control and correctional services. Her practice-based research expertise includes reflection and learning challenges, relational agency and interpretive practice, development and logics of work activities, activity theories, and sustainability. Laura's recent studies include service networks, robotic surgery and work on digital platforms. Besides Finland, Seppänen works in education in Brazil and Switzerland. She leads the FIOH part of a consortium, "Smart Work in Platform Economy", and participates in an EU-RISE-funded consortium, "Improving collaborative practice between correctional and mental health services". Laura is on the editorial board of the journal *Outlines: Critical Practice Studies*, and she has more than 70 scientific publications.

Steven P. Vallas is Professor of Sociology at Northeastern University in Boston. He has written and edited books and articles on various issues on workplace change, including shifts in technology, new forms of work organization, and socio-demographic shifts at work. His work has appeared in leading sociological journals. Most recently he is writing on the instabilities that neoliberalism generates, especially as precarious work spreads throughout the economy. He serves as editor of *Research in the Sociology of Work*.

Maija Vähämäki (D. Sc. Econ & Bus. Adm.) works as a university teacher of management and organization at the University of Turku's School of Economics. She has a wide working experience from both private and public sector organizations in Finland and abroad. She also worked for four years as a project manager in developmental projects for the media and graphic arts industries. In her doctoral thesis (2008) she applied participative action research to study knowledge management and organizational learning. Her research interest covers topics of organizational learning, dialogue in organizational development, workplace relationships, and qualitative research methods. Her latest research interests are in conflict management, learning of first-time managers, and doctoral supervisory relationship as an LMX-relation.

John Zysman is Professor Emeritus of Political Science at the University of California, Berkeley, and co-founder of the Berkeley Roundtable on the International Economy (BRIE). He has written extensively on national policy and corporate strategy. He is the author or editor of numerous books, scholarly articles, and journal special issues. His interests also include comparative politics, Western European politics, political economy, and the impacts of computation on society.

Part I
Introduction

Digital Work in the Platform Economy

Seppo Poutanen, Anne Kovalainen, and Petri Rouvinen

Introduction

This book is an outcome of three years of research on the different aspects of digital and platform work in this era of the platform economy. Over its 10 chapters, the volume takes an interdisciplinary approach, in which philosophy, economics, psychology, social psychology, sociology, education sciences, and public health are used and combined for analyzing the dimensions of digital work in the platform era. Based on both primary and secondary materials and sources, in-depth analyses of both qualitative and quantitative data, and several types of fieldwork materials, including seminars and policy briefs, the authors analyze the many current features of a working life where digitalization and new phenomena such as platform work are emerging. The common denominator for all chapters is examining the different facets of work in the era of digitalization and the platform economy.

By platform economy, most researchers refer to the birth and development of multisided markets, which can have direct (same side) and/or indirect (opposite side) network effects. Although there is no single agreed-upon definition of "platform economy", the most common definition of platform economy describes platforms as digital market places where buyers and sellers meet. The more complex definition of platforms and platform economy takes into account the technical aspects of digital platforms that create new and change current economic and societal circumstances through technologies. New aspects of worker-employer relationships can be identified when looking at technology as more than just a platform enabler, as discussed in Chapters 1 and 2. The platformization of work—meaning work that is offered, accepted, and performed increasingly through digital platforms—in many cases also means the taskification of work. Taskification refers to piecemealing (slicing) work activity into smaller activities and tasks, which can, for example, be performed by AI. These tasks can partially be dissected from actual professional work (e.g. Susskind and Susskind, 2015).

Taskification may dissect the familiar activities we often think of as 'work' or 'professional work'.

The diversity of work arrangements, as a result of globalization and digitalization and their presence in the society and economy alike, mingled with the changing subjective notions of work, have raised questions on how we understand, examine, explain, and conceptualize work in the current platform era. Generally, work enhances innovation and common good and adds value to companies and corporations. Work also means income (i.e., living wage), but not necessarily for everybody. Work should mean equal, worthy living and thus refer to identity-related aspects and issues. However, work also maintains and sometimes reinforces unequal power relations. Further, it carries and rebuilds individual and societal social status and connects individuals to various social networks and social structures. New arrangements in the form of atypical jobs, for example, created and re-enforced by digitalization, carry the seeds of change for organizations and institutions alike. In this context, the platformization of work includes the taskification of work and jobs (Vallas and Kovalainen, 2019), but also platform-mediated expertise (e.g., Kane et al., 2019) that determines its shape and format.

In this volume, we focus on some of the changes brought on by the digitalization and platformization of work, and as a result, discuss some of the reasons why changes such as digitalization at large are relevant and important for the future theorization of platform work. Through detailed case study analyses using a variety of datasets, we shed light on the multitude of changes in contemporary working life. While many of the empirical cases originate in Finland, the conceptualizations used and many of the identified and analyzed features carry no national labels but are global in nature. Finland, as one of the Nordic welfare countries, offers some advantages for these multi-prism analyses of working life, such as access to reliable and robust data.

Given the diversity of sources for mapping out the contemporary changes in working life and the objectives of this book, we provide a multifaceted picture of the changes in the platform economy era, offering empirical evidence on key aspects. However, it is tempting to restrict "the researcher's gaze" to analyses of digital work and the platform economy concerning only online gig workers, delivery riders, or new startups and entrepreneurs in the gaming industry. There is indeed an abundance of studies addressing these groups, for good reason, as these groups underline the novelty and importance of the topic. However, these examples do not give the full picture of the digital platform economy, which is currently developing and creating its framework. Our book thus takes a wider perspective, not limiting the analysis to one or two groups. The different aspects of the digital economy, which is at the core of most changes in current working life, are at the heart of this book.

Changing Work, Changing Categories

The classical research canon on work and employment provides limited support for understanding how platformization currently shapes the conditions and future of work and employment. The impacts of technology in general and of digitalization in particular are complex and do not "treat" work and jobs in a similar manner. While the platform economy is currently emerging and transforming work, there is no real basis to argue that all work is being transformed into tasks or becomes contingent (Susskind and Susskind, 2015; Sundararajan, 2015). Further, the changes that technologies bring are massive but very often gradual and invisible. In addition, they are adopted and implemented in institutions, organizations, and structures that often are not designed for rapid changes or development.

Despite the slow adoption of new technologies by organizations and institutions, we cannot avoid the intensity of the technology effects to the (a) content of work, (b) birth and death of work, and (c) transformations in work. Therefore, this edited volume includes several chapters addressing these three issues. Technology does not change the division between paid and unpaid work, but they change the very nature of unpaid work, relating it to those structural societal inequalities that are affected by technology in a myriad of ways. Therefore, even if the platform economy is still a relatively small part of developed countries' economies, its impact ranges beyond national borders. Digital labor platforms transcend national borders, with many variations, online and offline work orders, and crowdsourcing platforms.

Indeed, the question is whether the division into "employed" and "self-employed" or "workers" and "entrepreneurs" necessarily relates to future types of contracts. The new forms of "dependent contractors" and "dependent own-account workers" no longer fit the subcontracting models of the industrial phase but, rather, require a new definition/classification based on the post-industrial and post-service taskification models of work, where the power relations between "contractors," form and length (temporality) of tasks, and skills required are considered. However, the issues of the work and digital platform economy are topical and, therefore, the systematization of the various features of digital platform work is crucial for further analyses. Two of the chapters in this volume clarify the different types of digital and platform work by systematizing the new facets and features of work in general.

The argument is often that if the phenomenon of the digital platform economy is still minor (e.g., in comparison to normal employment), there should not be the need for new categorizations; then again, for example, new categorizations are too many to make a meaningful distinction between gig and platform workers (e.g., Eurofound, 2018). However, while the workforce may still be comparatively limited in this field, it disguises features becoming more common in the so-called "normal" work relationships. Being self-employed and an independent contractor is not a new feature, but having an app monitoring and regulating your "entrepreneurial freedom" certainly is.

In discussions, the assumption is often that many, if not most, of those who work using platforms are contingent workers (Wood et al., 2019). Contingent workers are those who do not have an implicit or explicit contract for ongoing employment. The share of contingent work has increased in Europe, with the share of such work being around 14% of the workforce, typically including more women than men and younger rather than older employees (Eurofound, 2017). The question is, how does Finland relate to the rest of Europe and to the United States? The types of work conducted as contingent work differ significantly, and alternative employment arrangements (online work) are not as frequent as in the United States. The share of temporary work in the United States is around 5% of the workforce, similar to European statistics (BSL, 2017). Further, the alternative employment arrangements in the United States (i.e., independent contractors, on-call workers, temporary help agency workers, and workers employed by contract companies) accounted for around 11% of all employees in 2017 (CPS, 2018). An emerging type of work, electronically mediated work, defined as short jobs or tasks that workers find through mobile apps that both connect them with customers and arrange payment for the tasks was measured in the United States in 2018 by Labor Statistics. According to the data, compared with workers in general, those who engaged in electronically mediated work were more likely to have a bachelor's degree or higher (CPS, 2018). However, the discrepancy between the data on online gig workers and these statistics underlines different methodologies in the data collection.

In any case, electronically mediated and platform workers are not the only terms used for people who work under emerging contracts. Other terms are also used, such as "online gig workers," "e-lancers," "sharing economy workers," "on-demand economy workers," and "electronically intermediated workers," among others. A key aspect is how to understand and relate this to the theorizing of work. The issues in the classifications of platform economy and platform work are complex and discussed in two chapters in this volume.

A more extensive comparison on the development of occupational structures, for example, reveals changes within occupational structures and, to an increasing degree, between occupations. The differences between occupational groups increase in the United States and Canada (Acemoglu and Autor, 2010) as well as in Europe (Goos et al., 2009), particularly so that the number of occupations with the lowest qualification levels increased. This polarization of occupations also became visible in Europe in the 2010s. A significant part of this polarization and the related changes have been accelerated not only by an increase in living standards, which has created new service sector occupations, but mostly by the development of technology, which has shifted routine and repeatable tasks to machines through automation. Occupational mobility, particularly upward, has nevertheless not grown. Specifically, studies of longtime series have shown the speed of technological development and its impact on occupations to have been slower than expected, especially over the past few decades (Atkinson and Wu, 2017). Given this development, platformization may also increase the digital divide.

As the platform economy is still seeking its shape, the exact projections of the number of individuals working on platforms and the nature of their work contracts are bound to be amiss. This may also concern the classification of individuals working for different platforms. The recent classifications of work in the platform (e.g., Kenney and Zysman, 2019), sharing (e.g., Sutherland and Hossein Jarrahi, 2018), and gig economies (Kalleberg and Dunn, 2016) relate the forms of work to control and the nature of platforms. However, platforms evolve and transform, and, hence, so does the work performed, its conditions, competition, and control mechanisms. Much of this shape seeking, however, is controversial and underlines the difficulty of capturing platforms and the effects of platform work: the changes in algorithms affect the compensation systems and the use of reputational algorithms, while legal and political struggles over regulatory policies shift the nature of operations.

An increasingly important part of the digitally wired platform economy is the increase in the outsourcing of the work at the corporate level that was previously performed "in-house" in corporations and in the public sector. Large corporations use startups for "trial-and-error" as a type of innovation-building activity, thus outsourcing part of their core functions. Therefore, the effects of digitalization, as evidenced in the studies on platform work and digitalization of work in this volume, are neither one-directional nor simplistic, but complex and multilayered.

It has been predicted—and highly criticized—that some human work will disappear (Frey and Osborne, 2017), and it has also been equally predicted that, rather than disappearing, a significant share of the work now performed by people will be carried out through automation or by robots and machines (Brynjolfsson and MacAfee, 2014), as the new machine age arrives. Although several studies have found that the globally transforming platform economy reduces human work and, in the future, will also eradicate certain types of work, technology also has its constant role to play in the creation of new work. As a result of digitalization, almost all work—and that carried out outside actual platform work—can be redefined and "taskified." Taskification means work is divided into smaller units and tasks than before, some of which can be taken care of by algorithmic decision-making (e.g. Jacobs and Karen, 2019), while some of the tasks will continue to be performed by humans. Technological development and digitalization are thus bound to change the nature and content of work. This change will also produce weaker, diverging positions related to social security and, for example, occupational healthcare. Hence, several aspects to digitalization and changes in work in the platform era are needed, and this book aims to serve this purpose.

References

Acemoglu, D. and Autor, D. (2010). Skills, Tasks and Technologies: Implications for Employment and Earnings. *NBER Working Paper No. 16082*. Cambridge, MA: NATIONAL BUREAU OF ECONOMIC RESEARCH. Available at: www.nber.org/papers/w16082 [Accessed 16 June 2019].

Atkinson, R. D. and Wu, J. (2017). False Alarmism: Technological Disruption and the U.S. Labor Market, 1850–2015. *Information Technology & Innovation Foundation ITIF*, May, pp. 1–28. Available at: www2.itif.org [Accessed 16 June 2019].

Brynjolfsson, E. and MacAfee, A. (2014). *The Second Machine Age: Work, Progress, and Prosperity in a Time of Brilliant Technologies*. New York & London: W. W. Norton & Company, Inc.

BSL. (2017). *Employment Statistics 2017*. Bureau of Labor Statistics. Washington, DC: U.S. Bureau of Labor Statistics. Available at: www.bls.gov. [Accessed 15 July 2019].

CPS. (2018). *Labor Force Statistics of the Current Population Survey*. Washington, DC: U.S. Bureau of Labor Statistics. Available at: www.bls.gov. [Accessed 15 July 2019].

Eurofound. (2018). *Living and Working in Europe 2017*. Luxembourg: Publication Office of the European Union.

Frey, C. B. and Osborne, M. A. (2017). The Future of Employment: How Susceptible Are Jobs to Computerisation? *Technological Forecasting and Social Change*, 114(C), pp. 254–280.

Goos, M., Manning, A. and Salomons, A. (2009). Job Polarization in Europe. *American Economic Review*, 99(2), pp. 58–63.

Jacobs, J. A. and Karen, R. (2019). Technology-Driven Task Replacement and the Future of Employment. In: S. P. Vallas and A. Kovalainen, eds., *Work and Labour in the Digital Age. Research in the Sociology of Work*. Vol. 33. London: Emerald Publishing Ltd, pp. 43–60.

Kalleberg, A. L. and Dunn, M. (2016). Good Jobs, Bad Jobs in the Gig Economy. *Perspectives on Work*, 20, pp. 10–14. Available at: http://lerachapters.org/OJS/ojs-2.4.4-1/index.php/PFL/article/viewFile/3112/3087 [Accessed 4 May 2019].

Kane, G. C., Nguyen Phillips, A., Copulsky, J. R. and Andrus, G. R. (2019). *The Technological Fallacy: How People Are the Real Key to Digital Transformation*. Cambridge, MA & London: MIT Press.

Kenney, M. and Zysman, J. (2019). The Rise of the Platform Economy. *Issues in Science and Technology*, 32(3) Spring 2016. Available at: https://issues.org/the-rise-of-the-platform-economy/ [Accessed 13 June 2019].

Sundararajan, A. (2015). *The Sharing Economy: The End of Employment and the Rise of Crowd-Based Capitalism*. Cambridge, MA: MIT Press.

Susskind, R. and Susskind, D. (2015). *The Future of the Professions: How Technology Will Transform the Work of Human Experts*. Oxford: Oxford University Press.

Sutherland, W. and Hossein Jarrahi, M. (2018). The Sharing Economy and Digital Platforms: A Review and Research Agenda. *International Journal of Information Management*, 43, pp. 328–341. doi: 10.1016/j.ijinfomgt.2018.07.004.

Vallas, S. P. and Kovalainen, A. (2019). Taking Stock of the Digital Revolution. In: S. P. Vallas and A. Kovalainen, eds., *Work and Labour in the Digital Age: Research in the Sociology of Work*. Vol. 33. London: Emerald Publishing Ltd, pp. 1–17.

Wood, A. J., Graham, M., Lehdonvirta, V. and Hjorth, I. (2019). Networked but Commodified: The (Dis)Embeddedness of Digital Labour in the Gig Economy. *Sociology*. https://doi.org/10.1177/0038038519828906

Part II

New Facets of Work and Workers' Life in the Digital Platform Economy

1 Employment, Work, and Value Creation in the Era of Digital Platforms

Martin Kenney, Petri Rouvinen, and John Zysman

Introduction: Platforms Are Changing the Very Fabric of Modern Society

At least since the introduction of Intel's first microprocessor in 1971, rapidly evolving digitalization has provided an ever-growing number of tools that empower, but also sometimes nudge or force, individuals and organizations to change their behaviors. The widespread emergence of digital platforms is arguably the most revolutionary aspect of digitalization in the past decade. Digital platforms should be regarded as intermediaries that reorganize economic and social life (Srnicek, 2017; Kenney and Zysman, 2016; Barley, 2015; Orlikowski and Scott, 2015; van Dijck, 2013; Scott and Orlikowski, 2010).

In this chapter, we consider the international scene primarily through U.S.-based and globally prominent digital platforms in terms of the implications of their increasing adoption by users. In contrast to other scholars offering taxonomies of platform types (e.g., Fumagalli et al., 2018; Li et al., 2018), we present a taxonomy of work and value creation in the platform economy (Kenney and Zysman, 2016). Our taxonomy defines main groups that platform workers fall into.

Although our focus is work, we do not confine ourselves to digital labor market platforms that provide access to paid labor. This would dramatically understate the impact of platforms. Labor market platforms such as Upwork, Fiverr, and Uber are only a part of a larger story that is more complex and more significant. First, although some of the world's most valuable corporations are platform companies, firms and organizations in nearly every industry not only create websites but also build platforms that can manage their interface with the external market and society (Parker et al., 2016). Along with a long tail of smaller platform firms and startups that nurture new platforms, these are significant sources of direct and arm's-length employment and thus of platform work. Second, some platforms establish markets for digital content. In these markets, the virtual good—as opposed to the physical manifestation of the labor input that went into creating it—is traded. In these consignment markets, the authors license copies of their creations to platforms, allowing the plat-forms to manage monetization. Consignment markets existed before digi-tal markets, but platforms have reshaped their scale and scope. Our broad focus thus encompasses three categories of work: platform firm employ-ment, platform-mediated work, and platform-mediated content creation.

Because platforms often directly shape marketplace interactions, they have great potential to disrupt market structures (Zysman and Kenney, 2018; Kenney and Zysman, 2016). For example, the increasing centrality of platforms in the delivery of goods and services is changing the sectoral composition of economies, and thus has both substitution and budgetary effects. Some intermediation, such as wholesaling, might cease to exist as separate activities and be provided by a platform that also offers business-to-consumer (B-to-C) services. If a platform gains market share, a comparable non-platform provider is likely to have lost it: take the case of platforms such as Uber, Lyft, or Airbnb, which offer lower prices for transportation or lodging while expanding their market size (Parrott and Reich, 2018).

Digital platforms are changing the organization of competition, work, and consumption—and thus the very fabric of modern society. Yet the ulti-mate outcomes will be determined not by technology but rather by busi-ness strategies, consumer choices, and policy decisions. Further, although many of the largest platforms are global in scope, at least some aspect(s) of adoption and use will be shaped by national choices and characteristics.

Platforms Decrease Interaction Frictions and Enable New Interactions

In technical terms, we follow the definition of Ghazawneh and Henfrids-son (2015) of a platform of interest as "an extensible cloud-based software stack enabling multi-sided interaction among contractually independent parties." These are "software-based external platforms consisting of the extensible codebase of a software-based system that provides core func-tionality shared by the modules that interoperate with it and the inter-faces through which they interoperate." Thus, platforms of interest are those that are online, cloud-based, and accessible through a wide vari-ety of edge devices such as smartphones, personal computers, and—in the future—possibly other "things." Each platform provides boundary resources such as application programming interfaces (APIs) and soft-ware development kits to third parties to enable them to build further applications on the software for creating ecosystems of complementors.

However, platforms are not just software stacks; they are also gov-ernance structures. If a digital platform is designed properly, it attracts complementors—who form an ecosystem of service—as well as product providers—who operate through the platform. Nevertheless, this does not address the power that the platform owner has over the ecosystem participants who make asset-specific investments in a specific platform.

The ecosystem metaphor implies that the successful platform owner often "taxes" ecosystem participants for their use. This metaphor also omits the possibility of the platform owner frequently finding himself/herself in a position to absorb valuable functionality or resources from complementors. The platform owner can often unilaterally change not only the share of income accruing to the various participants—for example, by subsidizing one side of the platform with income from the other side—but also the rules of participation in the ecosystem, as has recently been seen on Facebook, Amazon, Google, and other platforms.[1]

A platform not only controls but also actively shapes its participants' user interfaces and their access to other participants. This is in the best interest of most users when, for example, the content on the platform is curated, or when version control is handled appropriately. However, this also gives the platform a certain degree of power over participants. As the platform grows and interaction with it intensifies, it accumulates large and growing volumes of information.

Platforms exploit key features of digital technologies to decrease interaction frictions or even facilitate interactions that could not have occurred before. Because platforms establish multisided markets, they can have either or both direct (same side) and indirect (opposite side) network effects. Thus, the sheer number of transactions performed by a platform not only improves it but also allows decreasing costs due to scale. This implies an initial chicken-and-egg problem that the platform provider must solve: there is no incentive to join a platform that does not already have many participants. Network effects, combined with scale and scope effects of digital technologies, can often lead to the creation of winner-take-most markets that can be dominated and controlled by one or two firms. This domination depends on the particular markets. For example, online remote work has a larger variety of platforms, often separated into particular verticals. Other sectors such as travel initially had many online entrants, but the markets were consolidated through acquisitions, thus creating high levels of concentration.

Looking at the most popular platforms internationally suggests that, so far, we have largely seen a "Silicon Valley" version of platforms (except in China, which has its own dynamics), in which during the early stage, startups are structured to pursue growth at all costs to achieve market dominance.[2] Although some experiments with a variety of alternative organizational principles have taken place, nearly all of the most widely adopted platforms have been introduced by for-profit companies that are our focus in this chapter.

Platform Work Taxonomy

In this section, we extend the platform work taxonomy proposed by two authors of this chapter (Kenney and Zysman, 2019b).[3] The core strength of this taxonomy is that it distinguishes between work generated by platform companies on the one hand and work in the platform ecosystem on the other. The first, smaller set consists of workers who create and maintain the platforms. The second, larger set consists of workers in the platform ecosystems, whom we further divide into those undertaking platform-mediated work and those performing platform-mediated content creation. We also include uncompensated user-generated content (Terranova, 2000).

A common mistake when considering work in the platform economy is considering it only in terms of employment. Because of platform ecosystems, the vast majority of the individuals receiving income are not employed by the platform firms or by any firm. For example, millions of individuals or small limited liability corporations are Apple App Store and Google Play operators; Lyft and Uber drivers; Airbnb hosts; Amazon Marketplace, eBay, Etsy, and Instagram vendors; YouTubers; Amazon book publishers; and Kickstarter- and Indiegogo-funded project creators. They all generate income through platforms. These vast, dependent ecosystems are difficult to measure but have recently received attention from various statistical agencies and private sector research institutions (Allard and Polivka, 2018; Farrell and Greig, 2016). Finally, an enormous and perhaps impossible-to-measure population comprises workers building websites meant to be discovered by Google, managing their firm's social media strategy, and updating their LinkedIn profiles—all of whom are creating value for digital platforms. In Figure 1.1, we present a taxonomy so that the number of income generators can be empirically measured.

Platform Firms

At the center of the ecosystems are the firms operating these platforms. Many domains have just one or a few dominant firms. Nonexistent or minimal direct competition places these firms in excellent positions to extract value from one or more sides of the platforms, and their profit margins can be abnormally high (e.g., Apple, Facebook, Google, and Microsoft).

Platform Firm Employees: Venture Labor

The term "venture labor" (Neff et al., 2012) refers to the platform firm's founders and employees; if successful, these firms grow into large corporations. Their employees comprise only a small proportion of the individuals receiving income in platform ecosystems. Particularly during economic booms, the established platform companies offer not only high compensation but also remarkable benefits for their direct employees. Many startups are funded to establish platforms in various sectors. These startups are predicated upon attracting talented employees who can

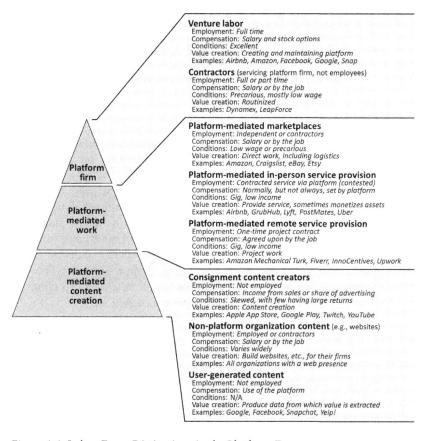

Venture labor
Employment: *Full time*
Compensation: *Salary and stock options*
Conditions: *Excellent*
Value creation: *Creating and maintaining platform*
Examples: *Airbnb, Amazon, Facebook, Google, Snap*

Contractors (servicing platform firm, not employees)
Employment: *Full or part time*
Compensation: *Salary or by the job*
Conditions: *Precarious, mostly low wage*
Value creation: *Routinized*
Examples: *Dynamex, LeapForce*

Platform-mediated marketplaces
Employment: *Independent or contractors*
Compensation: *Salary or by the job*
Conditions: *Low wage or precarious*
Value creation: *Direct work, including logistics*
Examples: *Amazon, Craigslist, eBay, Etsy*

Platform-mediated in-person service provision
Employment: *Contracted service via platform (contested)*
Compensation: *Normally, but not always, set by platform*
Conditions: *Gig, low income*
Value creation: *Provide service, sometimes monetizes assets*
Examples: *Airbnb, GrubHub, Lyft, PostMates, Uber*

Platform-mediated remote service provision
Employment: *One-time project contract*
Compensation: *Agreed upon by the job*
Conditions: *Gig, low income*
Value creation: *Project work*
Examples: *Amazon Mechanical Turk, Fiverr, InnoCentives, Upwork*

Consignment content creators
Employment: *Not employed*
Compensation: *Income from sales or share of advertising*
Conditions: *Skewed, with few having large returns*
Value creation: *Content creation*
Examples: *Apple App Store, Google Play, Twitch, YouTube*

Non-platform organization content (e.g., websites)
Employment: *Employed or contractors*
Compensation: *Salary or by the job*
Conditions: *Varies widely*
Value creation: *Build websites, etc., for their firms*
Examples: *All organizations with a web presence*

User-generated content
Employment: *Not employed*
Compensation: *Use of the platform*
Conditions: *N/A*
Value creation: *Produce data from which value is extracted*
Examples: *Google, Facebook, Snapchat, Yelp!*

Platform firm
Platform-mediated work
Platform-mediated content creation

Figure 1.1 Labor Force Distinctions in the Platform Economy

work long hours in the hope of building a successful business. If the firm succeeds, the founders and early employees can reap fabulous returns due to their stock holdings.

Platform Firm Contractors

Platform firms typically have many workers who work via either short-term direct employment or temporary help firms' arm's-length contracts.[4] These temporary employees and contractors can work remotely or on site and directly with venture laborers but nearly always receive lower pay, fewer benefits, and less job security. The sheer breadth of the activities that the contractors undertake is noteworthy. Many are what Irani (2015) calls "data janitors" who work both on- and offsite to perform not only coding but also search engine result monitoring, data cleaning and organization, vetting of uploaded material for prohibited content, and many other tasks (Gillespie, 2018). For example, in 2012, it was reported that Google Maps employed 7,100 people, of whom 1,100 were full-time employees and 6,000 were contractors (Carlson, 2012). A recent Bloomberg news article estimated that Google has as many contractors as regular employees (Bergen and Eidelson, 2018).

Platform-Mediated Work

The work discussed in the previous section concentrates on the platform itself. Organizations and individuals performing platform-mediated work are integrated into the platform's ecosystem and are often called platform complementors. This work depends upon the platform, and those doing the work are subject to the platform's rules and regulations. We identify two distinct types of platform-mediated work. First, platforms often establish marketplaces that facilitate the sale of goods and services; consider eBay and Etsy. Although the good or service may be delivered offline, the transaction is initiated on an online platform. Second, platform-mediated labor markets allow potential customers to contract for labor that may be provided either in person or remotely.

Platform-Mediated Marketplaces

Platform-mediated marketplaces were one of the earliest internet websites. Initially, many retailers stocked their own inventory, but with a few exceptions—the most notable of which is Amazon—most of them failed or were acquired. Amazon, which has acquired several failed retailers, was the most powerful survivor of the retail conflagration that hit the entire internet sector when the dotcom bubble collapsed. Despite the collapse, over the past 15 years, retail has gradually moved online; today, approximately 9 percent of all U.S. retail purchases are completed using online intermediaries. This has been growing by approximately one percentage point a year over the same 15-year period (Census Bureau, 2018). The trend is global.

Online marketplaces have several permutations. For example, Amazon is both an online retailer on its own account and a platform-mediated marketplace hosting other sellers—both businesses and private individuals. However, Expedia serves merely as an intermediary between travelers and their needs for accommodation and transportation. One profound implication of platform-mediated marketplaces and online sales is that an increasing proportion of sales is initiated online. Typically, online retailing has higher sales per employee, even when compared to highly efficient competitors such as Walmart (Wigglesworth, 2017). Online retailing dramatically affects the viability of physical retail outlets (Townsend et al., 2017). Although employment in physical retail is expected to increase, the rise will likely be concentrated in warehousing and logistics. Therefore, work in retail stores that employ college students and moderately educated individuals may be replaced by warehouse work that has little need for workers with a college education. Because many retailers on platforms such as eBay, Etsy, and Amazon are independent, some production and storage could shift to private homes. Small-scale providers depend on platforms for customer engagement, logistics, and several other aspects of their businesses. Warehouse work is more easily automated, creating further possibilities of the displacement of workers. This has implications for labor in terms of types and locations.

The character of work related to platform-mediated marketplaces is typically different from venture labor. For example, back-end fulfillment, for instance in Amazon's warehouses and even more so at outsourced fulfillment firms such as Dynamex, offers demanding working conditions with low pay and meager benefits. Although platforms such as Etsy or eBay offer sales outlets and opportunities for income generation, the responsibilities for fulfillment and buyer satisfaction fall upon the vendor, who is a free agent. Some vendors can build sound businesses on these sites, but most earnings are precarious. These businesses are also susceptible to competition, changes in the strategies of the platform owner, fickle consumer tastes, and any misfortunes that may befall the vendors.

Platform-Mediated In-Person Service Provision

In-person services have been provided by both corporate and independent contractors. An increasing proportion has been reorganized as digital intermediaries because of digital platforms. Work contracted through such labor platforms can be considered temporary one-off "gig" work. The most discussed example is Uber, which welcomes both casual and full-time drivers with minimal vetting. This easy entry of drivers is vitally important because it exposes the drivers to competition from other drivers who are willing to provide the service at even lower prices. Part-time drivers can enter the market for short periods when they need income and thus drive down wages for full-time drivers or direct competitors such as taxicab drivers (Hall and Krueger, 2018). During periods with the highest demand, new drivers can flow into the market and drive down prices while satisfying demand when full-time drivers would normally be busy (Hua and Ray, 2018; Dubal, 2017). This distinction between those who enter the market idiosyncratically but not full time or as a career and those who plan to use the platform for a full-time, permanent source of income is critical (Hua and Ray, 2018). By dissolving entry barriers, these platforms create competition between platform and non-platform providers (regular taxis) and between part-time and full-time platform providers, thereby depressing earnings for all.

Although much of the focus has been on Uber and Lyft, other platforms have attempted to organize such gig work. TaskRabbit, which allowed workers to bid on various chores, is an example of less successful in-person labor platforms. It was eventually sold to Ikea. Other variations on the Uber model include delivery services such as DoorDash in the United States and Deliveroo in Europe. Another variation is Airbnb, through which owners of real estate can rent their homes in the short term. While it provides income, this work is precarious and competition threatens to lower prices. How many of these firms will succeed is uncertain as even the highly touted Uber loses enormous amounts of money (Conger, 2018).[5]

Platform-Mediated Remote Contracting

Using telecommunications networks and internal firm platforms to contract for remote workers has a long history (e.g., Dossani and Kenney, 2009). A recent change is that firms and individuals are increasingly willing to contract freelance workers online. The platforms offering this work are quite diverse, as are the tasks for which buyers contract. They range from low-skill micro-tasks such as labeling images for Amazon Mechanical Turk (Ross et al., 2018) to highly skilled projects such as search engine optimization of a customer's website via Upwork (Pajarinen et al., 2018). Another site offering highly skilled work is InnoCentive, where customers requiring sophisticated problem-solving portray it as a challenge, offering a prize for the individual or team with the best solution (Lewin and Zhong, 2013).

Remote work provision can offer an alternative to outsourcing to a large service provider. Equally important, department-level managers can hire labor without increasing headcounts or making long-term commitments. It also allows managers to access temporary labor to meet fluctuating demand. The limits of such outsourcing cannot be easily measured, but constant efforts are made to find new tasks that can be discharged remotely through the mediation of a digital platform. Here again, it is hard to estimate how many individuals receive income through work platforms. However, in a 2018 Securities and Exchange Commission filing, Upwork (2018) claimed to operate the largest online global marketplace for freelance workers. For the year ending June 30, 2018, it had a gross services volume of $1.56 billion, and 375,000 freelancers completed nearly 2 billion projects in more than 180 countries.[6] Upwork is the largest of these firms, which are many and provide a broad range of services distinguished by size, location, and specialization.

Platform-Mediated Content Creation

Content, in all its manifestations, made the web valuable and in turn made Google, Facebook, LinkedIn, and (earlier) Yahoo! valuable companies.

We separate platform-mediated content creation into three categories. The first is user-generated content uploaded to platforms where the content and, in certain cases, the audience created for that content can be monetized. The second is content generated by existing organizations posted on the web or existing platforms as part of the organization's strategy. This process of content creation is an enormous source of employment, both directly and through contracting, but has been ignored in platform-related employment calculations thus far. The third is the gigantic volume of uncompensated user-generated content and data created as people surf the internet, interact on platforms such as Facebook and Instagram, and upload their information onto LinkedIn. This content is the core asset for many platform firms.

Consignment Content Producers

Platforms such as app stores, YouTube, and Amazon Publisher Services are marketplaces for virtual goods or content. The providers produce content that is monetized through the platform. In these consignment markets, the authors license a copy of their creation to the platform, which then offers it to its users. A platform specializing in content is worthless without creators; however, when the platform becomes dominant, much of the power shifts to the platform owner.

This category encompasses a wide range of activities. In cases such as the app stores, the content is often sold for a relatively nominal fee and the income is generated by means such as the in-app purchases that are prevalent in online games. In other venues, e.g., on YouTube, the creators generate revenue not only through advertising but also by monetizing their audiences in innovative ways such as crowd funding and (paid) personal appearances. The market for these products is skewed, with a few huge successes and a long tail of content that generates little income (Brynjolfsson and McAfee, 2011).

The consigner is effectively a freelance content producer. Consignment has long existed in the art world. However, internet platforms have dramatically increased opportunities for such business models. Before the existence of the internet and independent publishing, authors who wrote novels had to convince publishers to publish them. In the traditional publishing world, publishers were gatekeepers who selected only a few authors for publication. The remaining materials were never published and thus had no opportunity to prove their market value. Internet-based independent publishing allows written materials rejected by traditional publishers or shelved with no consideration to be marketed. Effectively, these new content delivery platforms have lowered entry barriers, permitting excluded creators to enter and thus enlarging the market. Conversely, existing publishers and successful offline authors are threatened with a loss of market share, pricing control, and, eventually, displacement. The ultimate results of these new delivery methods are unclear. For example, the London-based *Guardian* suggests that mid-ranking authors with long-standing publishers are experiencing a significant loss of income (McCrum, 2014). Flappy Birds on the Apple App Store was a successful game that no software publisher would have backed because of its simplicity and crudeness.[7] New content, new distribution channels, and many new content creators have entered the market created through platforms.

Non-Platform Organization Content Producers

Nowadays, every firm and organization must create a website to communicate with customers, employees, communities, and constituencies. Google indexes and monetizes users' searches for these websites. The firms must be indexed by Google to be found: it is the librarian for the internet. Today, what Google cannot find effectively does not exist. To illustrate, Nike's website provides a plethora of online materials, including public relations, advertising, sales, and investor information. It is a virtual location constructed by paid employees (though portions of the site may allow users to post comments, photos, etc.). A search for Nike on Google may trigger an advertisement by either Nike or another firm, and the appearance of this advertisement triggers a micropayment to Google. In an economic sense, Nike's work represents free labor for Google, while for Nike, it is a cost of doing business. The workers building websites are creating value for their employers but are also creating value for Google.

The number of paid employees and contractors working on the digital content of existing organizations is unknown, but—among the categories we consider here—it is far larger than those employed by the platforms.

User-Generated Content

On many of the most valuable platforms—including Facebook, Google, GitHub, LinkedIn, Snapchat, Twitter, Yelp, and Instagram—users either upload content or generate content-like virtual products (e.g., GitHub's open source software) when using the platform (Lanier, 2013; Terranova, 2000). The platform incurs the costs of providing the service. Platforms add value to this content by categorizing, storing, and serving it as well as making it discoverable. Although end users provide the content for free, platforms develop strategies for monetizing it (Lambrecht et al., 2014), primarily through advertising or selling it only via premium access.

The salient feature of online value creation is the enormous volume of what has been termed "free labor," that is, the exchange of user-generated content and user information for access to a service that is then monetized via the analysis and sale of either captured data or user access to third parties such as advertisers. Most importantly, unlike radio or television, the internet is bidirectional and provides a record of virtually all online activities (Huberty, 2015). Platform companies "mine," repurpose, and monetize user-generated data that has little value before it is recorded, curated, analyzed, and delivered via a suitable business model.

Observations on the Platform Labor Taxonomy

By developing a taxonomy of work, we elucidate the dimensions of value creation that are enabled. Digital platforms are rapidly becoming intermediaries in many sectors and reshaping those sectors and their work, value creation, and value capture. If Marc Andreessen was correct in his observation that "software is eating the world" (Andreessen, 2011), we might go further and say that platforms are reorganizing the economic world and, by extension, the world of work. We might go even further and say that the conventional word "work" is no longer meaningful. It may be better to think about human activities in terms of value creation and compensation for it.

Consignment content production continues to grow rapidly as the world's consumption patterns shift to online delivery. New sports categories such as fantasy sports played on online platforms have emerged, a phenomenon that is also transforming the way in which traditional sports are monetized. Consider, for example, the e-sports real-time gaming platform Twitch.tv that broadcasts e-sports (and, increasingly, other types of content). What is most interesting is that, in addition to players, an entire ecosystem of commentators has emerged (Johnson and Woodcock, 2019). Here again, both the players and commentators are complementors in the ecosystem, but for our purposes, what is important is that they are generating income.

In addition to the income from advertising, YouTubers develop extra-platform opportunities for income generation. Further, though each genre of YouTube videos exhibits certain patterns or, shall we say, "recipes," there are differences in terms of income generation. For example, music or skills-oriented videos often offer premium classes for an enrollment fee. A multitude of product placement strategies can be employed. In other cases, a YouTube star can develop a more traditional entertainment career, including live performances. Finally, some YouTubers have developed their own clothing or cosmetic brands. Sometimes, these platform ecosystem complementors post to multiple platforms, including YouTube, Instagram, Twitter, and Facebook. If they have a web store, it might be on Amazon or created using Shopify.

It has long been an axiom in economics that it is difficult to measure the impact of the value created by digital technological developments in terms of gross domestic product (Crafts, 2018; Brynjolfsson and Kahin, 2000).

Implicit in our taxonomy is the difficulty of determining how work should be measured, because measurement difficulties are proliferating.

The first difficulty is that although the McKinsey Global Institute (Manyika et al., 2016) found between 20 percent and 30 percent of the U.S. population to be engaged in some independent or gig work, much of it is not connected with an online platform. This is an important distinction; identifying independent work is one thing, but proving that total independent work has grown because of digitalization is another. More recently, Abraham et al. (2018) explored the problems that governments confront when trying to measure the gig economy. Reinforcing the McKinsey Global Institute's findings, the authors discovered that traditional job surveys, because of wording that focuses on traditional employment relationships, may not elicit information from respondents who receive income from nontraditional income-generating activities, such as YouTubers, other social media influencers, or someone with a small eBay sales operation. They illustrate this by noting that tax filings show an increase in nontraditional income whereas household surveys do not (Abraham et al., 2018).[8] These studies might lead to the conclusion that much of the income generated from platform-related activities is supplemental; however, ample evidence indicates that in the labor markets organized by the larger platforms, many individuals depend upon platform-derived income (Farrell and Greig, 2016). Some studies have attempted to estimate the number of individuals operating on a platform (Eurofound, 2018). This strategy may be ineffective since so many platforms exist and many of those are so opaque that measurement of employment, particularly income, would be difficult.

The second difficulty in measurement is that labor statistics are not straightforward in terms of analysis. Understanding the meaning and measuring the number of jobs (opportunities for earning income) created by the platforms outside of direct full-time employment is difficult. Even harder is assessing whether the new jobs are better paying or of higher quality than the previous jobs. So how can we decide whether working on these platforms is good or bad? Almost the entire body of existing research suggests that a significant proportion of the gig economy workforce affirmatively enjoys and seeks such employment (Schor, 2017; Manyika et al., 2016; Barley and Kunda, 2004). However, many others have little choice but to work through a digital platform. This dilemma is best illustrated by Lyft, whose drivers appear to enjoy driving for the company but often are part-timers working for extra income or sometimes just to keep busy. In the case of these drivers, the work appears voluntary and temporary. Similarly, some Airbnb hosts offer their properties out of necessity, others for the pleasure of meeting new people, and yet others for monetizing their properties. In each case, the motivations are different, and thus, drawing a single, universal conclusion is difficult. What seems certain is that an increasing percentage of the labor force derives at least some income from digital platforms. This is true even without including those who create and curate websites and the billions of people who create uncompensated content that is monetized by the platform firms.

Conclusion: Business Strategies, Consumer Choices, and Policy Decisions Determine Ultimate Outcomes

The platform economy is not merely fissuring the workplace (Weil, 2014) but also reorganizing the relations, locations, and activities involved, creating a new and expanding set of arrangements in which individuals can generate income. Some have argued that digital technology is blurring the boundaries of the firm (Yoo et al., 2010), and, from the perspective of work, the permutations of task division and organizational and spatial location have increased dramatically. The tests used for judging whether someone undertaking a task for a firm is an employee or a contractor now seem ill-suited for the purpose. For example, a spate of litigation has argued about whether an Uber driver is an employee or an independent contractor (Sanders and Pattison, 2016).[9] This issue is so vexing that some have called for a new legal category for such workers (Hagiu and Biederman, 2015). The fixation on platform-mediated in-person service provision ignores the other categories that we have enumerated, thus confirming our argument that fissuring does not capture the vast dispersion in the forms of work underway (Kenney and Zysman, 2019b).

Yet, all popular platforms share one commonality: the power of platform owners. They are in a strategically advantaged position to absorb resources from the ecosystems spawned by platforms that they partly share with the employees considered essential for the platforms' success. Platforms redefine power balances between businesses but also the relationships between the firm and labor. The platform owner has tremendous power in relation to members of the ecosystem, who depend on the platform in several ways. First, the platform can change the algorithms determining its operations at will (Lessig, 1999). Second, on most platforms, the algorithms determining payment and content acceptability are private and not publicized to ecosystem complementors, thus keeping them in a constant state of uncertainty (Scolere et al., 2018). Third, in ecosystems such as app stores or the Amazon Marketplace, the platform owner can offer a product that competes with that of an ecosystem member and favor that product on the platform. Fourth, the platform owner has a panoptic view of all activities on the platform and thus can shift nearly any parameter in a way that favors the platform's ability to extract value from the ecosystem. Each of these types of power affects not only labor and work but also markets, terms of competition, and social dynamics. An Uber driver who can be disqualified as a driver by an unknown algorithm will lose income immediately. There is no need for notice; the app simply stops working. YouTubers can have their videos demonetized without receiving any explanation. Not only can they be forbidden to monetize new videos, but previous videos that earned income can also get demonetized. This effectively devalues their entire portfolios, not simply the offending video. In this economic system, labor is evermore precarious, has no recourse for grievances except the firm, and is often uncertain what the decision criteria are.

The taxonomy of labor for the platform economy shows that, in each category, the organization of work and value creation differs. Therefore, a fixation on only one or the other of the platforms—most commonly exemplified by Uber and Amazon—fails to provide a comprehensive perspective on labor in the platform economy. The controversies over giant firms, from Facebook and Amazon to Uber and Airbnb, signal the profound impacts of platforms on our economy, society, and income distribution. The ultimate configuration and disposition of work and the beneficiaries of the value created by these platforms will be determined by policy decisions. The power and ability of these platforms to extract such an enormous portion of the social surplus will prompt a political response. The exact character of the changes driven by the move to a platform economy cannot be known in advance. Yet, given the rising income inequality, though not due solely to the rise of these platforms, these changes may lead to increasingly tense and disruptive social and political relations. A better understanding of the roles of different kinds of labor in the platform economy is imperative for addressing the future of work. Finally, we may need to shift from thinking about a world of traditional employment to thinking about one in which income and relative shares of the value created form a better basis to reflect contemporary economics.

Notes

1 Cutolo and Kenney (2019) have referred to the platform ecosystem members as "dependent entrepreneurs."
2 There are a few exceptions, such as Spotify and Booking.com. On the globalization of Chinese platform firms, see Jia et al. (2019).
3 Other platform categorizations include Fumagalli et al. (2018) and Forde et al. (2017).
4 For a more general discussion of the temporary help industry, see Hyman (2018). For a discussion of the complicated and contradictory perceptions of these contract employees, see Barley and Kunda (2004).
5 For further discussion of the ability of these new entrants to lose enormous amounts of money and tip the market, see Kenney and Zysman (2019a).
6 If the number of freelancers is divided by income, the average income per freelancer was approximately $4,160. This suggests that the average freelancer is working part-time and also relying on other sources of income.

7 At the height of its popularity, the very simple and even crude Flappy Birds game was estimated to earn $50,000 per day through in-app purchases before the game creator removed it from the Apple App Store.
8 See also Allard and Polivka (2018).
9 Since then, some regulations have been put in place (e.g., Khouri, 2018; Morris, 2018).

References

Abraham, K. G., Haltiwanger, J. C., Sandusky, K. and Spletzer, J. R. (2018). Measuring the Gig Economy: Current Knowledge and Open Issues. *NBER Working Papers*, *24950*. Available at: www.nber.org/papers/w24950.pdf [Accessed 19 April 2019].

Allard, M. D. and Polivka, A. E. (2018). Measuring Labor Market Activity Today: Are the Words Work and Job Too Limiting for Surveys? *Monthly Labor Review*, November. https://doi.org/10.21916/mlr.2018.26.

Andreessen, M. (2011). Why Software Is Eating the World. Available at: https://a16z.com/2011/08/20/why-software-is-eating-the-world/ [Accessed 5 April 2019].

Barley, S. R. (2015). Why the Internet Makes Buying a Car Less Loathsome: How Technologies Change Role Relations. *Academy of Management Discoveries*, 1(1), pp. 5–34. https://doi.org/10.5465/amd.2013.0016.

Barley, S. R. and Kunda, G. (2004). *Gurus, Hired Guns, and Warm Bodies: Itinerant Experts in a Knowledge Economy*. Princeton: Princeton University Press.

Bergen, M. and Eidelson, J. (2018). Inside Google's Shadow Workforce. *Bloomberg News*, [online]. Available at: www.bloomberg.com/news/articles/2018-07-25/inside-google-s-shadow-workforce/ [Accessed 19 April 2019].

Brynjolfsson, E. and Kahin, B. (eds.) (2000). *Understanding the Digital Economy: Data, Tools, and Research*. Cambridge, MA: MIT Press.

Brynjolfsson, E. and McAfee, A. (2011). *Race Against the Machine: How the Digital Revolution Is Accelerating Innovation, Driving Productivity, and Irreversibly Transforming Employment and the Economy (Kindle edition)*. Boston: Digital Frontier Press.

Carlson, N. (2012). Apple Has ~7,000 Fewer People Working on Maps Than Google. *Business Insider*. Available at: www.businessinsider.com/apple-has-7000-fewerpeople-working-on-maps-than-google-2012-9/ [Accessed 19 April 2019].

Census Bureau. (2018). Quarterly Retail E-Commerce Sales, 3rd Quarter. [online] *Census Bureau*. Available at: www.census.gov/retail/mrts/www/data/pdf/ec_current.pdf [Accessed 19 April 2019].

Conger, K. (2018). Losses Persist in Uber's March Toward an I.P.O. *New York Times*, [online] p. B5. Available at: www.nytimes.com/2018/08/15/technology/ubers-losses-continue-in-march-toward-initial-public-offering.html [Accessed 19 April 2019].

Crafts, N. (2018). The Productivity Slowdown: Is It the "New Normal"? *Oxford Review of Economic Policy*, 34(3), pp. 443–460. https://doi.org/10.1093/oxrep/gry001.

Cutolo, D. and Kenney, M. (2019). Dependent Entrepreneurs in a Platform Economy: Playing in the Gardens of the Gods. *BRIE Working Papers*,

2019–03. Available at: https://brie.berkeley.edu/sites/default/files/brie_working_paper_2019-3.pdf [Accessed 19 April 2019].

Dossani, R. and Kenney, M. (2009). Service Provision for the Global Economy: The Evolving Indian Experience. *Review of Policy Research*, 26(1/2), pp. 77–104. https://doi.org/10.1111/j.1541-1338.2008.00370.x.

Dubal, V. B. (2017). The Drive to Precarity: A Political History of Work, Regulation, & Labor Advocacy in San Francisco's Taxi & Uber Economies. *Berkeley Journal of Employment & Labor Law*, 38(1), pp. 73–135. https://doi.org/10.15779/Z38KW57H5S.

Eurofound. (2018). *Employment and Working Conditions of Selected Types of Platform Work*. Luxembourg: Publications Office of the European Union.

Farrell, D. and Greig, F. (2016). *Paychecks, Paydays, and the Online Platform Economy: Big Data on Income Volatility*. New York & Washington, DC: JPMorgan Chase & Co. Institute Reports.

Forde, C., Stuart, M., Joyce, S., Oliver, L., Valizade, D., et al. (2017). *The Social Protection of Workers in the Platform Economy*. Brussels: EU Directorate General for Internal Policies, Policy Department A: Economic and Scientific Policy, IP/A/EMPL/2016-11.

Fumagalli, A., Lucarelli, S., Musolino, E. and Rocchi, G. (2018). Digital Labour in the Platform Economy: The Case of Facebook. *Sustainability, MDPI, Open Access Journal*, 10(6), pp. 1–16. Available at: www.mdpi.com/2071-1050/10/6/1757/pdf.

Ghazawneh, A. and Henfridsson, O. (2015). A Paradigmatic Analysis of Digital Application Marketplaces. *Journal of Information Technology*, 30(3), pp. 198–208. doi: 10.1057/jit.2015.16.

Gillespie, T. (2018). *Custodians of the Internet: Platforms, Content Moderation, and the Hidden Decisions That Shape Social Media*. New Haven: Yale University Press.

Hagiu, A. and Biederman, R. (2015). Companies Need an Option Between Contractor and Employee. *Harvard Business Review* [online]. Available at: https://hbr.org/2015/08/companies-need-an-option-between-contractor-and-employee/ [Accessed 19 April 2019].

Hall, J. V. and Krueger, A. B. (2018). An Analysis of the Labor Market for Uber's Driver-Partners in the United States. *ILR Review*, 71(3), pp. 705–732. doi: 10.1177/0019793917717222.

Hua, J. and Ray, K. (2018). Beyond the Precariat: Race, Gender, and Labor in the Taxi and Uber Economy. *Social Identities*, 24(2), pp. 271–289.

Huberty, M. (2015). Awaiting the Second Big Data Revolution: From Digital Noise to Value Creation. *Journal of Industry, Competition & Trade*, 15(1), pp. 35–47. doi: 10.1007/s10842-014-0190-4.

Hyman, L. (2018). *Temp: How American Work, American Business, and the American Dream Became Temporary*. New York: Penguin.

Irani, L. (2015). Justice for "Data Janitors." *Public Books*. Available at: www.publicbooks.org/justice-for-data-janitors/ [Accessed 17 April 2019].

Jia, K., Kenney, M. and Zysman, J. (2019). Global Competitors? Mapping the Internationalization Strategies of Chinese Digital Platform Firms. In: R. van Tulder, A. Verbeke and L. Piscitello, eds., *International Business in the Information and Digital Age. Vol. 13*. Bingley, UK: Emerald Publishing Limited, pp. 187–215.

Johnson, M. R. and Woodcock, J. (2019). "It's Like the Gold Rush": The Lives and Careers of Professional Video Game Streamers on Twitch.tv. *Information, Communication & Society*, 22(3), pp. 336–351. doi: 10.1080/1369118X.2017. 1386229.

Kenney, M. and Zysman, J. (2016). The Rise of the Platform Economy. *Science and Technology*, 32(3), pp. 61–69.

Kenney, M. and Zysman, J. (2019a). Unicorns, Cheshire Cats, and the New Dilemmas of Entrepreneurial Finance? *Venture Capital: An International Journal of Entrepreneurial Finance*, 21(1), pp. 35–50. doi: 10.1080/13691066.2018. 1517430.

Kenney, M. and Zysman, J. (2019b). Work and Value Creation in the Platform Economy. In: A. Kovalainen and S. Vallas, eds., *Work and Labor in the Digital Age (Research in the Sociology of Work, Vol. 33)*. Bingley, UK: Emerald Publishing Limited, pp. 13–41.

Khouri, A. (2018). Uber Drivers, Freelancers and Other Independent Contractors Are Getting a Tax Cut. Available at: www.latimes.com/business/la-fi-independent-contractors-tax-20180116-story.html [Accessed 19 April 2019].

Lambrecht, A., Goldfarb, A., Bonatti, A., Ghose, A., Goldstein, D., et al. (2014). How Do Firms Make Money Selling Digital Goods Online? *Marketing Letters*, 25(3), pp. 331–341. doi: 10.1007/s11002-014-9310-5.

Lanier, J. (2013). *Who Owns the Future?* New York: Penguin.

Lessig, L. (1999). *Code and Other Laws of Cyberspace*. New York: Basic Books.

Lewin, A. Y. and Zhong, X. (2013). The Evolving Diaspora of Talent: A Perspective on Trends and Implications for Sourcing Science and Engineering Work. *Journal of International Management*, 19(1), pp. 6–13.

Li, W. C. Y., Nirei, M. and Yamana, K. (2018). Value of Data: There's No Such Thing as a Free Lunch in the Digital Economy. *Paper presented at the Sixth IMF Statistical Forum, Washington, DC, November.*

Manyika, J., Lund, S., Bughin, J., Robinson, K., Mischke, J. and Mahajan, D. (2016). *Independent Work: Choice, Necessity, and the Gig Economy*. Available at: www.mckinsey.com/featured-insights/employment-and-growth/independent-work-choice-necessity-and-the-gig-economy [Accessed 17 April 2019].

McCrum, R. (2014). From Bestseller to Bust: Is This the End of an Author's Life? Available at: www.theguardian.com/books/2014/mar/02/bestseller-novel-to-bust-author-life/ [Accessed 19 April 2019].

Morris, D. Z. (2018). Uber Drivers Are Employees, New York Unemployment Insurance Board Rules. Available at: http://fortune.com/2018/07/21/uber-drivers-employees-new-york-unemployment/ [Accessed 19 April 2019].

Neff, G., Nardi, B. A., Kaptelinin, V. and Foot, K. A. (2012). *Venture Labor: Work and the Burden of Risk in Innovative Industries*. Cambridge, MA: MIT Press.

Orlikowski, W. J. and Scott, S. V. (2015). The Algorithm and the Crowd: Considering the Materiality of Service Innovation. *MIS Quarterly*, 39(1), pp. 201–216.

Pajarinen, M., Rouvinen, P., Claussen, J., Hakanen, J., Kovalainen, A., Kretschmer, T., Poutanen, S., Seifried, M. and Seppänen, L. (2018). *Upworkers in Finland: Survey Results. ETLA Reports*, 85. Helsinki: ETLA.

Parker, G. G., Van Alstyne, M. W. and Choudary, S. P. (2016). *Platform Revolution: How Networked Markets Are Transforming the Economy and How to Make Them Work for You*. New York: W. W. Norton & Company, Inc.

Parrott, J. A. and Reich, M. (2018). *An Earnings Standard for New York City's App-Based Drivers*. New York: Report for the New York City Taxi and Limousine Commission.

Ross, J., Irani, L., Silberman, M. S., Zaldivar, A. and Tomlinson, B. (2018). Who Are the Crowdworkers? Shifting Demographics in Mechanical Turk. *Conference on Human Factors in Computing Systems: Proceedings*, pp. 2863–2872.

Sanders, D. E. and Pattison, P. (2016). Worker Characterization in a Gig Economy Viewed Through an Uber Centric Lens. *Southern Law Journal*, 26(2), pp. 297–320.

Schor, J. B. (2017). Does the Sharing Economy Increase Inequality Within the Eighty Percent? Findings From a Qualitative Study of Platform Providers. *Cambridge Journal of Regions, Economy and Society*, 10(2), pp. 263–279. https://doi.org/10.1093/cjres/rsw047.

Scolere, L., Pruchniewska, U. and Duffy, B. E. (2018). Constructing the Platform-Specific Self-Brand: The Labor of Social Media Promotion. *Social Media + Society*, 4(3). https://doi.org/10.1177/2056305118784768.

Scott, S. V. and Orlikowski, W. J. (2010). Reconfiguring Relations of Accountability: The Consequences of Social Media for the Travel Sector. *Academy of Management Annual Meeting Proceedings*, (1), pp. 1–6. https://doi.org/10.5465/AMBPP.2010.54499679.

Srnicek, N. (2017). The Challenges of Platform Capitalism: Understanding the Logic of a New Business Model. *Juncture*, 23(4), pp. 254–257. https://doi.org/10.1111/newe.12023.

Terranova, T. (2000). Free Labor: Producing Culture for the Digital Economy. *Social Text*, 18(2), pp. 33–58. https://doi.org/10.1215/01642472-18-2_63-33.

Townsend, M., Surane, J., Orr, E. and Cannon, C. (2017). America's 'Retail Apocalypse' Is Really Just Beginning. Available at: www.bloomberg.com/graphics/2017-retail-debt/ [Accessed 19 April 2019].

Upwork. (2018). Prospectus for an Initial Public Stock Offering. Available at: www.sec.gov/Archives/edgar/data/1627475/000119312518291879/d575528d424b4.htm#toc575528_10/ [Accessed 19 April 2019].

van Dijck, J. (2013). *The Culture of Connectivity: A Critical History of Social Media*. New York: Oxford University Press.

Weil, D. (2014). *The Fissured Workplace*. Cambridge, MA: Harvard University Press.

Wigglesworth, R. (2017). Will the Death of US Retail Be the Next Big Short? Available at: www.ft.com/content/d34ad3a6-5fd3-11e7-91a7-502f7ee26895/ [Accessed 19 April 2019].

Yoo, Y., Henfridsson, O. and Lyytinen, K. (2010). The New Organizing Logic of Digital Innovation: An Agenda for Information Systems Research. *Information Systems Research*, 21(4), pp. 724–735. https://doi.org/10.1287/isre.1100.0322.

Zysman, J. and Kenney, M. (2018). The Next Phase in the Digital Revolution: Intelligent Tools, Platforms, Growth, Employment. *Communications of the ACM*, 61(2), pp. 54–63. doi: 10.1145/3173550.

2 Theorizing Work in the Contemporary Platform Economy

*Anne Kovalainen, Steven P. Vallas,
and Seppo Poutanen*

Introduction: Platformization Changes Societies, Economies, and Work

The rise of the platform economy has become a major source of debate in both advanced and developing economies. Driven by the spread of mobile devices, growing access to the internet, the availability of venture capital, and the economic strategies of many governments, internet-based economic transactions have rapidly grown during the last decade, a period in which Uber, Airbnb, Upwork, Mechanical Turk and many other platforms have risen to worldwide prominence. Though the effects of platforms are as yet uncertain, there is widespread agreement that the platform economy is likely to have far-reaching effects on the structure of the retail sector (as e-commerce "disrupts" brick-and-mortar stores), urban transportation (which is increasingly being shaped by private, for-profit firms), and consumption patterns (as the discourse of the "sharing economy" suggests). Social media platforms have enticed users on sites such as YouTube and Instagram to compete for prominence in the "attention economy," performing "aspirational labor" as a means of generating advertising revenues through their online activity (Duffy, 2016; van Dijck et al., 2018). Perhaps most far reaching are the potential changes the platform economy is likely to have on work and employment, as "gig" work becomes more prominent, even changing our very conception of what it means to have a "job" (Davis, 2016). One can glimpse the scale of these changes by comparing the most heavily capitalized firms in the world today with their counterparts of a few decades ago. Here one begins to see the growing prominence of the FAANGs—Facebook, Apple, Amazon, Netflix, and Google—firms that employ relatively few workers, own relatively little in the way of fixed capital, and very likely represent a new epoch in the development of contemporary capitalism (e.g., Gottfried, 2013; Smith, 2016; Srnicek, 2016; Schor and Attwood-Charles, 2017; Kalleberg and Vallas, 2017; Vallas and Kovalainen, 2019).

Platforms have also attracted interest for political and cultural reasons quite apart from their economic consequences (Zuboff, 2018; Frey and Osborne, 2013; Vallas, 2012, 2019; Acemoglu and Autor, 2010), perhaps because of their seeming omnipotence, their ability to manage workers algorithmically, and their skill at evading established forms of regulation (Thelen, 2018). These characteristics, along with a growing sense that machine learning, robotics, and artificial intelligence have outstripped societal controls, have imbued the debate over platforms with a highly polarized, often moralistic quality. Advocates see in the platform revolution an opportunity to establish a more entrepreneurial and inclusive economy; critics see instead a privately owned surveillance state that usurps the power of state planning agencies. Needed are analytical approaches toward the platform economy which are conversant with such issues, but not reducible to them. Needed are theoretically nuanced models of platforms, a necessary condition if we are to direct them down socially useful paths.

Yet such approaches are not readily available at present. Although there has been a surge of scholarly research on the dilemmas and challenges which platforms pose to workers, firms, and communities (Vallas, 2019; Schor and Attwood-Charles, 2017), this literature has developed in highly uneven ways. Much of the attention has been focused on the very largest global players—Uber, Airbnb, and MTurk as prime examples— potentially skewing our knowledge in arbitrary ways. Gender bias has been smuggled into the literature, as is evident in the general neglect of care work, a massive and largely female part of the platform economy that has received relatively little attention until recently (Ticona and Mateescu, 2018). Although scholars have used provocative analogies to portray the meaning of the platform revolution, e.g., seeing it as ushering in a backward-looking reversion to the putting-out system that characterized early capitalism (Kenney and Zysman, 2016), metaphors cannot substitute for the empirically grounded theoretical frameworks needed to make sense of the various types of platforms, their relation to the conventional economy, and their impacts on different segments of the labor market. In this chapter we hope to fill in this gap, contributing to the necessarily large task of theorizing the platform economy. In effect, we hope to provide an aerial reconnaissance of the field, providing an overview of the main lines of analysis that scholars will need to develop if we are to understand (and hopefully influence) the course which the platform revolution is likely to take in the coming period.

Prior to the growth of platformization and the app economy, the technological developments that transformed or changed production did not enable the "decoupling" of work and workers from the organization/institution. Because workers were connected to their organizational or institutional structures through their embeddedness within the firm and their spatial co-presence (e.g., DiTomaso, 2001; Brynjolfsson and McAfee, 2015), scholars could explore how new information and process control technologies were changing the interior operations of the firm. Now, however, platforms have seemed to accelerate the erosion of the Fordist firm. Now, platforms and apps mediate work digitally, they divide tasks and work in novel ways, and they also control the performance of workers' jobs through algorithmically governed structures that have lent work and employment entirely new features. The direction, allocation, and evaluation of work are increasingly accomplished digitally, with little transparency and few opportunities for informal negotiation.

These changes raise new issues regarding trust building in the decoupling of work and workers, legal questions regarding labor classification, structural changes affecting the role of regulatory bodies, and dilemmas for governments trying to balance scientific and technological innovation with social justice concerns. As platforms grow, they also raise questions about access to training, support for research and development, and the future course of the welfare state. Platforms and platformization are also increasingly involved in public goods production, such as in education (e.g., the massive open online courses, or MOOCs) and healthcare (apps for data gathering and use). In changing the consumption and production patterns towards consumers' "produsage" (Bruns, 2007), platforms also erode traditional employment contracts and earning logic, fostering a discourse of entrepreneurialism that often seems a poor fit with the actual role of platform workers. Moreover, platforms blur boundaries, not only between consumers and producers but also between workers and the self-employed, between work and non-work, and between market and non-market activity. This multitude of societal and economic changes provide the warrant for our reflections on the rhetorical and theoretical framings of work in this new platform economy.

Globally, public discussions on the changing nature of work echo some more general changes currently prevalent in economies and societies. The discussions range from politicized questions on the future labor supply (which broaches the issue of immigration, currently so inflamed) to the actual and projected changes in the demand for labor (and thus the question of technological unemployment). The contractual form of work based on occupational categories (such as the "professions" or the skilled crafts) may weaken, as new systems arise for consulting, freelancing, and independent contracting arrangements. Though the scale of such shifts is as yet unclear, some incipient signs are currently visible in the growing numbers of digital part-timers, workers engaged in micro-tasking, or freelancers. These contractual forms have in many cases led to greater flexibility for workers (who can make a wider range of choices about when and where to work), but also low levels of compensation, zero-hour contracts, greater income insecurity, and social isolation as well (Wood et al., 2019). Although there is a sense that platforms have accelerated the growth of these non-standard work arrangements, we have few detailed studies of where such changes have been felt most acutely, which occupations have benefited and which have been hurt, and how public policies can respond more proactively (Vallas and Kovalainen, 2019).

Research has shown a global increase in the types of work that do not fit any categories of paid employees. Digitalization brings a growing diversity in the categories and forms of work arrangements as well as employment patterns.[1] This is partly due to the fact that digital technologies enable the breaking down of work into tasks. These tasks—smaller jobs—may be skill-based but they often are also skill-biased. These new forms of skill-biased patterns are widespread globally (EC, 2019; Standing, 2010; OECD, 2006). There is a long tradition in research for addressing the effects of digitalization for work and the working life, from pioneering studies such as those of Braverman (1974), Adler (1992), Harrison (1994), and Barley and Kunda (2001), to those of Head (2005), Evans and Tilly (2016), and Beynon (2016). Many of these studies argue that technology in general and digital technologies will be eliminating some types of work and jobs. However, in many studies, the effects of technology are related to specific occupations and jobs, often industrial jobs. In a similar fashion, the consequences and effects of digitalization as implications for the workforce and its supply and demand have often been analyzed as separate from the technologies themselves. However, the service sector and its jobs are transforming as well. According to Evans and Tilly (2016), only a small subset of jobs can be defined as belonging to the capability-enhancing service sector, which can create "good" jobs and more work in the future.

The variety of ways in which platform work emerges has led to a growing number of typologies of platform work (e.g., Howcroft and Bergvall-Kåreborn, 2019; Kenney and Zysman, 2019), where the classifying aspects can be payment (yes/no), initiating actor (worker-initiated, requester-initiated), and, for some, control over the work. Mixtures of non-paid (or speculative) work are also often presented in these classifications, such as "playbor" (Kucklich, 2005) work, which is mixing the boundaries between work and leisure, or new crowdwork such as Top-Coder and InnoCentive (Howcroft and Bergvall-Kåreborn, 2019), where online competition communities compete for solutions in hope of gaining a reputation or gaining training for labor, as in coding competitions for girls (Poutanen and Kovalainen, 2017).

Vallas and Schor (2020), building on earlier work by Kenney and Zysman (2019), identify five types of platform work: architects and technologists (who design the apps and algorithms on which platforms rely); skilled crowdworkers (freelancers and consultants who contract for work via digital means); offline service providers (as in the app-based ride-hailing, courier, and home repair sectors); micro-taskers (unskilled crowdworkers, as on MTurk); and content producers or "influencers" (YouTube users performing "aspirational" labor). The point of their enumeration is to stress the enormous variety of conditions that characterize the work situations of platform workers today. Likewise, this enumeration is helpful in pointing out how unevenly developed the literature is. We have a flood of recent studies of offline service providers (Uber and Deliveroo being the prime examples), yet relatively few glimpses of the architects and technologists who design the "guts" of the platform revolution itself (for exceptions, see Neff, 2012; Kelkar, 2018). Equally important is the need for studies emphasizing the *relations* that exist between each category of workers (Irani, 2015), as well as the complex linkages that exist between each category and their equivalents in the conventional economy.

Given the background presented, it is necessary to determine what constitutes work and its conditions in the new, digitally wired platform economy and in what ways work is changing with the trumping of digitalization in all spheres of life. It is well known that both the labor markets and skills required are currently influenced by advanced automation and robotization everywhere, but in complex and nuanced ways that are not as yet well understood (e.g., Acemoglu and Restrepo, 2017). This influence is not necessarily one-dimensional or one-directional, as the diminishing of jobs hypothesis assumes. The shaping can be contradictory as well, as exemplified by spillover effects (e.g., Jacobs and Karen, 2019) and also loosely coupled experts' work (e.g., DiTomaso, 2001), or by new technologies servicing employers' surveillance needs (e.g., Ajunwa et al., 2017). Further, the increasing individualization of expert work and the need to brand oneself despite qualifications and skills (e.g., Vallas and Cummins, 2015) is enabled by the platformization of work. Equally important are the complex linkages among different platforms, as when Uber drivers use YouTube and other apps to carry out the direct action campaigns with which they act back on the algorithms that govern their earnings.

The Nature and Consequences of Platform Work

Although the actual size of the labor force that participates in platform work is relatively meager, the platform economy can implement far-reaching changes into virtually every facet of contemporary capitalism. For instance, e-commerce platforms have captured a growing share of the revenues once controlled by brick-and-mortar retail outlets. Capital platforms for lodging have rapidly encroached the hospitality industry. Platforms such as Uber and Lyft have usurped the market positions of taxi firms. Sites such as Upwork and Freelancer have accelerated the trend toward outsourcing, placing the global supply of labor at the disposal of firms at scales not previously possible. Social media firms such as Facebook and Instagram, which subsist on revenue from advertising and the sale of user data, have brought platforms into the most intimate realms of our everyday lives. Platforms such as Amazon Mechanical Turk provide an almost unlimited supply of gig workers, a sector that has shown unprecedented growth (Kuek et al., 2015). It is no exaggeration that the platform economy has begun to blur many taken-for-granted boundaries that once organized social life.

Although definitions vary widely, and being mindful of the enormous variation that exists across the types of platforms and the work situations they promote, it seems possible to identify a number of ideal-typical features that characterize platform work today.

1. By their very nature, platforms use *digital* means of production, relying on internet applications and mobile devices to mediate or "match" workers with consumers, whether these are commuters needing rides (Uber and Lyft), customers seeking delivery services (Postmates and Uber Eats), homeowners seeking repairs (TaskRabbit and Handy), firms outsourcing professional services (Upwork and Freelancer), or firms delegating human tasks that computers cannot yet perform (Amazon Mechanical Turk). Functioning as "two-sided markets" (Rochet and Tirole, 2003), platforms can grow only if they can attract and retain sufficient pools of both workers and consumers. This is why platforms must resort to a variety of inducements—bonuses, surge pricing, gamification, and even normative controls (Gerber and Krzywdzinski, 2019)—to maintain their labor supplies despite the nominal control workers retain with respect to their work schedules.

2. Platform firms almost always define themselves purely *as* intermediaries rather than employers, thus defining their workers as independent contractors or self-employed. Implied is a redistribution of financial, legal, and even bodily risks, all of which are externalized by the company to the service providers. In many societies, this means platform workers are not covered by minimum wage laws, occupational safety and health regulations, or social insurance systems. This has led many scholars to view platforms as reinforcing or accelerating the already-existing trend toward the precarization of employment (Davis, 2016; Kalleberg, 2011, 2018). Platforms often grow by undercutting the economic positions of conventional firms, which must shoulder the full cost of labor services, including the payment of payroll taxes and benefits. Because platforms evade the obligations related to employment, they may also potentially weaken the basis of the welfare state (Zanoni, 2019).

3. Platforms extend the logic of the "just-in-time" inventory system into the provision of labor services. Workers are no longer hired into *jobs* but merely hired to perform one-off *tasks* (Davis, 2016; Casilli and Posada, 2019). Because platforms reduce the transaction costs involved in the outsourcing of work, firms find it possible to use "crowdsourcing" in lieu of standard employment, "dis-integrating" or "fissuring" the labor processes that were previously integrated

(Weil, 2014). Theoretically, this exposes a growing proportion of the labor force to piece-rate payment and the income insecurity this can imply. This is why scholars often point to the putting-out system as an historical antecedent of platform work (Kenney and Zysman, 2016). Just as the most economically impoverished weavers were compelled to rent their looms from capitalist merchants, thus providing a double source of revenue for the latter, so are ride-hailing workers who do not own cars compelled to rent automobiles from Uber-contracted agencies, which requires them to work especially long hours to cover their costs (Manriquez, 2019). Food delivery workers, called "riders," are similarly lacking worker protection.

4. Platforms *individualize* the workforce they use or employ, in effect reversing the spatial agglomeration of labor that the advent of the factory system unleashed. Although workers often forge surrogate forms of solidarity in online forums and social media (Gray et al., 2016) and can even devise defensive applications on their behalf (as with platforms rating prospective clients or guarding against wage theft), platforms generally dissipate the relational spaces that material co-presence had provided, isolating workers (Wood et al., 2019). In many cases, workers are also positioned in competitive relation toward one another, such as on crowdworking sites, where they must bid against one another for work (Gerber and Krzywdzinski, 2019). The tasks are bid on globally, and workers may need to adjust their bidding to suit levels not corresponding to the standard living costs of their area/country.

5. By design, platforms employ *algorithmic* means of governing the operations of the labor processes they oversee, thus building the function of labor management into the digital technology itself. From the workers' viewpoint, this means the rules governing platform work (e.g., number of tasks which workers can reject or the rating levels they must maintain) are no longer subject to informal negotiation but are instead enforced by the very digital tools workers must use to complete their tasks. Even as platforms generate a wealth of data about workers' movements and activities, they share these data unevenly, generating information asymmetries that can limit the abilities of the workers to make informed choices about which tasks to accept (Rosenblat and Stark, 2016). Part of the work is governed by electronic performance monitoring (EPM), where individualized performance measures, such as GPS tracking and computer content and time usage, are being used (De Stefano, 2018). Job rewards, whether material or symbolic, can also be built into an app, involving not only compensation levels or bonuses but also the provision of special statuses, game-like inducements, and communal attachments that can serve to keep workers on the job. Key are the systems that aggregate the reputational scores workers have earned and make

the results visible to all prospective customers. Workers who fail to maintain acceptable ratings are often pushed downward in the queue (as with Upwork) or even "deactivated" (Uber) without explanation.

Although these five features apply to a broad spectrum of platforms, they do so in the most varied ways. The sources of such heterogeneity are complex, but several shared influences exist. First, there is the *varying degree to which workers depend on their platform income*. Although many accounts stress the uniformity with which platforms transform the nature of work (for better or worse), most empirical studies on platform work reveal globally substantial variations between the work situations of supplemental workers (who may work part time, often in combination with full-time "standard" work) and full-time or fully dependent workers (who are entirely reliant on their platform incomes for survival). This difference is likely to have profound consequences not only for the work orientations each group of workers will exhibit but also, more generally, for the regulatory policies each group is likely to support.

Second, there is the consideration whether the work is provided entirely *online* (as part of Upwork or Mechanical Turk, where workers perform as crowdworkers) or instead *performed in person or offline* (as with Uber and Handy workers, who are sometimes termed "gig workers," or as part of Upwork activities). This point has a powerful effect on the social context in which the work is performed; for instance, gig workers are brought into direct contact with the buyers of their labor services and can derive important sources of fulfillment that are denied to crowdworkers, who may suffer higher levels of social isolation as a result (e.g., Wood et al., 2018).

A third source of differences stems from *the level of skill, education, and qualifications* workers command. Although some accounts view platform workers as holding uniformly "contingent" positions (in that they are commonly paid by piece or project), some workers command skills that are sufficiently in demand to generate high employability levels. However, more research is needed on the inter-occupational variations in the effects of platform work, as such favorable outcomes are probably found among workers supplying technical services in graphical design and programming, for example. Changes in technology can of course weaken the positions of skilled crowdworkers, as is the case of translators or providers of transcription services, and technically qualified workers can suffer from skill obsolescence, especially given their lack of access to training programs such as those conventional employers often provide.

Within each category described here, the actual work and task specialization types may differ, creating variations within categories and differences among platform workers. For instance, for the online lawyer or medical expert, the taskification level of work may be high, as is the skill level, and tasks may be performed online with time pressure and limitations, among others. However, the same features except for the skill level—high taskification and time pressure in performance—are also valid for a food-delivery biker. The contractual nature of the work tasks on platforms and the taskification level of work are thus not restricted to simple tasks and singled-out actions but extend from low-skilled work tasks into highly specified and complex ones, such as those of legal professionals (e.g., Susskind and Susskind, 2015), where the demand for "narrow, highly specialized skills" may be very high and sporadic but not necessarily continuous or permanent.

Platforms perform the aforementioned five features in different ways and grades but at least two aspects are common: the control of the work and its conditions move away from the worker's grasp, and the commodification of personal skills and personal possessions is key for working and earning a living on platforms. Controlling for the various aspects of work is taken over from workers by platforms. The monetization of personal ownership (house, car, bicycle), and personal skills is a prerequisite but does not necessarily accumulate into wealth, as these prerequisites are used only when there are buyers on the platform.

The Meaning of Digital and Platformed Work

The new forms of production are exemplified through the rising number of platforms and consumption as work, that is, working consumers (Cova et al., 2011)—e.g., through bloggers' and vbloggers' virtual and identity work—add post-consumeristic features to the digital economy. These working consumers are even considered sources of growth in stagnating economies, particularly in respect of industrial platforms and the renewal of traditional industries. However, these effects on work are not restricted to advanced economies only, nor to visible production mechanisms. At the global scale, the conjecture is that the effects of the digitally wired economy are likely to affect work and labor in developing countries much more, and more severely, than those in the developed countries (e.g., Giuntella and Wang, 2019; Casilli and Posada, 2019). The effects extend not only to the amount of work or number of jobs but, more profoundly, to the content of work, the creation of new jobs, and the disappearance of old forms of work and ways of working.

Platforms support a specific kind of individualization of work and work tasks. As brought up, individualization is one of the distinct features of platformization. The individualization of work tasks, loss of collectivity and social dimension at work, and detachment from the workspace have both cultural and political percussions, and in fact this may undermine our notion of the shared public sphere and the social basis for social solidarity more generally. Informal forms of work take place at platforms: unpaid work is increasingly performed in connection and intertwined with the paid employment, as is the case with aspirational work, identity work, and work performed but not billed, for example, to maintain one's own job security.

Individualization has many facets. One of these is the characteristics of "do-alone-meet-no-one" work, which typically covers on-screen work performed at platforms. Because individualization is so important as a distinctive feature of late modernity (e.g., Beck and Lau, 2005), platform work seems likely to reinforce already existing tendencies that require actors to submit to quantified measures that judge, evaluate, and rank them in relation to one another in publicly visible ways. It can even be argued that performance rating systems on platforms foster what can be called "virtual catwalks," involving digital presentations and traces of presentations, track-records and self-representations, all available on line. These are accentuated in the rating procedures that so crucially are part of the platform functions and "attention economy" writ large. We argue that the constant rating in platform work may require emotional and identity work that can be stressful, as it is not necessarily a question of the skills or capabilities but the abilities to put them on display.

Hochschild's (1983) concept of emotional labor conceptualizes the emotionally draining service work (originally, that of flight attendants). Here, the offer of various features is assumed to create positive responses from the receivers of the service or act, where the act of displaying appropriate emotions is called emotional labor. For Hochschild, this was first and foremost a question of personal encounters between service providers and clients, taking place as emotional labor for service provisioning. "Identity work," for its part, is viewed as an emotional process similar to emotional labor, but achieved when selling the skills of workers (Vallas, 2012).

The rise of knowledge-intensive work and technological innovations have coincided with the rise of individualization, and the growth of precarious work that has taken place since the 1970s (Kalleberg, 2009, 2011). It has been argued that the rise of *societal individualism* and *cultural individualization*, both visible in the jobs and careers of the new economy, increasingly in the public sector (e.g., Sennett, 2008), have shifted the focus to individual achievements at work, thus ignoring several other aspects in knowledge-intensive work, such as emotional labor and "otherness" (Irani, 2019) in the literature (Ocejo, 2017; Sennett, 1998). Both emotional labor and identity work are performed at platforms through rating and on webpages where skills and capabilities are exhibited. The ways in which these performative actions rest on the new managerial language that transforms work into tasks through managerial practices, such as "branded clothing," "supplier agreements," and "contract termination" (Rosenblat, 2018), calls for more ethnographic analyses of the depth of this transformation.

Platformization of Economy and Society

Over the past few years, descriptors involving the transformation of work and the economy—such as the platform economy and its global growth, the gig or "on-demand" economy, gig work, and "algorithmic governance"—have entered the economic and socio-political discussion, as well as scientific discourse on labor and economy (see, e.g., Susskind and Susskind, 2015; Sundararajan, 2016; Horton et al., 2017). Much of this discussion is geared towards technological development and digitality, including artificial intelligence (AI) and robotization as "raisons d'etre" for job losses (Brynjolfsson and McAfee, 2014). The thought that work will simply shift from people to machines rather than be "replaced" with new work is based on the problematic notion that work itself would somehow be a permanent entity and that the work, or rather parts of it, or even the workplace, can be taken for granted in perpetuity (e.g., Weil, 2014).

Recent research on the platform economy and its developments has not only shown this to not be the case, but also indicated that platform work comes in many forms and does not automatically lead to specific types of labor market positions or to dead-end jobs (e.g., Pajarinen et al., 2018). This seems to be especially true when the adoption of platforms is well connected to public sector activities, such as active labor market policies or platforms operated by the public sector for mediating work. It is indeed the complexity of education, training, skills, and competences vis-à-vis the work tasks at hand that require processual and contextual analyses. Hence, instead of addressing only job losses, labor displacement, and technology, the reconfiguration of jobs and work and the actual processes through which these become platform work are key. Like platforms themselves, platform work is also changeable and precarious, extending to new areas and also shaping previous work.

It is convincingly argued in the literature that the emergence of platforms, as an economic model and as the actual platform economy, is likely to reorganize work and employment (Kenney and Zysman, 2019; Vallas and Kovalainen, 2019; Kalleberg and Dunn, 2016), not only in prestigious start-ups ("unicorns") but also in traditional institutions in healthcare, education, universities, and public services (Poutanen and Kovalainen, 2019). The rationale for this stems not only from the economic power of platforms or the new consumption patterns of individuals. In addition, firms and governments can invoke platforms as symbols of innovation, modernity, and growth. The symbolic power of platforms can, however, mask complexities and contradictions that are not easily resolved. For example, by favoring platform growth via tax preferences, governments can incentivize practices (such as the evasion of social regulations) that undermine support for the welfare state (Zanoni, 2019; Gillespie, 2010). Likewise, high tech firms can generate highly misleading images of their actual activities, as when start-ups define themselves as creative, technology-intensive firms, even as they rely on the most mundane forms of work—e.g., mTurk's "human intelligence tasks"—that are hidden behind the scenes (Irani 2015). The point here is that our very symbols of "innovation" and modernity can serve to reproduce premodern social practices.

Platforms have at least three different "shapes" or effects that are of importance when thinking about the future forms of work. First, *platformization affects both private and public institutions and structures.* As one example, hospitals use regional and national digital platforms when announcing for short-term posts and gig jobs for nurses and medical staff. In a similar manner, professionals use, for example, occupation-specific platforms when searching for new posts and positions. These types of mediating roles can assume a relatively passive role, and the jobs mediated through these platforms may not have gig work features. However, at other times platforms can actively shape the labor market even for skilled positions, as when they encourage the outsourcing of work to independent contractors, or foster complex linkages among automated hiring systems in lieu of human-controlled intermediaries.

Second, *the rise of platforms can potentially change the business model and the contents of work tasks even in parts of the "traditional" economy that seem distant from the digital revolution.* Universities are an interesting example of this latter case. They increasingly use MOOCs in their curricula but control the outcome (exam and degree) themselves. Some universities are beginning to use student-centered apps as digital guides for students to use when deciding which courses or programs might benefit them. Health care service organizations are beginning to use mobile devices to track the performance of care-givers in their employ. And local governments are beginning to use platforms to generate a sense of public involvement in and support for policy directions. Though a rhetoric of democracy often surrounds such uses, the realities may be quite different.

Third, *platforms actively alter the role that trust plays in societal and economic transactions.* It is true that commercial apps have addressed the problem of "stranger trust," using reputation measurement systems to generate higher levels of comfort with the use of unknown drivers, hosts, and service providers. But we may thus ask if the reputational algorithms suffice here. Indeed, there is growing evidence that the generation of trust implicitly conforms to existing sociodemographic inequalities. Airbnb guests are known to rate apartments substantially lower when they are located within lower-status neighborhoods; women receive significantly fewer offers on freelancer websites than do men; and consumers are less likely to bid on products sold on eBay when the seller gives a minority-dominated address (Besbris et al. 2015).

In the Western world, the era of institutionalized collective bargaining has, for example, transformed the general understanding of how to think about work and rights and earnings in relation to work, but the present diversification of jobs, work, and tasks has led to a real-world situation where work and its benefits are no longer precise units to be bargained for collectively. Analogically, national employment policies are no longer distinguishably "national" due to globalization and digitalization. There is a stark difference from the employment policies developed and analyzed in the 1990s (e.g., Christiansen et al., 1999) and the employment policies and their analysis today (e.g., Card et al., 2017).

Overall, platforms change what we know as the traditional worker-employer relationship. The emergence of platform work also intensifies the discussions on the boundaries of employment positions and their nature. This contractual position is an important aspect in the redefinitions of employee versus dependent own-account worker vis-à-vis the "entrepreneurialism" in neoliberal market economies. In this volume, Kenney and Zysman (2019) take up the question on the variety of platforms and whether that variety should be reflected in job categories. They argue that a shift from the traditional employment analyses is needed for the analyses of income and relative shares of value to form a better viewpoint for considering the contemporary economy. As such, it is crucial to ask whether the relative shares of value are measurable in similar terms to those requesting work and those performing it in terms of stability of work or contractual continuity, for example.

As stated, at platforms, the work/employment status can be highly volatile and, indeed, from policy perspectives, this controversial employment status challenges the existing employment models, as pointed out earlier in this chapter and in empirical studies, such as those by Pesole et al. (2018) and Aloisi (2016). Irrespective of the types of platforms, work is taskified and the differences between self-employed, own-account workers and workers in paid employment become hyped, but eventually merge due to the dependency in task performance and the features listed previously. Work-related platforms mediate the abilities and capabilities of those offering their skills as responses to the supply of tasks and the defined job activities. The conduct of the work takes place independently of the platform and leads to the contracting of required skills between the provider and the buyer/supplier of tasks. Whether such a contract fulfills the requirements of an employment contract is under scrutiny from many nation-states' legal institutions.

When the means and ways of working are changing, it is apt to ask whether the classical theories of work are still relevant today. The increasing variety in the relationships between individuals who work and sell their work and the buyers of their work adds to the complexity of theorizing work. Still, several aspects have not lessened their value over time: one's moral worth and dignity still derives from one's (paid) labor (e.g., Slater, 1998; Gorz, 1982; Beck, 2000; Pugh, 2015) and the ways the cultural capital of the worker becomes transformed into monetized value (Bourdieu, 1984). The claims of decoupling work from the social standing or societal value of an individual (Gorz, 1982) did resonate with Fordism, but the transition from manufacturing to service or "non-material" industries, among others, complicated long-standing debates over deskilling and labor control. The labor process discussions of the 1990s increasingly brought up globalization and outsourcing and off-shoring as examples of the effects of globalization (see, e.g., Leonardi and Bailey, 2017), sense-making (Weick, 1995), blurring of boundaries of work/non-work times, but were often silent about the transformation of large scale shifts affecting the distribution of work in both time and space (e.g., Barley et al., 2017).

Analyses of "non-standard forms of work and employment" (e.g., Kalleberg, 2016; Standing, 2010) have focused on important aspects of precarity and the precariousness of work for a relatively long time. Apart from "casualization" (Standing, 2010), seen as a salient part of twenty-first-century neoliberalism, the experiences and documentation of insecurity and precarity are worldwide and highly visible in the contemporary research on work (Smith, 2016; Wood et al., 2019). The multidimensionality of platform work, which ranges from casualization to the co-operativist style of community-oriented platforms and regulated markets, makes it difficult, however, to explain the transformation of platforms under one framework.

In the wake of the technological boost, the cultural aspects of understanding work emerged in new ways. The discussion on the new capitalism (e.g., Sennett, 2008), intensity of market and marketization, variety of socio-cultural approaches to work, and new cleavages such as exclusions, unemployment, and entrepreneurial selves at work and relations between consumption and work became the new fields of interest. These new fields of interest merge into transformations such as the growth of the gig economy, short-termism, and entrepreneurial self and platform economies, which have drastically changed the ways new and old jobs are arranged and organized (e.g., Poutanen and Kovalainen, 2020; Vallas and Kovalainen, 2019). Kalleberg and Dunn (2016) have argued that the jobs in the gig economy differ from what we traditionally have thought of as "good jobs." They do so because of the change in the logic of how economies function. Crowd-based innovations are one example: as argued by Powell (2017), Craigslist and other related services have abolished classified advertisements as a source of revenue for newspapers. The eBay and Amazon have for their part altered the retail business model, etc.

Much of the research underlining technological development as the key element in societal and economic changes (e.g., Brynjolfsson and McAfee, 2017) often relates the changes in the working life to what is called the *technological regime* that imposes changes due to technological rationality. The emphasis on institutions, in that the technological changes are adopted due to *institutional regimes* (e.g., Baldwin, 2016) whereby changes are imposed by national ecosystems and policies due to the global competition rationality, takes a different view on the technological imperative. The research addressing the rapid and highly unpredictable consequences of technological changes seldom considers the political economy or cultural perspectives. Rather, as pointed out by Codagnone et al. (2019), technological regime research often relies on platforms' own data and ignores workers' experiences. By including in the analyses such people as gig workers, riders, MTurkers, and others (Irani, 2015; Scholz, 2016; Schor, 2017; Srnicek, 2016), the research on work has re-addressed the agencies of economic change.

Platform Regulation and Regulative Measures

The mobile platform development means that the legal structures and protection legislation are also under scrutiny (De Stefano, 2018; Prassl, 2018; Lehdonvirta, 2016). It is clear that "control," as a classical means for distinguishing types of work, is a legally and organizationally vital feature of platform work, despite the platform not being an employer. Still, using control as a distinguishing marker for work/non-work makes the classifications markedly important, not only because the algorithms represent a new control mechanism, but also because platforms are introducing other, more powerful surveillance tools that relate to the panopticon disposition enabled by technologies and the built-in asymmetries that blur the "visuals" of workers in relation to their choices and possibilities at platforms.

Platforms are not transparent but create constraints to workers due to information asymmetries. Here, Uber and food-delivery platforms provide examples of the "fog" of workers (e.g., Codagnone et al., 2019; Rosenblat, 2018; Rosenblat and Stark, 2016), which for the platform is instead a panopticon situation. Further, new forms of surveillance to monitor and regulate workers have been introduced through platform work. Wearable gadgets, programs that register online and offline activity during the working day, GPS tracking, screenshots, and keystroke monitoring are examples of control mechanisms also increasingly used in ordinary work outside platforms and in recruitment (Greene and Ajunwa, 2019; De Stefano, 2018; Veen et al., 2019). With new technology, new forms of discrimination become possible.

The employment relationship is based on the three main prerogatives. First, there exists the power to assign work tasks and orders in relation to these tasks and directives to employees. Second, in relation to the first prerogative, there exists the power to monitor both the performance and compliance with these orders. Third, in relation to the previous two prerogatives, there exists the power to sanction improper performance or any disobedience (e.g., ILO, 2010). Of these three key elements, managerial and direction power are present in most platform work, as are supervision and control power. Additionally, the coordination of work with the platform, which relates to the supervision power of an employer, is high and at least episodic, if not constant, in most platform work. All these criteria are traditionally seen as related to employment status, not to self-employment status. The increasing use of independent or dependent contractors at platforms creates an odd contracting situation, where so-called worker surveillance mechanisms (wearable technologies, on-screen shots, etc.) are spreading to the surveillance of allegedly independent contractors and produce data for the platforms. Zuboff (2018) calls this surveillance capitalism, where surveillance is not a technology but a logic that imbues technology and "commands it into action" (Zuboff, 2018, p. 14). Surveillance is thus no longer digital but a logic in action.

Conclusion: Which Direction for the Platform Economy?

Platforms are changing individuals' ways of earning money and placing private property and personal resources at the center of earnings—we talk about the "monetizing" of property or, in more vernacular terms, "making money" using own one's car or house for transportation or lodging, respectively. The larger picture shows that the patterns individuals face reflect the trends in the labor markets. The labor market policies in most countries have been deregulatory (e.g., Thelen, 2014) since the 1990s and in the United States since the 1970s, although the pressures are currently channeled in differing ways. The pressures refer to, for instance, cost pressures of employers being shifted to employees though lower employee protection. Related to protection is also the degree of overtime activities as part of control and regulation mechanisms.

The concentration/dispersion and profit making of the digital economy are the factors that differentiate the operating methods of the digital economy, but not the sole criteria for classifying work. The term "sharing economy" is most often linked to predominantly positive perceptions, and it can, at its best, become a locally functional, trust-based network of equals that increases a community's cohesion. However, it can just as easily enable renting, selling, and profit-seeking. The timeliness of the phenomenon is also the reason research has presented the transportation platform Uber, hospitality platform Airbnb, and freelancing platform for professionals Upwork as fresh forms of the sharing economy, challenging the old-fashioned corporatist operating logic (e.g., Dula and Kuo Chuen, 2018). Each one of the aforementioned globally operating platform economy companies has become the object of serious questions about their earnings logic and ethics in relation to, for example, the rights and possibilities of those working on the platforms (e.g., Prassl, 2018) or the rise in cities' general costs of living and rents (Wachsmuth et al., 2018).

The platform economy generally refers to an online marketplace of digitally organized work, tasks, skills, goods, and services, whether as an individual business or a business cluster. The platform can function locally or globally and can be open or closed. Platforms' significance and positions within the operations of different companies vary. The core business of a platform economy company can consist of a reliable and sufficiently interesting pairing of sellers and buyers of goods and services (Etsy, Amazon, BlaBlaCars, Tinder). The platform economy is varying: it can consist of both the use of platforms in the organization of public sector infrastructure and of the value that platforms can create for traditional business operations. Examples of the traditional creation of value and its expansion include platform companies (ridesharing and ride-hailing services) bought by the automobile industry (Daimler, BMW). Digitalization has brought the traditional automobile industry face-to-face with the need not only to reorganize its own industrial production, but also to control the new "mobility markets" created and produced by the platform economy, such as mobility sharing, transportation services, and forms by which to share transportation. In the same proactive manner, public sector development produces platform-like solutions for working. However, the nature of the employment relationship is not dependent on the nature of the platform work.

The positions that national platforms, and particularly platforms tied to a language or local services, have in the consumer sector are indirectly dependent on the popularity and use of that platform among consumers. The permanence and popularity of platforms are globally significant, and market control is presumably the goal of all platform businesses. Given that the nature of a platform is to be omnipotent—due to which it is not bound to the sale of only one or a single type of product or service—the platform is free to expand and increase the range of its operations in a variety of ways; consequentially, when successful, the platform business tends to change the structure and future of any industry and to quickly introduce technology into traditional industry sectors, changing their work arrangements.

On platforms, digitality creates the basis for the new operations and work, while global or local competition and legislation are the preconditions for operations. This is why the platform economy also transforms and changes. Therefore, platform work does not lend itself easily to "old" classifications of good or bad jobs. Most classifications on the nature of platforms and platform work, as well as the changes in work, require revising (Kalleberg, 2011). Platform work can be online work carried out digitally (examples include Amazon's Mechanical Turk), or offline work for which performance is achieved competitively, such as work requiring specific expertise, that is carried out online (e.g., design work carried out on the Upwork platform). There is also platform work, mostly offline in one's own time or in the form of physical labor (care, cleaning, transportation, or messenger work managed and supervised with the help of an app). The nature of the latter work's content does not change much even if managerial and supervisory duties transfer under digital management.

An examination and analysis of platform work without defining the platform in question is problematic because the nature of platform work and tasks and the way in which these are carried out are dependent on at least one of the following: the nature of the platform, qualification and skill requirements, and nature of the work performances bought through the platform. Including solely the platform in the analysis of work is thus not enough, given that platform work is, in addition to the platform, dependent on the types of skills and work offers the platform monetizes. The monetizing of messenger work does not necessarily take place on the same platform that monetizes skills in writing algorithms or artistic design. Hence, rather than developing theories on "the" implications of platform work, we need to capture the growing heterogeneity of work and employment in the wake of the platform revolution. The question then becomes, how can we explain the sources of the variations platforms impose on individuals, work, and employment relations? Further, what is the role of the regulatory institutions, professional associations, educational structures, and trade unions?

Platform companies and companies that offer platform-mediated work create different ways of working. Platform companies are built on platform creation and maintenance, which is defined as either venture or contractual labor. Platform-mediated work, on the other hand, may be contractual, independent, performance-based, or continuous labor. Kenney and Zysman (2019) further separate the aforementioned platform-mediated content production, which is typically, for instance, entertainment industry work but does not fulfill the hallmarks of an employment or independent contractual relationship. The classification of a work performance's degree of digitality allows us to examine that work's independence and nature of its digitality. However, it is perhaps even more important to look beyond the degree of digitality and search for features common in platform work and the degrees of variety of the five features previously outlined in this chapter.

The rate at which new technology develops and changes is not, by itself, sufficient for the prediction of how technology for different tasks, on one hand, and the labor market, on the other, will develop in the future (e.g., Bessen, 2018). Thelen (2014, 2018) suggests these social choices that societies "make" are largely dependent on the institutional landscape in which platforms are introduced. However, as platforms are evolving, so are their workers, with cooperative platforms, for example, which might provide an influential model for public service provision in many countries, and with resistance movements such as the #slaveroo movement, and legal cases for judicial decisions both in the United States and Europe. When theorizing platform work, needed are in-depth analyses of the mobilization of stakeholders, the regulatory frameworks each proposes, and the rhetoric each uses to form coalitions on their own behalf. These dynamics, after all, are likely to shape the nature of the platform economy in the generations to come.

Note

1 Digitalization, which has enabled the development of platforms, changes not only the contents of almost all work but also the way work gets done. Indeed, the boundaries between work and non-work have become malleable and are redrawn in everyday life and work practices. The market relations subsume many of those unpaid activities that are not considered work, and leave many activities that would entitle those compensations usually connected to work outside the definition of work. Even by narrowing down the definition of work to those activities that are market related and paid, it is crucial to recognize work is not merely a function of specific activities but includes non-market activities and labor reproduction.

References

Acemoglu, D. and Autor, D. (2010). Skills, Tasks and Technologies: Implications for Employment and Earnings. *NBER Working Paper 16082*. Cambridge, MA: National Bureau of Economic Research. Available at: www.nber.org/papers/w16082 [Accessed 27 March 2019].

Acemoglu, D. and Restrepo, P. (2017). Robots and Jobs: Evidence from US Labor Markets. *NBER Working Paper No. 23285*. Cambridge, MA: National Bureau of Economic Research. Available at: www.nber.org/papers/w23285 [Accessed 27 March 2019].

Adler, P. S. (1992). *Technology and the Future of Work*. Oxford: University Press on Demand.

Ajunwa, I., Crawford, K. and Schultz, J. (2017). Limitless Worker Surveillance. *California Law Review*, 105, pp. 735. Available at: https://ssrn.com/abstract=2746211. [Accessed 15 April 2019].

Aloisi, A. (2016). Commoditized Workers: Case Study Research on Labor Law Issues Arising from a Set of "On-Demand/Gig Economy" Platforms. *Comparative Labor Law and Policy Journal*, 37(3), pp. 620–653.

Baldwin, R. (2016). *The Great Convergence: Information Technology and the New Globalization*. Cambridge, MA: Harvard University Press.

Barley, S. R., Bechky, B. A. and Milliken, F. J. (2017). The Changing Nature of Work: Careers, Identities and Work-Lives of the 21st Century. *Academy of Management Discoveries*, 3(2), pp. 111–115.

Barley, S. R. and Kunda, G. (2001). Bringing Work Back In. *Organization Science*, 12, pp. 75–94.

Beck, U. (2000). *Brave New Work of Work*. Cambridge: Polity.

Beck, U. and Lau, C. (2005). Second Modernity as a Research Agenda: Theoretical and Empirical Explorations in the "Meta-Change" of Modern Society. *British Journal of Sociology*, 56(4), pp. 525–557.

Besbris, M., Faber, J. W., Rich, P., and Sharkey, P. (2015). Effect of neighborhood stigma on economic transactions. *Proceedings of the National Academy of*

Sciences, 112(16), pp. 4994–4998; first published April 6, 2015 https://doi.org/10.1073/pnas.1414139112.

Bessen, J. (2018). *AI and Jobs: The Role of Demand. NBER Working Paper Series 24235.* Available at: www.nber.org/papers/w24235 [Accessed 26 March 2019].

Beynon, H. (2016). Beyond Fordism. In: S. Edgell, H. Gottfried and E. Granter, eds., *The Sage Handbook of Work and Employment.* Los Angeles, London, New Delhi, Singapore, and Washington, DC: Sage Publications, pp. 306–328.

Bourdieu, P. (1984). *Distinction: A Social Critique of the Judgement of Taste.* Translation R. Nice. London: Routledge and Kegan Paul.

Braverman, H. (1974). *Labor and Monopoly Capital: The Degradation of Work in the Twentieth Century.* New York: Monthly Review Press.

Bruns, A. (2007). Produsage: Towards a Broader Framework for User-Led Content Creation. In *Proceedings Creativity & Cognition.* Washington, DC. Available at: http://eprints.qut.edu.au/6623/1/6623.pdf [Accessed 15 April 2019].

Brynjolfsson, E. and McAfee, A. (2014). *The Second Machine Age: Work, Progress, and Prosperity in a Time of Brilliant Technologies.* New York: W. W. Norton & Company, Inc.

Brynjolfsson, E. and McAfee, A. (2015). Will Humans Go the Way of Horses. *Foreign Affairs*, 94(4), pp. 8–14.

Brynjolfsson, E. and McAfee, A. (2017). *Machine, Platform, Crowd: Harnessing Our Digital Future.* New York and London: W. W. Norton & Company, Inc.

Card, D., Kluve, J. and Weber, A. (2017). What Works? A Meta Analysis of Recent Active Labor Market Program Evaluations. *Journal of the European Economic Association*, 16(3), pp. 894–931.

Casilli, A. and Posada, J. (2019). The Platformization of Labor and Society. In: M. Graham and W. H. Dutton, eds., *How Networks of Information and Communication Are Changing Our Lives (2nd edition).* Oxford: Oxford University Press, pp. 293–306.

Christiansen, J., Koistinen, P. and Kovalainen, A. (1999). Introduction. In: J. Christiansen, P. Koistinen and A. Kovalainen, eds., *Working Europe: Reshaping European Employment Systems.* Aldershot, Brookfield, Singapore, and Sydney: Ashgate, pp. 3–15.

Codagnone, C., Karatzogianne, A. and Matthews, J. (2019). *Platform Economics: Rhetoric and Reality in the "Sharing Economy."* Bingley, UK: Emerald Publications Ltd.

Cova, B., Dalli, D. and Zwick, D. (2011). Critical Perspectives on Consumers' Role as "Producers": Broadening the Debate on Value Co-Creation in Marketing Processes. *Marketing Theory*, 11(3), pp. 231–241.

Davis, G. F. (2016). *The Vanishing American Corporation: Navigating the Hazards of a New Economy.* Oakland, CA: Berrett-Koehler Publishers.

De Stefano, V. (2018). *"Negotiating the Algorithm": Automation, Artificial Intelligence and Labour Protection.* Geneva: International Labour Office.

Di Tomaso, N. (2001). The Loose Coupling of Jobs: The Subcontracting of Everyone? In: I. Berg and A. L. Kalleberg, eds., *Sourcebook of Labor Markets: Evolving Structures and Processes.* New York: Kluwer Academic/Plenum Publishers, pp. 247–70.

Duffy, B. E. (2016). The Romance of Work: Gender and Aspirational Labour in the Digital Culture Industries. *International Journal of Cultural Studies*, 19(4), pp. 441–457.

Dula, C. and Kuo Chuen, D. L. (2018). Reshaping the Financial Order. In: D. L. Kuo Chuen and R. Deng, eds., *Handbook of Blockchain, Digital Finance, and Inclusion, Vol. 1: Cryptocurrency, FinTech, InsurTech, and Regulation*. Elsevier Inc., pp. 1–18. https://doi.org/10.1016/C2015-0-04334-9.

EC. (2019). *The Impact of the Digital Transformation on EU Labor Markets: Report of the High-Level Expert Group*. Brussels: European Commission.

Evans, P. and C. Tilly. (2016). The Future of Work: Escaping the Current Dystopian Trajectory and Building Better Alternatives. In: S. Edgell, H. Gottfried and E. Granter, eds., *The Sage Handbook of Work and Employment*. London: Sage Publications, pp. 651–671.

Frey, C. B. and Osborne, M. A. (2013). *The Future of Employment: How Susceptible Are Jobs to Computerisation? Working Papers*, Oxford University.

Gerber, C. and Krzywdzinski, M. (2019). Brave New Digital Work? New Forms of Performance Control in Crowdwork. In: S. P. Vallas and A. Kovalainen, eds., *Work and Labor in the Digital Age (Research in the Sociology of Work, Vol. 33)*, London: Emerald Publishing Limited, pp. 121–143.

Gillespie, T. (2010). The Politics of Platforms. *New Media & Society*, 12(3), pp. 347–364.

Giuntella, O. and Wang, T. (2019). *Is an Army of Robots Marching on Chinese Jobs?* IZA Institute of Labor Economics. IZA DP 12281.

Gorz, A. (1982). *Farewell to the Working Class: An Essay on Post-Industrial Socialism*. London: Pluto.

Gottfried, H. (2013). *Gender, Work, and Economy: Unpacking the Global Economy*. Cambridge, UK: Polity Press.

Gray, M. L., Suri, S., Ali, S. S. and Kulkarni, D., (2016). The Crowd Is a Collaborative Network. *In Proceedings of the 19th ACM Conference on Computer-Supported Cooperative Work & Social Computing*, pp. 134–147, ACM.

Greene, D. and Ajunwa, I. (2019). Platforms at Work: Automated Hiring Platforms and Other New Intermediaries in the Organization of Work. In: S. P. Vallas and A. Kovalainen, eds., *Work and Labor in the Digital Age (Research in the Sociology of Work, Vol. 33)*, London: Emerald Publishing Limited, pp. 50–65. Available at: https://doi.org/10.1108/S0277-283320190000033005 [Accessed 13 August 2019].

Harrison, B. (1994). *Lean and Mean: The Changing Landscape of Corporate Power in the Age of Flexibility*. New York: Basic Books.

Head, S. (2005). *The New Ruthless Economy: Work & Power in the Digital Age*. Oxford: Oxford University Press.

Hochschild, A. (1983). *The Managed Heart: Commercialization of Human Feeling*. Berkeley, CA: University of California Press.

Horton, J., Kerr, W. R. and Stanton, C. (2017). Digital Labor Markets and Global Talent Flows. *NBER Working Paper Series 23398*. Available at: www.nber.org/papers/w23398 [Accessed 11 May 2018].

Howcroft, D. and Bergvall-Kåreborn, B. (2019). A Typology of Crowdwork Platforms. *Work, Employment and Society*, 33(1), pp. 21–38.

Irani, L. (2015). Difference and Dependence Among Digital Workers: The Case of Amazon Mechanical Turk. *South Atlantic Quarterly*, 114(1), pp. 225–234.

Irani, L. (2019). *Chasing Innovation: Making Entrepreneurial Citizens in Modern India*. Princeton, NJ: Princeton University Press.

Jacobs, J. A. and Karen, R. (2019). Technology-Driven Task Replacement and the Future of Employment. In: S. P. Vallas and A. Kovalainen, eds., *Work and Labour in the Digital Age. (Research in the Sociology of Work, Vol. 33)*. London: Emerald Publishing Ltd, pp. 43–60. Available at: https://doi.org/10.1108/S0277-283320190000033004. [Accessed 15 August 2019].

Kalleberg, A. L. (2009). Precarious Work, Insecure Workers: Employment Relations in Transition. *American Sociological Review*, 74(1), pp. 1–22.

Kalleberg, A. L. (2011). *Good Jobs, Bad Jobs: The Rise of the Polarized and Precarious Employment Systems in the United States 1970s to 2000s*. New York: Russell Sage.

Kalleberg, A. L. (2016). Good Jobs, Bad Jobs. In: S. Edgell, H. Gottfried and E. Granter, eds., *The Sage Handbook of the Sociology of Work and Employment*. Thousand Oaks, CA: Sage Publications, pp. 111–128.

Kalleberg, A. L. (2018). *Precarious Lives: Job Insecurity and Well-Being in Rich Democracies*. Cambridge, UK: Polity Press.

Kalleberg, A. L. and Dunn, M. (2016). Good Jobs, Bad Jobs in the Gig Economy. *Perspectives on Work*, 20(1), pp. 10–14.

Kalleberg, A. L. and Vallas, S. P. (2017). Probing Precarious Work: Theory, Research, and Politics. In: A. L. Kalleberg and S. P. Vallas, eds., *Precarious Work. Book Series: Research in the Sociology of Work*. Bingley, UK: Emerald Publishing, pp. 1–30.

Kelkar, S. (2018). Engineering a Platform: The Construction of Interfaces, Users, Organizational Roles, and the Division of Labor. *New Media & Society*, 20(7), pp. 2629–2646.

Kenney, M. and Zysman, J. (2016). The Rise of the Platform Economy. *Issues in Science and Technology*, 32(3), p. 61.

Kenney, M. and Zysman, J. (2019). Work and Value Creation in the Platform Economy. In: S. P. Vallas and A. Kovalainen, eds., *Work and Labour in the Digital Age (Research in the Sociology of Work, Vol. 33)*. London: Emerald Publishing Ltd, pp. 13–41. Available at: https://doi.org/10.1108/S0277-283320190000033003 [Accessed 16 August 2019].

Kucklich, J. (2005). Precarious Playbour. *Fibreculture Journal, 5*. Available at: http://journal.fibreculture.org/issue5/kucklich_print.html [Accessed 10 January 2019].

Kuek, S. C., Paradi-Guilford, C., Fayomi, T., Imaizumi, S., Ipeirotis, P., Pina, P. and Singh, M. (2015). *The Global Opportunity in Outline Sourcing*. Washington, DC: The World Bank.

Lehdonvirta, V. (2016). Algorithms That Divide and Unit: Delocalisation, Identity and Collective Action in Microwork. In: J. Flecker, ed., *Space, Place and Global Digital Work*. London: Palgrave Macmillan, pp. 53–80.

Leonardi, P. M. and Bailey, D. E. (2017). Recognising and Selling Good Ideas: Network Articulation and the Making of Offshore Innovation Hub. *Academy of Management Discoveries*, 3(2). https://doi.org/10.5465/amd.2015.0151.

Manriquez, M. (2019), Work-Games in the Gig-Economy: A Case Study of Uber Drivers in the City of Monterrey, Mexico. In: S. P. Vallas and A. Kovalainen, eds., *Work and Labor in the Digital Age (Research in the Sociology of*

Work, Vol. 33). London: Emerald Publishing Limited, pp. 165–188. Available at: https://doi.org/10.1108/S0277-283320190000033010 [Accessed 16 August 2019].

Neff, G. (2012). *Venture Labor: Work and the Burden of Risk in Innovative Industries*. Cambridge, MA: MIT Press (Acting with technology).

Ocejo, R. E. (2017). *Masters of Craft: Old Jobs in the New Urban Economy*. Princeton and Oxford: Princeton University Press.

OECD. (2006). *Getting Skills Right: Assessing and Anticipating Changing Skill Needs?* Paris: OECD.

Pajarinen, M., Rouvinen, P., Claussen, J., Hakanen, J., Kovalainen, A., Kretschmer, T., Poutanen, S., Seifried, M. and Seppänen, L. (2018). *Upworkers in Finland: Survey Results*. Helsinki, Finland: ETLA Reports 85.

Pesole, A., Urzí Brancati, M. C., Fernández-Macías, E., Biagi, F. and González Vázquez, I. (2018). *Platform Workers in Europe: Evidence from COLLEEM Survey: JRC Reports*. Luxembourg: European Commission.

Poutanen, S. and Kovalainen, A. (2017). *Gender and Innovation in the New Economy—Women, Identity, and Creative Work*. New York: Palgrave Macmillan.

Poutanen, S. and Kovalainen, A. (2019). Gig Science Marches Onward. *Discover Society* DS 68. Available at: https://discoversociety.org/2019/05/01/gig-science-marches-onward/ [Accessed 12 February 2019].

Poutanen, S. and Kovalainen, A. (2020). *Skills, Creativity and Innovation in the Digital Platform Era: Analyzing the New Reality of Professions and Entrepreneurship*. London and New York: Routledge.

Powell, W. W. (2017). A Sociologist Looks at Crowds: Innovation or Invention? *Strategic Organization*, 15(2), pp. 289–297.

Prassl, J. (2018). *Humans as a Service: Promise and Perils of Work in the Gig Economy*. Oxford: Oxford University Press.

Pugh, A. J. (2015). *The Tumbleweed Society*. Oxford: The Oxford University Press.

Rochet, J-C. and Tirole, J. (2003). Platform Competition in Two-Sided Markets. *Journal of the European Economic Association*, 1(4), pp. 990–1029.

Rosenblat, A. (2018). *Uberland: How Algorithms Are Rewriting the Rule of Work*. Oakland, CA: University of California Press.

Rosenblat, A. and Stark, L. (2016). Algorithmic Labor and Information Asymmetries: A Case Study of Uber's Drivers. *International Journal of Communication*, 10, p. 27.

Scholz, T. (2016). *Uberworked and Underpaid: How Workers Are Disrupting the Digital Economy*. Cambridge, UK: Polity Press.

Schor, J. (2017). Does the Sharing Economy Increase Inequality Within the Eighty Percent? Findings From a Qualitative Study of Platform Providers. *Cambridge Journal of Regions, Economy and Society*, 10, pp. 263–279.

Schor, J. and Attwood-Charles, W. (2017). The "Sharing" Economy: Labor, Inequality, and Social Connection on For-Profit Platforms. *Sociology Compass*, 11(8), p. e12493.

Sennett, R. (1998). *The Corrosion of Character: The Personal Consequences of Work in the New Capitalism*. New York: W. W. Norton & Company, Inc.

Sennett, R. (2008). *The Craftsman*. Yale and London: Yale University Press and Allen Lane.

Slater, D. (1998). *Work/Leisure*. In: C. Jenks, ed., *Core Sociological Dichotomies*. London, Thousand Oaks, and New Delhi: Sage Publications, pp. 391–404.

Smith, V. (2016). Employment Uncertainty and Risk. In: S. Edgell, H. Gottfried and E. Granter, eds., *The SAGE Handbook of the Sociology of Work and Employment*. Los Angeles, London, New Delhi, Singapore, and Washington, DC: Sage Publications, pp. 367–384.

Srnicek, N. (2016). *Platform Capitalism*. Cambridge, UK: Polity Press.

Standing, G. (2010). The International Labour Organization. *New Political Economy*, 15(2), pp. 307–318.

Sundararajan, A. (2016). *The Sharing Economy: The Endo of Employment and the Rise of Crowd-Based Capitalism*. Cambridge, MA: MIT Press.

Susskind, R. and Susskind, D. (2015). *The Future of the Professions: How Technology Will Transform the Work of Human Experts*. Oxford: Oxford University Press.

Thelen, K. (2014). *Varieties of Liberalization and the New Politics of Social Solidarity*. Cambrigde: Cambridge University Press.

Thelen, K. (2018). Regulating Uber: The Politics of the Platform Economy in Europe and the United States. *Perspectives on Politics*, 16(4), pp. 938–953.

Ticona, J. and Mateescu, A. (2018). Trusted Strangers: Carework Platforms' Cultural Entrepreneurship in the On-Demand Economy. *New Media & Society*, 20(11), pp. 4384–4404.

van Dijck, J., Poell, T. and de Vaal, M. (2018). *The Platform Society*. Oxford: Oxford University Press.

Vallas, S. P. (2012). *Work: A Critique*. London and Malden, MA: Polity Press.

Vallas, S. P. (2019). Platform Capitalism: What's at Stake for Workers? *New Labor Forum*, 28(1), pp. 48–59.

Vallas, S. P. and Cummins, E. R. (2015). Personal Branding and Identity Norms in the Popular Business Press: Enterprise Culture in an Age of Precarity. *Organization Studies*, 36(3), pp. 293–319.

Vallas, S. P. and Kovalainen, A. (2019). Introduction Taking Stock of the Digital Revolution. In: S. Vallas and A. Kovalainen, eds., *Work and Labor in the Digital Age (Research in the Sociology of Work. Vol. 33)*. London: Emerald Publishing, pp. 1–12. Available at: https://doi.org/10.1108/S0277-283320190000033001 [Accessed 17 August 2019].

Vallas, S. P. and Schor, J. B. (2020). What Do Platforms Do? Understanding the Gig Economy. *Annual Review of Sociology*, 46.

Veen, A., Barratt, T. and Goods, C. (2019). Platform-Capital's "Appetite" for Control: A Labour Process Analysis of Food-Delivery Work in Australia. *Work, Employment and Society*, pp. 1–19. doi: 10.1177/0950017019836911.

Wachsmuth, D., Chaney, D., Kerrigan, D., Shillolo, A. and Basalaev-Binder, R. (2018). *The High Cost of Short-Term Rentals in New York City*. New York: McGill University.

Weick, K. E. (1995). *Sensemaking in Organizations*. New York: Sage Publications.

Weil, D. (2014). *The Fissured Workplace*. Cambridge, MA: Harvard University Press.

Wood, A. J., Graham, M., Lehdonvirta, V. and Hjorth, I. (2019). Good Gig, Bad Gig: Autonomy and Algorithmic Control in the Global Gig Economy. *Work, Employment and Society*, 33(1), pp. 56–75.

Zanoni, P. (2019). Labor Market Inclusion Through Predatory Capitalism? The "Sharing Economy," Diversity, and the Crisis of Social Reproduction in the Belgian Coordinated Market Economy. In: S. P. Vallas and A. Kovalainen, eds., *Work and Labor in the Digital Age (Research in the Sociology of Work, Vol. 33)*, London: Emerald Publishing Limited, pp. 145–164. Available at: https://doi.org/10.1108/S0277-283320190000033009 [Accessed 17 August 2019].

Zuboff, S. (2018). *The Age of Surveillance Capitalism: The Fight for a Human Future at the New Frontier of Power*. New York: Profile.

3 Workers' Health, Wellbeing, and Safety in the Digitalizing Platform Economy

Annina Ropponen, Jari J. Hakanen, Mervi Hasu, and Laura Seppänen

Introduction—Workers in Focus

This chapter builds on the assumption that platform work involves an individual who performs tasks (i.e., is a worker) in task-driven circumstances (i.e., working conditions) and that the interplay between worker and environment has effects on the individual's health, safety, and wellbeing. Altogether, these three aspects are influenced by laws and regulations, but they may also differ in various societies. We follow Eurofound's (2018) definition of platform work: it is a form of employment that uses an online platform to enable organizations or individuals to access other organizations or individuals to solve problems or to provide services in exchange for payment. Thus, in this chapter, the focus is not on other aspects of new forms of work (e.g., effects of digitalization itself on salaried work or various types of unpaid crowdwork) but rather on the work characteristics of platform work and their potential effects on the health, safety, and wellbeing of those individuals working in platforms. Platform work is varied and consists of online work, in which tasks are carried out completely via the internet, and on-demand work, which offers and assigns local work activities (e.g., graphic design) through digital platforms. The tasks in both types of work can be either routine or sophisticated, requiring expertise (see Chapter 9 by Seppänen and Poutanen in this book). Another aspect influencing platform work characteristics and the wellbeing and health of platform workers is the fact that an individual may have a main job or other employment type along with platform work (Berg et al., 2018). Those who undertake work at platforms can be distinguished roughly based on three sets of characteristics (Pesole et al., 2018). Platform workers in one group perform their work for motivational rewards such as attractive pay, interesting work, and a means of income. The motivations of the second group of platform workers are related to flexibility and autonomy. See Pichault and McKeown (2019) for an analytical approach to autonomy in platform work. The platform workers in the third group are those who have difficulty finding standard work, prefer part-time work, or have health issues.

We utilize the job demands–resources (JD-R) model as a conceptual framework (Demerouti et al., 2001; Schaufeli and Taris, 2014). Until now, working conditions that characterize different tasks in platform work and influence wellbeing, motivation, health, and safety have been rarely investigated. Instead, more is known about what drives people to undertake "gig" work or assignment in platforms (e.g., additional income, flexible work hours) than what drives their engagement when they are working in platforms. Hence, in this chapter, the theoretical framework of the JD-R model helps us to understand and capture the essential work characteristics of platform work. We describe the effects of platforms on work, demands, and resources in platform work, and their associations with platform workers' wellbeing, health, and safety.

Work Change Due to the Digitalizing Platform Economy

Work change is evident from the economic indicators for the online gig economy developed to track online labor projects (Kässi and Lehdonvirta, 2016). This Online Labour Index shows that the highest demand for labor is skilled work, including software development, technology, and creative and multimedia tasks. Another example, from a recent report by Eurofound, introduced three vectors of change of work—automation, digitalization of processes, and coordination by platforms—that lead to a transformation of work and employment (Fernández-Macías, 2018). For tasks and occupations, technological advances mean that the distribution of tasks and occupational structure change. In practice, each new technology alters some process(es) and therefore, changes associated tasks. Technology (i.e., digitalization) may alter conditions of work, as it may change requirements and physical, psychological, and environmental working conditions. For conditions of employment, issues related to contracts and social contract of the work (stability, opportunities for development, and pay) are affected directly and indirectly by technology. For industrial relations, the current way of collaborating between workers and employers will change in many ways, although the effects of technology are usually indirect and indeterminate (Fernández-Macías, 2018).

According to Eurofound (Mandl and Biletta, 2018), platform work includes several features: the organization of paid work through online platforms; the involvement of three parties (online platform, client, and worker); the use of platforms to conduct specific tasks or solve specific problems; the operation of platforms as a form of outsourcing/contracting out; breaking work down into tasks; and providing services on an on-demand basis. This means that a large variation of tasks can be performed through platforms in a variety of sectors and types of services. For workers, this means increasing heterogeneity in platform work (Kässi and Lehdonvirta, 2016). The fact is that the level of pay in platforms is in general low and insecure—although higher prices are available for larger tasks, for services delivered offline, or for tasks with higher skills requirements (Mandl and Biletta, 2018). Nonetheless, platform workers resemble self-employed workers and freelancers. Therefore, one of the effects of digitalizing platform work has been changes in employment (Schaible et al., 2017). Those with higher education and in skilled occupations now have access to work globally, but work has also become more temporary and compartmentalized. In other words, workers are involved in the digital economy at any time from any place. This means that migration involves not the physical movement of humans anymore, but rather virtual labor migration. In virtual labor migration, work crosses national borders through online capital, labor, and information transfers.

Platform work leads to diversity of work content and work arrangements. One of the potential benefits of platform work is that it can include socially marginalized groups, including the unemployed, geographically isolated, and refugees (Johnston and Land-Kazlauskas, 2018; De Stefano, 2016). Platform work could be an opportunity for disabled workers as well as those with time constraints, that is, individuals with health problems or care responsibilities for whom the increased control over when and how much they work is an important precondition for work (Berg et al., 2018). On the other hand, in many tasks in the platform economy, the structure of work can include aspects that have negative influence on workers, such as unpredictability of schedules, inconsistent or irregular earnings, unreliable long-term employment prospects, isolation in cases in which work is undertaken at home via computers, and limited opportunities for career development (Johnston and Land-Kazlauskas, 2018; De Stefano, 2016; Newell et al., 2009; Tremblay, 2003). Hence, the platform economy includes an increasing fraction of work performed by workers who work for companies, even via an app, with no set schedule and paid on a per-job basis. These workers exist both in so-called blue-collar jobs, such as bicycle couriers and Uber drivers, and white-collar jobs, including language proofreading, graphic design, and coding (Kässi and Lehdonvirta, 2016).

Conceptual Framework to Identify the Key Drivers for Wellbeing, Health, and Safety in Platform Work

The effects on worker's wellbeing, health, and safety in the era of digitalization and platforms have not been widely studied yet except for workers' protection (Huws et al., 2018; Vandaele, 2018). Based on the findings among traditional contingent workers, both fatal and non-fatal injuries may be associated with lack of training and fear of job loss, but may also be affected by employment in high-hazard sectors such as construction and agriculture (Foley et al., 2014). In addition, some motivating factors for working in platforms have been identified, including difficulty finding a regular job, health issues, and preference for working part-time and having control over working time (Pesole et al., 2018). Thus, research in this field and a theoretical framework to understand the key elements in platform work are crucial.

According to the JD-R model, psychosocial work characteristics in any work can be divided into two broad categories: job resources and job demands. The JD-R model defines job demands as those physical, psychological, social, or organizational aspects of work that require sustained physical and/or psychological (i.e., cognitive or emotional) effort and therefore are associated with certain physiological and/or psychological costs, which may result in stress and burnout. By contrast, job resources refer to those aspects of work that help meet various demands at work, enable goals to be achieved, and promote learning and growth as well as engagement and motivation at work (Schaufeli and Bakker, 2004; Demerouti et al., 2001). The JD-R model also posits that demands and resources evoke two different but related processes: a health impairment process from demands at work through strain at work (burnout), and a motivational process from job resources through motivation (work engagement). Both are assumed to impact important organizational and employee-related outcomes, such as safety consequences like injuries and accidents (Nahrgang et al., 2011), innovativeness (Hakanen et al., 2008a), sickness absence (Schaufeli et al., 2009), and mental health (Hakanen and Schaufeli, 2012).

The most important work characteristics—that is, job demands and job resources—are likely to vary according to the type of work, industry, and organizational context. Thus, in contrast to other influential stress and motivational models and theories such as the demand-control model (Karasek and Theorell, 1990) or the effort-reward imbalance model (Siegrist, 1996), the key drivers of wellbeing and motivation are not predetermined but are considered to be context dependent. Therefore, the JD-R model can be used to study, identify, and develop key working conditions in tasks that are different to platform work. The aforementioned job demands at work can be considered as hindrance demands, that is, they tend to constrain or interfere with employees' work and have negative consequences for wellbeing (job stress, loss of motivation) and performance (Lepine et al., 2005). By contrast, learning new techniques and skills and managing cognitive load in some platform work can act as a challenge to job demands, meaning that job demands may require effort and be stressful for platform workers and at the same time have positive consequences for motivation, engagement, and performance.

Like traditional work in organizations, work in the platform economy is different and therefore, job resources and job demands vary according to the work and task. This explains the range in the platform work literature and whether certain work characteristics are typically considered existing or lacking. For example, key job demands and job resources may vary depending on the online labor markets: the outcome of a work task is electronically transmittable, or, in mobile labor markets, the delivery of a service is based on physical presence (Codagnone et al., 2016). The work can further be split into that consisting of microtasks—that is, relatively quick and routine cognitive tasks—and self-contained (mini) projects that are somewhat longer lasting and cognitively more challenging. Another distinction has been made between on-location platform-determined routine work, on-location worker-initiated moderately skilled work, and online contestant specialist work, each of which contains different types and amounts of job demands and resources (Eurofound, 2018).

Consequently, platform work differs in terms of employee wellbeing resulting from them: High job demands and lack of resources are a breeding ground for stress and burnout at work (Hakanen et al., 2008b); high resources and moderately high level of challenge demands boost work engagement (Bakker et al., 2007; Hakanen et al., 2005); and lack of both demands and resources is likely to lead to experiences of a motivational state of boredom at work (Reijseger et al., 2013). These types of wellbeing in turn characterize to what extent platform workers find their jobs meaningful and, in the longer term, how healthy they stay.

Demands and Resources of Platform Work

Next, based on the literature, we discuss the typical job demands and job resources that have been identified in a range of platform jobs.

Job Insecurity

Due to a wide variety of work performed through platforms, which include transportation and services among others, a number of health and safety risks and demands are evident, such as road traffic safety, interaction with the public, and use of household cleaning agents (Huws et al., 2017). Both long waiting and working hours may lead to prolonged sitting times or hours at the screen, which may be linked to musculoskeletal or eye strain. Furthermore, job insecurity, which is linked to poor overall health, may affect digitalizing platform workers (Howard, 2017; Cummings and Kreiss, 2008) due to the fact that looking for work requires a lot of time (Berg et al., 2018). A factor that may play a role in these health risks is the effect of income; that is, gig workers with higher income may be less prone to health and safety risks as their work includes less physical strain.

Physical Work Environment, Time Pressure, and Harassment

While physical job demands and risks in on-location platform work, like salaried work, remain, they may embed new meanings in platform work.

A different kind of job demand concerns the physical work environment; for example, bike couriers may occasionally experience high-paced demands and tough biking in bad weather conditions and be at risk of accidents (Huws et al., 2017). Food couriers constantly need to balance traffic safety risks with speed, considering that speed performance is the basis of its categorization as workers (Seppänen et al., 2018). Owing to image and fluency of work, platform companies may voluntarily offer freelancers resources such as team support or safety instruction. In services performed on location (e.g., delivery, housekeeping), harassment is another potential demand that platform workers may encounter (Wisterberg, 2017). For example, workplace harassment is a well-known risk to health and wellbeing (Nielsen et al., 2012).

Isolation

Isolation is a job demand related to the way in which tasks and projects in the digitalizing platform economy are arranged. Many platform tasks, regardless of the industry, are performed separately from—and often in competition with—fellow workers, without face-to-face contact with colleagues or supervisors, which leads to lack of either social support or discussion of work concerns (Tran and Sokas, 2017). These social contacts may also be complicated by the anonymity of communication between workers, clients, and the platform staff as well as being perceived as not having "own voice" (Huws et al., 2017). Another influential factor may be remote work (i.e., working elsewhere rather than at the office, albeit in close contact with a supervisor and colleagues), which may lead to increased time pressure and stress owing to lack of support and contact, or unclear expectations of results (Ojala and Pyöriä, 2013). Lack of social support is a well-known risk factor for health and wellbeing (Ojala and Pyöriä, 2013).

Competition

The structure of the digitalizing platform economy evidently intensifies the competition among workers on platforms, which may lead to workers not being willing to cooperate with one another. In addition, potentially opportunistic behavior may exist, whereas the major role of reputation and ratings affects workers' interest in exercising collaboration (De Stefano, 2016). Nonetheless, the ease of termination via a simple deactivation or exclusion from a platform or app may increase feelings of instability related to non-standard forms of work. Another demand is the constant connection to platforms and apps, which enables companies to monitor workers and which may cause pressure and stress. Moreover, given the unpredictability of job assignments, another typical demand in platform jobs is work—family/non-work conflicts. In addition, some tasks in platform work include heavy competition and a constant experience of being controlled, monitored, and rated, which may cause job stress. The number of clients, the number of tasks, and algorithmic management all affect the speed, deadlines, and ratings to keep up with decent income while competing with others. Hence, autonomy in platform work can lead to overwork, lack of sleep, and tiredness if a worker fails to self-regulate the work (Pesole et al., 2018; Wood et al., 2018).

Cognitive Load

Digitalizing platform work may also lead to heavy job demands, which is cognitive load. According to a foresight paper by the Institute for the Future for the University of Phoenix Research Institute (Davies et al., 2011), the management of cognitive load requires the ability to discriminate and filter information for importance, as well as to understand how to maximize cognitive functioning using a variety of tools and techniques. Today, because of both digitalization and new technologies, platform workers are faced with lots of information in multiple formats and from multiple sources, which has potential to hit the limit of cognitive overload. Both platforms and workers are challenged to filter a huge amount of data and to focus on what is important. A reason may be the financial insecurity of platform work, which requires monitoring of various sites, performing simultaneous tasks, and controlling various sources of information at the same time. New techniques are needed to manage cognitive overload. For example, some methods of social filtering—ranking, tagging, or other means of transforming metadata to information—would help distinguish relevant information from less relevant information.

Variety and Possibilities for Skills Creation

Platform work also provides other positive aspects for health and safety. Variety—that is, varied nature of work and clients—can be a resource (Huws et al., 2017). Furthermore, the potential for creating skills development opportunities, facilitating learning-by-doing, and gaining valuable experiences and positive feedback have been listed as positive aspects of platform work (Fernández-Macías, 2018). In other words, these are resources known to boost engagement in and meaningfulness of an individual's work. The opportunity to realize substantial gains in personal productivity through the adaptation of service provision to an individual's personal working patterns or even work capacity adds to the positive aspects of this activity (Fernández-Macías, 2018). Because of heterogeneity, the same characteristics can act as either demands or resources in different kinds of platform work. For instance, Finnish freelancers working through Upwork, a global platform enhancing exchange of skilled work, can learn marketing and entrepreneurial skills (see Chapter 9 by Seppänen and Poutanen in this book).

Wellbeing and Health in Platform Jobs Resulting From Different Types of Job Demands and Job Resources

The combination of different challenges and/or hindrances to demands, job resources, and/or lack thereof contributes to the wellbeing and health of platform workers. Relatively high levels of challenging job demands (e.g., demand for learning new skills) and valued job resources (e.g., support when needed) are likely to enhance work engagement. By contrast, high levels of hindrances and lack of resources may lead to stress and even burnout symptoms in the long term. Somewhat differently, lack of challenges and resources (combined with hindrances) may trigger feelings of boredom in platform jobs. Consequently, whether a platform worker feels engaged or bored/stressed has implications for the individual's mental and physical health.

In addition, work engagement is likely to play an important role in platform work in which the worker is constantly evaluated and ranked, and therefore, is willing to pursue being the best to earn income and receive further tasks. Work engagement has been found to relate to greater financial returns even among employees who sell fast food (Xanthopoulou et al., 2009). It is also known that work engagement predicts commitment and that both are linked with more energy and less loading after the working week (Salanova et al., 2014; Sonnentag et al., 2008). Nonetheless, commitment might not be without cost: high commitment to work could lead to longer working hours. Perhaps platform workers could benefit from the finding that positive feelings about work are associated with a lower chance of worse sleep quality and alertness (Salanova et al., 2014; Sonnentag et al., 2008).

Need for Self-Management and Self-Regulation to Balance Job Demands and Resources

Autonomy Paradox

Based on this chapter and a review of the literature on platform work (Eurofound, 2018; Fernández-Macías, 2018; Pajarinen et al., 2018; Pesole et al., 2018; Huws et al., 2017), platform work is characterized by extremes between heavy and light job demands and resources (Pichault and McKeown, 2019). For instance, autonomy or job control (Karasek and Theorell, 1990) is a core psychosocial factor at work, which plays an important role in health and wellbeing at work (Nijp et al., 2012; Niedhammer et al., 2006). Flexibility, or the possibility of combining work with childcare, other care responsibilities, studies, or restricted work ability, is one of the main positive characteristics of digitalizing platform work (Huws et al., 2017). In online platform work, workers may freely choose their location.

Meanwhile, the digitalizing platform economy faces an autonomy paradox (Shevchuk et al., 2019; Pichault and McKeown, 2019), which is the discrepancy between flexibility and real experience in time use. This means that even though platform workers have the possibility of scheduling flexible working hours, they choose to work at unsocial hours (evenings, nights, or even weekends) to optimize their financial income, or they are forced to work unsocial working hours owing to time differences with clients. Hence, high job autonomy and flexible working hours lead to unsocial working hours. This may have several consequences that are not only related to the well-known health effects of night work, but also for work-life balance and wellbeing (Shevchuk et al., 2019; Pesole et al., 2018). Our own research (Hasu et al., 2018) shows that initiatives to imitate platform organizing are emerging even in public sector back-office administrative tasks, although presently, this trend is among salaried employees with traditional employment contracts. Increased self-management and self-regulation are required, as the work is full-time telework from home, tasks are picked from a digitalized queue of tasks, the system allows flexible working hours, workers are monitored online via the system, and payments are partially performance-related. Consequently, a worker needs to balance demands and recourses daily, including at nighttime, particularly in an extreme case in which a worker combines work for a public employer with one or two private entrepreneurial activities, and sometimes a demanding hobby.

Unpredictability

Furthermore, digitalizing platform work is characterized by a relatively wide range of unpredictability (Huws et al., 2017). Unpredictability is not only associated with tasks, but also with clients, and the way they should interact. Unpredictability sometimes leads to long waiting hours and sometimes long working hours, and is accompanied by stress related to the response and rating of the performance. For instance, in some types of platform work, long working hours and having to be available for work all the time to earn a decent income are important job demands; although too few task assignments—that is, too few job demands—are an even more typical feature of many platform jobs. Moreover, these two types of demands may co-occur, when there are too few tasks, and the platform worker has to be on call and needs to work longer hours to get an assignment, which implies long waiting times, unpredictability of schedules, and unsocial work hours (i.e., working at night or on weekends). A specific feature of platform work is that scheduling gets complicated (increases unpredictability), as the work is broken into small pieces, namely, tasks (Grossman and Woyke, 2015). Tasks can be paid for on hourly rates, but workers may be scheduled to carry out tasks by algorithms that optimize the schedule for the client or the platform. This may lead to a situation of multiple and simultaneous tasks at the same time for a worker. Scheduling several tasks may lead to compromises at daily levels of time use, namely, limiting time for leisure or sleep to manage to complete all tasks within time limits. On the other hand, these kinds of busy periods may be followed by shortages of tasks, where the uncertainty of earning an income increases and efforts must again be undertaken to obtain more tasks.

Algorithmic Management

One of the important factors in the role of self-management in digitalizing platform work is algorithmic management, which involves platform-based rating and reputation systems (Wood et al., 2018) now used for motivating and controlling human behavior (Lee et al., 2015). Due to algorithmic management, which typically means supply-demand control algorithms, workers at the digitalizing platform economy are rated by their clients and/or by the platform on the completion of tasks. Consequently, those with the best scores and the most experience can receive more work due to clients' preferences and the platforms' algorithmic ranking of workers. Nonetheless, this emphasizes the need for maintaining a high average rating and good accuracy scores, and if they are not maintained, algorithms can lead to a situation in which work is filtered away from those with low ratings, risking the ability to make a living. From a self-management perspective, workers can work flexibly if they can maintain a good quality service, as the evaluation is done at delivery. The long-term motivational effect of ratings is still unknown. An external ratings device could weaken the intrinsic motivation that workers may have and change the meaning that they attribute to their behavior (Lee et al., 2015). Another question concerns the transparency of the algorithm. Worker cooperation with the assignment is influenced not only by the source of the assignment (i.e., human vs. algorithm) but also how the assignment is presented and regulated. Transparency in algorithmic work assignments helps workers to create better work strategies and workarounds (ibid.)

Boundaries Between Work and Leisure Time

Although there is little research on platform workers' working hours, tasks, and wellbeing, it may be assumed that recent reports of modern working life would apply. For example, a recent study (Ropponen et al., 2018) based on a volunteer sample of employees in knowledge-intensive expert work indicated that organization of work (i.e., working hours, timing of work, and stress-related factors) plays an important role in the associations between work, health, and wellbeing (Nijp et al., 2012; Kompier, 2006). Studies based on employees indicate that associations between the characteristics of work, health, and wellbeing are mixed; that is, flexibility may promote as well as compromise health and wellbeing (Ojala et al., 2014; Nijp et al., 2012; Kattenbach et al., 2010; Grönlund, 2007). One explanation for the mixed findings is that schedules for work tasks set by the workers themselves may prove to be unrealistic, leading to increased workload and eventually to negative consequences for health, wellbeing, and work-life balance (Grönlund, 2007). A realistic assumption is that this also plays an influential role in digitalizing platform work. The known importance of the boundaries between work and leisure time for recovery and sleep applies to all types of work—including platform work. The possibility of keeping work and leisure time separate enables detachment from work during leisure time, which is important for recovery, especially when an employee is engaged or heavily stressed.

Furthermore, an important aspect for platform workers is the vicious circle between sleep quality and alertness, detachment and recovery, and working hours (Ropponen et al., 2018). This means that associations exist in both directions—from day of work to the next morning, as well as from the preceding evening and morning to the next day for unreasonable and unnecessary tasks (Sonnentag and Lischetzke, 2017), recovery and work performance (Binnewies et al., 2009), and recovery from job stress (Sonnentag and Fritz, 2015).

Discussion and Insights for the Future

There is a growing body of literature of platform work revolving around its economic, sociological, and legal issues. In this chapter, we focused on workers in the platform. Using the theoretical framework of the JD-R model, we aimed to identify and illustrate the potential characteristics (i.e., job demands and resources) of platform work and their potential impacts on wellbeing, health, and safety. This chapter is a foundation for more theoretically based empirical research on platform workers.

Based on earlier studies, work characteristics—that is, job demands and job resources—were expected to vary and to be context dependent. A review of reports on platform work (Eurofound, 2018; Fernández-Macías, 2018; Pajarinen et al., 2018; Pesole et al., 2018; Huws et al., 2017) indicated that platform work is characterized by their heavy job demands and resources, but in many cases there are periods in which those same demands and resources are lacking. While job demands in some types of platform work, including long working hours and having to be available for work all the time to earn a decent income are important, even more typical of platform jobs is having too few task assignments—that is, too few job demands. To add complexity, these two types of demands may co-occur, when too few tasks require that the platform worker be on call and work longer hours to get an assignment, which implies long waiting times, unpredictability of schedules, and unsocial work hours. The shifting and even simultaneity of too many and too few tasks and working hours reflects the fluctuations in platform work, which is a core characteristic of this work type and affects organizational and worker-related outcomes such as safety consequences, including injuries and accidents (Nahrgang et al., 2011), innovativeness (Hakanen et al., 2008a), sickness absence (Schaufeli et al., 2009), and mental health (Hakanen and Schaufeli, 2012), either directly or through the assumptions of the JD-R model. In this regard, job demands and job resources evoke two different but related processes according to the JD-R model: a health impairment process from demands at work through strain at work (burnout), and a motivational process from resources through motivation (work engagement).

In future research, it would be valuable to study different types of platform jobs using the JD-R model as a theoretical framework to capture an overall picture of work characteristics that impact wellbeing, health, and occupational safety. Another important future research avenue would be to analyze to what extent platform workers are able to proactively craft their work or tasks to make them fit better with preferences, values, and strengths (Wrzesniewski and Dutton, 2001) and even to craft their careers in the long term. Another aspect that merits attention is the possibility of platform work gaining access to collective knowledge and, at the same time, instruments aimed at invoking and adapting such knowledge for the purposes of work (Säljö, 2010). This means that more attention should be paid to how workers change technologies to attain new goals—that is, reinvent platforms—and whether their reinvention pattern is performance oriented (more adaptive and present) or mastery oriented (more expansive and future oriented) (Nevo et al., 2016).

Work changes at the worker level. It seems that full-time, permanent employment will be supplemented with increasing numbers of temporary, part-time, and independent contracting jobs. The independent or self-employed category of jobs, which refers to the so called "non-standard" work, have been forecast to continue to grow (Taylor et al., 2017) although their extent is still relatively marginal (Dølvik and Jesnes, 2017). In practice, this poses the challenge of how we classify workers and, even more importantly, for labor regulations (Garben, 2017). The differences in the legal standards of a worker and a contractual worker need to be clarified. This is important for all levels of stakeholders—workers, employers, and occupational health and safety institutions—and for society to identify those who work through various new digital channels (i.e., freelance work) or who generate novel economic activity to include all new forms of work. In this chapter, we did not consider the representation of platform workers, but that is a future research option that would require in-depth analysis.

It is argued that in the future, more work will comprise tasks (i.e., gigs) rather than jobs for an increasing number of individuals. This means that a larger number of individuals will not go to work and, consequently, will not have an employer. Instead, work will consist of performing tasks that are coordinated through online platforms and compensated through digital transfers. This leads to a situation in which self-employed freelancers work in a larger, more competitive labor market to support themselves (Eurofound, 2018). This questions the rights and protections of those performing the work (Stewart and Stanford, 2017), as it poses challenges to traditional models for regulating work and setting minimum standards.

A recent report by Eurofound (Fernández-Macías, 2018) notes that platform workers are usually considered self-employed/freelancers who do not receive company benefits such as human resource measures, including training, mentoring, and coaching. In addition, job security and social protection may be lacking. Platform workers also face lack of information about employers and tasks to be performed (i.e., availability and content of tasks), lack of a reliable dispute resolution system (i.e., who protects workers if they are not paid), risk of privacy violation owing to the need to disclose personal information without proper guarantee of confidentiality, and lack of support from managers and colleagues.

Perhaps the main characteristic of the digitalizing platform economy shaping workers is the fact that the companies treat those working for them as independent and they have no employment rights. Except in the UK, workers in the digitalizing platform economy are part of the self-employed who are entitled to basic rights such as paid holidays, a minimum wage, and protection from discrimination (Taylor et al., 2017). In a UK government report (Taylor et al., 2017), four key labor market challenges were identified. Among them, the main one affecting workers was jobs to match their skills profile. For example, in the UK, there is a rising proportion of workers with high-level qualifications. Consequently, there is demand for jobs with high-level qualifications. Furthermore, less-than-optimal utilization of available skills is probably linked to the need to increase productivity. The other labor market challenge was new business models (i.e., platform work), by which technology facilitates matching supply and demand (sellers and buyers of goods and services) for new ways of making money. This gives workers possibilities for flexibility and control over how they work, but it also addresses concerns about the suitability of the current employment law framework to cover the needs of people actively choosing to work outside the traditional employment model (Taylor et al., 2017).

There is consensus that platform workers need support, especially in terms of health, safety, and wellbeing. However, the means of doing so vary. For instance, commercial or NGO platforms have been established for this purpose (Grossman and Woyke, 2015). Meanwhile, there are aspirations for increased regulation (Eurofound, 2018). However, there is also a particular need to find means to support platform workers. Here, the focus has turned from the outcome to the process of policymaking. This requires implementing participatory, open-ended forms of intervention for innovation to find solutions that are acceptable and sustainable for platform workers, companies, and societies (Schot and Steinmueller, 2018).

Conclusions

In this chapter, we described the effects of platforms on work, demands, and resources in platform work and their associations with platform workers' wellbeing, health, and safety. Evidently, work in the platform economy provide both demands and resources—and quite often also lack challenging job demands and resources—for a variety of tasks and gigs and for those who perform them—that is, workers. As stated by the European Commission, the platform economy should recognize the need to ensure fair working conditions and to protect both workers and consumers (2016). Doing so would result in platform workers staying engaged, well, and healthy regardless of the type of platform work.

References

Bakker, A. B., Hakanen, J. J., Demerouti, E. and Xanthopoulou, D. (2007). Job Resources Boost Work Engagement, Particularly When Job Demands Are High. *Journal of Educational Psychology*, 99(2), pp. 274–284.

Berg, J., Furrer, M., Harmon, E., Rani, U. and Silberman, M. S. (2018). *Digital Labour Platforms and the Future of Work: Towards Decent Work in the Online World*. Geneva: International Labour Office.

Binnewies, C., Sonnentag, S. and Mojza, E. J. (2009). Daily Performance at Work: Feeling Recovered in the Morning as a Predictor of Day-Level Job Performance. *Journal of Organizational Behavior*, 30(1), pp. 67–93.

Codagnone, C., Abadie, F. and Biagi, F. (2016). The Future of Work in the "Sharing Economy": Market Efficiency and Equitable Opportunities or Unfair Precarisation. *JRC Science for Policy Report EUR 27913 EN*, Institute for Prospective Technological Studies.

Cummings, K. J. and Kreiss, K. (2008). Contingent Workers and Contingent Health: Risks of a Modern Economy. *Jama*, 299(4), pp. 448–450.

Davies, A., Fidler, D. and Gorbis, M. (2011). *Future Work Skills 2020*. Phoenix: Institute for the Future for the University of Phoenix Research Institute.

Demerouti, E., Bakker, A. B., Nachreiner, F. and Schaufeli, W. B. (2001). The Job Demands-Resources Model of Burnout. *Journal of Applied Psychology*, 86(3), pp. 499–512.

De Stefano, V. (2016). The Rise of the "Just-in-Time Workforce": On-Demand Work, Crowd Work and Labour Protection in the "Gig-Economy." *Comparative Labor Law & Policy Journal*, 37(3), pp. 471–504.

Dølvik, J. E. and Jesnes, K. (2017). *Nordic Labour Markets and the Sharing Economy: Report From a Pilot Project: TemaNord.* Copenhagen: Nordic Council of Ministers.

Eurofound. (2018). *Employment and Working Conditions of Selected Types of Platform Work.* Luxembourg: Publications Office of the European Union.

European Commission. (2016). *A European Agenda for the Collaborative Economy.* Available at: https://eur-lex.europa.eu/legal-content/EN/TXT/?uri=COM%3A2016%3A356%3AFIN [Accessed 6 April 2019].

Fernández-Macías, E. (2018). *Automation, Digitalisation and Platforms: Implications for Work and Employment.* Luxembourg: Eurofound, Publications Office of the European Union.

Foley, M., Ruser, J., Shor, G., Shuford, H. and Sygnatur, E. 2014. Contingent Workers: Workers' Compensation Data Analysis Strategies and Limitations. *American Journal of Industrial Medicine*, 57(7), pp. 764–775.

Garben, S. (2017). *Protecting Workers in the Online Platform Economy: An Overview of Regulatory and Policy Developments in the EU.* Available at: https://osha.europa.eu/en/tools-and-publications/publications/regulating-occupational-safety-and-health-impact-online-platform/view [Accessed 23 October 2018].

Grönlund, A. (2007). Egenkontroll som friskfaktor och riskfaktor: Det gränslösa arbetet i Västeuropa och Sverige. *Arbetsmarknad & Arbetsliv*, 13(2), pp. 11–25.

Grossman, N. and Woyke, E. (2015). *Serving Workers in the Gig Economy: Emerging Resources for the On-Demand Workforce.* Boston: O'Reilly Media.

Hakanen, J. J., Bakker, A. B. and Demerouti, E. (2005). How Dentists Cope With Their Job Demands and Stay Engaged: The Moderating Role of Job Resources. *European Journal of Oral Sciences*, 113(6), pp. 479–487.

Hakanen, J. J., Perhoniemi, R. and Toppinen-Tanner, S. (2008a). Positive Gain Spirals at Work: From Job Resources to Work Engagement, Personal Initiative and Work-Unit Innovativeness. *Journal of Vocational Behavior*, 73(1), pp. 78–91.

Hakanen, J. J. and Schaufeli, W. B. (2012). Do Burnout and Work Engagement Predict Depressive Symptoms and Life Satisfaction? A Three-Wave Seven-Year Prospective Study. *Journal of Affective Disorders*, 141(2–3), pp. 415–424.

Hakanen, J. J., Schaufeli, W. B. and Ahola, K. (2008b). The Job Demands-Resources Model: A Three-Year Cross-Lagged Study of Burnout, Depression, Commitment, and Work Engagement. *Work & Stress*, 22(3), pp. 224–241.

Hasu, M., Käpykangas, S., Saari, E. and Korvela, P. (2018). Toimistotyöntekijä automaation kynnyksellä—Tekstinkäsittelijöiden työelämäarjen profiilit digitalisoidussa kokoaikaisessa kotietätyössä [Office Worker in the Edge of Automation. Employees' Worklife Profiles in Digitized Full-Time Teleworking at Home]. *Työelämäntutkimus* [*Worklife Research Journal*], 16(4), pp. 251–274. (In Finnish).

Howard, J. (2017). Nonstandard Work Arrangements and Worker Health and Safety. *American Journal of Industrial Medicine*, 60(1), pp. 1–10.

Huws, U., Spencer, N. H. and Syrdal, D. S. (2018). Online, on Call: The Spread of Digitally Organised Just-in-Time Working and Its Implications for Standard Employment Models. *New Technology, Work and Employment*, 33(2), pp. 113–129.

Huws, U., Spencer, N. H., Syrdal, D. S. and Holts, K. (2017). *Work in the European Gig Economy. Research Results from the UK, Sweden, Germany, Austria, The Netherlands, Switzerland & Italy*. Brussels, Belgium: FEPS—Foundation for European Progressive Studies, UNI Europa, Hertfordshire Business School, University of Hertfordshire.

Johnston, H. and Land-Kazlauskas, C. (2018). Organizing On-Demand: Representation, Voice, and Collective Bargaining in the Gig Economy. *Conditions of Work and Employment Series No. 94*. Geneva: International Labour Office.

Karasek, R. A. and Theorell, T. (1990). *Healthy Work: Stress, Productivity and the Reconstruction of Working Life*. New York: Basic Books.

Kässi, O. and Lehdonvirta, V. (2016). *Online Labour Index: Measuring the Online Gig Economy for Policy and Research*. Available at: https://mpra.ub.uni-muenchen.de/74943/ [Accessed 5 April 2019].

Kattenbach, R., Demerouti, E. and Nachreiner, F. (2010). Flexible Working Times: Effects on Employees' Exhaustion, Work—Nonwork Conflict and Job Performance. *Career Development International*, 15(3), pp. 279–295.

Kompier, M. A. (2006). New Systems of Work Organization and Workers' Health. *Scandinavian Journal of Work, Environment & Health*, 32(6), pp. 421–430.

Lee, M. K., Kusbit, D., Metsky, E. and Dabbish, L. (2015). Working With Machines: The Impact of Algorithmic and Data-Driven Management on Human Workers. *Proceedings of the 33rd Annual ACM Conference on Human Factors in Computing Systems*, Seoul, Republic of Korea: ACM.

Lepine, J. A., Podsakoff, N. P. and Lepine, M. A. (2005). A Meta-Analytic Test of the Challenge Stressor-Hindrance Stressor Framework: An Explanation for Inconsistent Relationships Among Stressors and Performance. *The Academy of Management Journal*, 48(5), pp. 764–775.

Mandl, I. and Biletta, I. (2018). *Overview of New Forms of Employment—2018 Update*. Luxembourg: Eurofound, Publications Office of the European Union.

Nahrgang, J. D., Morgeson, F. P. and Hofmann, D. A. (2011). Safety at Work: A Meta-Analytic Investigation of the Link Between Job Demands, Job Resources, Burnout, Engagement, and Safety Outcomes. *Journal of Applied Psychology*, 96(1), pp. 71–94.

Nevo, S., Nevo, D. and Pinsonneault, A. (2016). A Temporally Situated Self-Agency Theory of Information Technology Reinvention. *MIS Quarterly*, 40(1), pp. 157–186.

Newell, S., Robertson, M., Scarbrough, H. and Swan, J. (2009). *Managing Knowledge Work and Innovation*. London: Palgrave Macmillan.

Niedhammer, I., Chastang, J-F., David, S., Barouhiel, L. and Barrandon, G. (2006). Psychosocial Work Environment and Mental Health: Job-Strain and Effort-Reward Imbalance Models in a Context of Major Organizational Changes. *International Journal of Occupational and Environmental Health*, 12(2), pp. 111–119.

Nielsen, M. B., Hetland, J., Matthiesen, S. B. and Einarsen, S. (2012). Longitudinal Relationships Between Workplace Bullying and Psychological Distress. *Scandinavian Journal of Work, Environment & Health*, 38(1), pp. 38–46.

Nijp, H. H., Beckers, D. G., Geurts, S. A., Tucker, P. and Kompier, M. A. (2012). Systematic Review on the Association Between Employee Worktime Control and Work-non-Work Balance, Health and Well-Being, and Job-Related

Outcomes. *Scandinavian Journal of Work, Environment & Health*, 38(4), pp. 299–313.

Ojala, S., Nätti, J. and Anttila, T. (2014). Informal Overtime at Home Instead of Telework: Increase in Negative Work-Family Interface. *International Journal of Sociology and Social Policy*, 34(1/2), pp. 69–87.

Ojala, S. and Pyöriä, P. (2013). Kotona Työskentelyn Yleisyys ja Seuraukset: Suomi Eurooppalaisessa Vertailussa [Generality and Consequences of Working at Home: Finland in European Comparison]. *Työpoliittinen aikakauskirja* [*Employment Policy Journal*] 1, pp. 53–64. (In Finnish).

Pajarinen, M., Rouvinen, P., Claussen, J., Hakanen, J. J., Kovalainen, A., Kretchmer, T., Poutanen, S., Seifried, M. and Seppänen, L. (2018). *Upworkers in Finland: Survey Results. ETLA Report 85*. Helsinki: ETLA.

Pesole, A., Urzí Brancati, M. C., Fernández-Macías, E., Biagi, F. and González Vázquez, I. (2018). *Platform Workers in Europe: JCR Science for P Report*. Luxembourg: European Commission.

Pichault, F. and Mckeown, T. (2019). Autonomy at Work in the Gig Economy: Analysing Work Status, Work Content and Working Conditions of Independent Professionals. *New Technology, Work and Employment*, 34(1), pp. 59–72.

Reijseger, G., Schaufeli, W. B., Peeters, M. C., Taris, T. W., Van Beek, I. and Ouweneel, E. (2013). Watching the Paint Dry at Work: Psychometric Examination of the Dutch Boredom Scale. *Anxiety, Stress & Coping*, 26(5), pp. 508–525.

Ropponen, A., Härmä, M., Bergbom, B., Nätti, J. and Sallinen, M. (2018). The Vicious Circle of Working Hours, Sleep, and Recovery in Expert Work. *International Journal of Environmental Research and Public Health*, 15(7), p. 1361.

Salanova, M., Del Libano, M., Llorens, S. and Schaufeli, W. B. (2014). Engaged, Workaholic, Burned-out or Just 9-to-5? Toward a Typology of Employee Well-Being. *Stress Health*, 30(1), pp. 71–81.

Säljö, R. (2010). Digital Tools and Challenges to Institutional Traditions of Learning: Technologies, Social Memory and the Performative Nature of Learning. *Journal of Computer Assisted Learning*, 26(1), pp. 53–64.

Schaible, S., Fischer, C., Seufert, J. and Fuest, K. (2017). *How Digitization Will Affect Tomorrow's World of Work: 12 Hypotheses: Digitalization Threatens Jobs: Digitalization Creates Jobs*. Stuttgart, Germany: Roland Berger GmbH.

Schaufeli, W. B. and Bakker, A. B. (2004). Job Demands, Job Resources, and Their Relationship With Burnout and Engagement: A Multi-Sample Study. *Journal of Organizational Behavior*, 25(3), pp. 293–315.

Schaufeli, W. B., Bakker, A. B. and Van Rhenen, W. (2009). How Changes in Job Demands and Resources Predict Burnout, Work Engagement, and Sickness Absenteeism. *Journal of Organizational Behavior*, 30(7), pp. 893–917.

Schaufeli, W. B. and Taris, T. W. (2014). *A Critical Review of the Job Demands-Resources Model: Implications for Improving Work and Health. Bridging Occupational, Organizational and Public Health: A Transdisciplinary Approach*. Dordrecht: Springer Netherlands.

Schot, J. and Steinmueller, W. E. (2018). Three Frames for Innovation Policy: R&D, Systems of Innovation and Transformative Change. *Research Policy*, 47(9), pp. 1554–1567.

Seppänen, L., Hasu, M., Käpykangas, S. and Poutanen, S. (2018). On-Demand Work in Platform Economy: Implications for Sustainable Development. In: S. Bagnara, S. Tartaglia, S. Albolino, T. Alexander and Y. Fujita, eds., *20th*

Congress of International Ergonomics Association (IEA 2018). Basel: Springer Nature.

Shevchuk, A., Strebkov, D. and Davis, S. N. (2019). The Autonomy Paradox: How Night Work Undermines Subjective Well-Being of Internet-Based Freelancers. *ILR Review*, 72(1), pp. 75–100.

Siegrist, J. (1996). Adverse Health Effects of High-Effort/Low-Reward Conditions. *Journal of Occupational Health Psychology*, 1(1), pp. 27–41.

Sonnentag, S., Binnewies, C. and Mojza, E. J. (2008). "Did You Have a Nice Evening?" A Day-Level Study on Recovery Experiences, Sleep, and Affect. *Journal of Applied Psychology*, 93(3), pp. 674–684.

Sonnentag, S. and Fritz, C. (2015). Recovery from Job Stress: The Stressor-Detachment Model as an Integrative Framework. *Journal of Organizational Behavior*, 36(S1), pp. S72–S103.

Sonnentag, S. and Lischetzke, T. (2017). Illegitimate Tasks Reach into Afterwork Hours: A Multilevel Study. *Journal of Occupational Health and Psychology*, 23(2), pp. 248–261.

Stewart, A. and Stanford, J. (2017). Regulating Work in the Gig Economy: What Are the Options? *The Economic and Labour Relations Review*, 28(3), pp. 420–437.

Taylor, M., Marsh, G., Nicol, D. and Broadbent, P. (2017). *Good Work: The Taylor Review of Modern Working Practices*. London: Government of the United Kingdom.

Tran, M. and Sokas, R. K. (2017). The Gig Economy and Contingent Work: An Occupational Health Assessment. *Journal of Occupational and Environmental Medicine*, 59(4), pp. e63–e66.

Tremblay, D. (2003). Telework: A New Mode of Gendered Segmentation? Results from a Study in Canada. *Canadian Journal of Communication*, 28(4), pp. 3–23.

Vandaele, K. (2018). Will Trade Unions Survive in the Platform Economy? Emerging Patterns of Platform Workers' Collective Voice and Representation in Europe. *ETUI Research Paper—Working Paper*.

Wisterberg, E. (2017). I Spent Two Weeks Delivering for Uber Eats and Made $4.4 per Hour. Available at: www.breakit.se/artikel/7599/i-spent-two-weeks-delivering-for-uber-eats-and-made-4-4-per-hou [Accessed 25 October 2018].

Wood, A. J., Graham, M., Lehdonvirta, V. and Hjorth, I. (2018). Good Gig, Bad Gig: Autonomy and Algorithmic Control in the Global Gig Economy. *Work, Employment and Society*, 33(1), pp. 56–75.

Wrzesniewski, A. and Dutton, J. E. (2001). Crafting a Job: Revisioning Employees as Active Crafters of Their Work. *The Academy of Management Review*, 26(2), pp. 179–201.

Xanthopoulou, D., Bakker, A. B., Demerouti, E. and Schaufeli, W. B. (2009). Work Engagement and Financial Returns: A Diary Study on the Role of Job and Personal Resources. *Journal of Occupational and Organizational Psychology*, 82(1), pp. 183–200.

Part III

Challenges to Skills and Capabilities in the Digital Platform Economy

4 Vocational Education Goes to Industry

Future Skills at Work Derive From Novel Models of Cooperation

Kaisa Hytönen and Anne Kovalainen

Introduction

The current state of working life is characterized by complexity and rapid, extensive, and permanent change. The driving forces changing economies, societies, and working life are largely related to new technological developments and breakthroughs (Brynjolfsson and McAfee, 2015; Davies et al., 2011; Palonen et al., 2014; Talwar and Hancock, 2010). Digitalization is one of the key transformative engines (Kenney et al., 2015; Kenney et al., Chapter 1 in this book) driving the constant need for the renewal of skills, especially among professionals. Digitalization does not have one single, fixed definition but is usually defined as the way in which many domains, such as working lives and private lives in society, are restructured around digital communication and media infrastructures. Today digitalization is profoundly part and parcel of all activities, including work and economy. Digitalization and other significant changes and developments challenge professionals who face novel professional complexities and entirely new skill requirements, as well as educational systems and workplaces that generate the need to rethink and transform the ways in which competencies are cultivated over lifetimes in the face of accelerating change.

Technological advancements are often assumed to reduce employment, but more often than not, they alter the actual nature of work (Vallas and Kovalainen, 2019). It is, therefore, of utmost importance to explore and understand the ways in which educational institutions react to and accommodate the growing needs and changing requirements of technologically driven working life. These increasing needs also require inputs from companies. In this chapter, we examine this matter, first, by discussing the new educational needs of a technologically driven society; second, by taking a look at the strengthening interfaces between education and working life; and third, by introducing an educational design called a company-driven vocational education and training program, where the interface between education and working life is strong and intensive. We use a global company, KONE Elevators Ltd., as the subject of a case study. Based on our recent studies, we examine whether this educational design of KONE that is organized in close partnership with the industry is able to support the development of the individual competencies that are necessary for future working life, and how the interconnections between education and working life are constructed in a sustainable manner (see Hytönen and Kovalainen, 2018)

New Educational Needs of a Technologically Driven Society

Rapid technological developments transform existing professions and work, organizations, work environments, and ways of working. Technological developments also lead to the emergence of new occupations and professional fields (Davies et al., 2011; Palonen et al., 2014; Seppänen et al., 2018). It has been estimated that in the next 10 to 15 years, one-third of the currently employed workforce is likely to be replaced by computer-controlled equipment and that many people will work in jobs that do not exist yet (Pajarinen and Rouvinen, 2014). It is indeed well known that the increasing complexity of technological development concerns all sectors and all kinds of work (Brynjolfsson and McAfee, 2015). Therefore, keeping education relevant in a technology-driven society is one of the major challenges in the field of education, and will remain so in the years to come (Facer, 2011; Johnson et al., 2016).

Recent scientific and societal discussions have emphasized the need to deepen the interconnections between working life and different levels of the educational system in order to meet the growing needs for changes in working life and to increase the availability of flexible education and training designs (e.g., Billett and Henderson, 2011; Harteis et al., 2014; Hytönen, 2016; Kenney and Zysman, 2016; Susskind and Susskind, 2015; Vallas and Hill, 2018). Working life is often seen as separate and distant from educational processes and institutions. Traditionally, educational institutions aim to provide a theoretical knowledge base for employees, prior to their employment careers; workplaces, for their part, are important places for the development of professional practices and learning at work. This rather rigid division between education as a "preparatory" mechanism and working life as an "implementation site" of the knowledge gained from educational institutions is no longer valid.

Extensive international studies, such as the PIAAC program's examination of adult proficiency with information-processing and working life skills along with their utilization in work (e.g., Hämäläinen et al., 2019), and the recent small-scale and national studies, have all shown the need for a better understanding of working life and the strengthening of interfaces and new modes of cooperation between education and working life (e.g., Berner, 2010; Costley and Lester, 2012; Endedijk and Bronkhorst, 2014; Hytönen, 2016; Lamb et al., 2015; Siivonen, 2016). As technological developments especially call for closer and more strategic cooperation between education and business to anticipate and respond to future competence and capability needs, it is of utmost importance to systematically examine and rethink the roles and responsibilities of individuals, educational institutions, the labor market, and working life, and the relationships among them in socio-technical futures (Kwiek, 2009).

Professions with an emphasis on designing, developing, and producing technology are often located at the intersection of several professional domains and the interface of different knowledge cultures. Therefore, standard educational designs or solutions for learning and cultivating expertise are often missing (Carlile, 2004; Edwards, 2010; Vest, 2008). An agile labor market requires responsive education, training, and at-work-learning systems (e.g., Susskind and Susskind, 2015) as technological disruptions drive change and entail a faster pace of business and new expectations for ways of working. Companies need to be able to transform business according to the changing technological environment. Here, a competent and skilled workforce holds a key position.

According to some researchers, employees' technological knowhow is so important that they talk of "new experts," whose skills can be developed within companies only through the application of technology (e.g., Autor et al., 2003; Susskind and Susskind, 2015; Larson, 2013; Kaplan, 2011). Such expertise may be related to the use and analyses of a specific kind of big data, etc. In general, however, only a few workplaces are able to provide opportunities to improve conceptual and other knowledge-laden aspects of professional competencies, and thereby provide opportunities to learn novel skills and the complex expertise necessary to suit the changes in working life (Harteis et al., 2014). Therefore, especially in technologically driven fields, there is a growing need for new kinds of efforts to bridge and combine expertise, knowledge, and practices of educational institutions and workplaces. But how to combine in more agile ways the changing needs of the working life and the educational curriculum and contents? This may call for a closer dialogue and collaboration between institutions.

New forms of cooperation among educational institutions, working life organizations, and industry can yield answers to meet future educational challenges by generating novel learning solutions as well as developing and distributing new kinds of competencies, innovations, and cutting-edge expertise. The new forms are seen to have the potential to provide flexible forums for professional development and cultivating skills as well as environments for sharing and receiving critical knowledge through different types of expertise and professional cultures, as many working professionals face the need to continuously gain new skills and competencies and to update their expertise or even change the nature and focus of their professional profiles (Hakkarainen et al., 2004; Knorr Cetina and Reichmann, 2015; Kessels and Kwakman, 2007; Nerland, 2012; Ohlsson, 2011; Redecker et al., 2010; Roxå et al., 2011; Saari et al., Chapter 8 in this book). In addition, new interactions at the interface of education and working life can accommodate the needs of companies and can open up opportunities for enhancements in a number of key areas, such as increased competitiveness, better operational efficiency, enhanced productivity and performance, and tools for intelligent and strategic decision-making (e.g., Sundararajan, 2016).

Strengthening Interfaces Between Education and Working Life

How interactions at the interfaces of professional education and working life are constructed in a rapidly changing, technologically driven society is a globally significant question, not least because of the transnational nature of business in the wake of technology. At the national level, different kinds of educational designs are currently adopted in order to tackle the complexity of contemporary working life and to find solutions to the internationally significant phenomenon of how to create and strengthen the interface between education and working life, and to provide possibilities for professionals to update and expand their expertise in quick and flexible ways.

We are interested in finding out whether the state-organized and subsidized education has potential to collaborate with private sector companies, in order to deliver specific or designed teaching that gives career opportunities extending beyond one company. This question is particularly interesting for countries where the education at the population level is high, and where the education system is extensive. For instance, in Finland, different kinds of professional specialization programs and educational programs for further professional development have been established at a higher education level. They are financed by the state and organized by universities, including universities of applied sciences, together with working life organizations. These educational programs aim to generate competence in areas of specialized expertise for which no market-based education exists, and to address the acute shortage of skilled employees in emerging and technology-driven fields. They are available for those who have completed a degree and have already entered their working lives. For example, a training design called Academic Apprenticeship Education was established in Finland in 2009 to address the requirements of the future education of those professionals who are already pursuing tasks involving professional expertise but must expand their skills and competencies and update their expertise (Hytönen, 2016). This training design is geared toward fields such as technical fields that are located at the interface of universities, and working life organizations that are often multi-scientific and rapidly changing in nature, and constantly cope with complexity by capitalizing on both scientific and practical knowledge (Hytönen et al., 2016).

Other examples of new, nationally developed interactions between academic educational institutions and working life include a system called "Postdocs in Companies" (PoDoCo) (e.g., Kunttu et al., 2018) and "Professors of Practice" at universities (e.g., Frølich et al., 2018). PoDoCo is a joint initiative of Finnish universities, industry, and foundations that supports the employment of young doctors in the private sector. It also aims to enhance long-term competitiveness and the strategic renewal of companies. It is funded together by the PoDoCo foundation pool and companies. An internationally renowned system of Professors of Practice, for one, has recently been introduced at many Finnish universities. It aims to relate the two knowledge "worlds" of academic and working life together. The position of Professor of Practice is based not on a person's academic merit but, rather, on professional merits and experience from outside the academic world. Therefore, it provides an opportunity to engage highly qualified private or public sector experts at universities. The system aims to strengthen cooperation between universities and representatives of working life by providing a mechanism through which practical experience and know-how are transferred and integrated into the academic community.

Even though different kinds of partnerships between education and industry have only recently emerged in the fields of higher and continuing professional education, they are internationally typical of vocational education and training (Billett and Henderson, 2011; Endedijk and Bronkhorst, 2014; Poortman et al., 2014). For example, the German vocational education and training system, also known as a dual model, is based on a strong corporatist skill formation system and the continuing high need for skilled labor especially in manufacturing industries (Busemeyer and Trampusch, 2012). The dual system is characterized by cooperation mainly between small and medium-sized companies and publicly funded vocational schools. Cooperation is regulated by law. The German dual model is often referred to as a model for the Nordic labor markets and apprenticeship training.

In the UK, echoing the need to lower youth unemployment, policies governing employment and training at work were reversed in the 2010s. Apprenticeships were transformed into full-time paid jobs, incorporating on-the-job and off-the-job training. As part of the vocational education system, apprenticeships were made available to those aged over 16 years, and from the beginning, a nationally recognized certificate was assigned to the system. Apprenticeships are currently available at various educational levels and take at least one year to complete—longer for higher qualifications (e.g., Pullen and Clifton, 2016). In Norway, Denmark, and Switzerland, the vocational education and training system is characterized by stakeholder networks in which companies are strongly involved. These networks aim to improve access to training jobs and the quality of learning, especially in workplaces.

In Finland, the vocational education and training system is predominantly school-based. Education is organized mainly through institutions but also as apprenticeship training that is a parallel route to obtaining a vocational degree. On-the-job training conducted at workplaces is included in school-based education. In Finland, the ongoing reforms of vocational education and training aim to make secondary-level vocational training more centered on skills and working life as well as increasing the extent of cooperation between the actors in working life and educational institutions.

As all previous international examples show, the educational value of connecting learning within educational institutions with practice-based workplace experiences has been acknowledged both in research and in policy. However, recent research has revealed that actual cooperation and partnership between education providers and workplaces may be very limited (Graf, 2013; Mikkonen et al., 2017). It has been emphasized that the models of vocational education and training are often fixed and inflexible in practice and are therefore ineffective in answering the growing needs for change in working life. In the following section, we discuss these challenges further and introduce an educational design that we call "company-driven vocational education." We examine whether this specialized educational design, which is organized by a company, is able to sustainably construct the interface and interconnections between education and working life and to flexibly support the development of individual competencies needed for future working life (Hytönen and Kovalainen, 2018).

Company-Driven Vocational Education: The Case of KONE Elevators Ltd.

A multifaceted example of the long-standing system of company-driven vocational education can be found in Finland. KONE Elevators Ltd. is one of the world's leading companies in the elevator and escalator industry. KONE was founded in 1910, and despite its origins in a machine shop in Finland, it has become a global leader in the elevator and escalator industry, operating in over 60 countries around the world. It provides elevators, escalators, and automatic building doors, solutions for maintenance and modernization, and other business services. The rapid technological developments and digitalization (including advancements in connectivity, mobility, and computing power) have had a strong impact on the company's field of business, promulgating new processes, new integrated technologies and connectivity, and new benchmarks for customer service.

KONE has its own Industrial School, set up in 1951 to ensure the continued availability of a qualified workforce in its specialized field. In Finland, company-driven vocational education has been organized since the early twentieth century in professional and vocational training establishments, starting at the time when the general education system in the country was not considered adequate to ensure the continued availability of skilled employees. Since then, vocational education and training have largely shifted to educational establishments, with only a few specialized vocational institutes organizing training in companies. At present, 19 specialized vocational institutions are members of the Association of the Finnish Industrial Academies, the umbrella organization for these institutions. Primarily, training provided in companies does not fall within the scope of the educational administrations' degree programs. The KONE Industrial School is the only specialized Finnish vocational institution that provides students with a degree program. Globally, there are several examples of company-based education systems, such as Sony's Technology Training Courses (see also Freeman and Soete, 1997). However, these are often based on the needs of the companies and focus on at-work learning.

The KONE Industrial School trains elevator engineers for KONE and provides technical training for its staff. The Industrial School is a specialized vocational institute under the supervision of the Finnish National Agency for Education. Therefore, it follows the national educational legislation and regulations, and is provided funding by the Finnish state. The Industrial School provides a two-year training program in elevator engineering, which gives elevator engineers a vocational qualification. The training program corresponds to the requirements of KONE's business operations and takes the form of advanced training provided in an institution of vocational education.

We focused on KONE as our case study in order to examine the ability of the company-driven vocational education while also taking the new challenges posed by the changing work-life paradigm into account. The results of the case study are reported in further detail in Hytönen and Kovalainen (2018). We interviewed 12 people in the spring of 2017. The focus of our case study was not on examining the students of the elevator engineering training program, but rather on examining how the training program prepared its participants for their future careers from the perspective of those who had participated in the elevator engineering training program at various times and continued working with KONE. A total of 10 interviewees had worked as elevator engineers or maintenance engineers after graduating from the elevator engineering training program and later progressed to other jobs (e.g., management, planning, sales) in the company (N1–N10). The years in which they had begun their studies in the Industrial School varied from 1986 to 2016. The number of years of working in the company varied from 2 to 43. One interviewee worked in a managerial position at KONE Industrial School, and one interviewee worked in human resources management at KONE Elevators Ltd. (N11 and N12). The interviews covered the education and training in elevator engineering as provided in the Industrial School, the educational background and the work history of the participants, their careers with KONE, their views on the elevator sector, the changes taking place within the sector, and future prospects. Data were analyzed through qualitative content analysis.

Constructing the Interconnections Between Education and Working Life

When we examine how the interconnection of education and working life is constructed in company-driven vocational education, our case study opens up room for several interesting elaborations. Earlier studies have revealed that even though learning in vocational education and training often takes place both in a vocational school and in a company, these two environments often remain separate (Fürstenau et al., 2014). For example, the actual integration of learning experiences is often limited. The goals, interests, and priorities of specialized companies may not always go hand in hand with the goals set for education, and the availability of sustainable traineeships may be limited. Supervisors in workplaces often have no pedagogical competence, and there may not be sufficient time available to guide trainees (Billett, 2008; Fürstenau et al., 2014; Hytönen et al., 2016). According to earlier studies, vocational education and training promotes rapid and seamless transitions from education to work and decreases youth unemployment, but its positive employment effect diminishes later on in a person's career (Forster et al., 2016; Hanushek et al., 2017).

Our case study shows that in the case of company-driven vocational education and training, the connection between the company and training is very close. In our study, this comes across in many different ways and at various levels. The close connection helps overcome many of the aforementioned problems in bridging education and the workplace. The students of the KONE Industrial School engage with the company at an early stage, even before the program begins, because this anticipated future workforce needs to determine the number of places offered for study. The training program for elevator engineering is usually held annually. About 200 people apply for the training program each time. A smaller group is selected to participate in the entrance exam and, eventually, about 15–20 students are chosen for the training program from each such cohort. The company's supervisors participate in the student selection process as they select future employees for their own units: "It's not so much a case of the school's representatives choosing the students for the school, but more a case of the KONE supervisors choosing the workers for themselves"

(N12). Thus, supervisors are committed to developing their students' skills through the course of the training program.

The interviews revealed that with regard to job security and benefits, the distinction between general vocational education and training and the KONE Industrial School training is remarkable. KONE aims to provide permanent jobs for its graduates. During the training period, students are paid a student salary, in accordance with the applicable collective wage agreement, and are covered by KONE's occupational healthcare policy. Therefore, the students' careers in the company can be said to have begun at the start of the training program itself: "In a way, you start working with the company by first going to the school to study for a couple of years" (N11). Students participate in the company's activities and operations right from the beginning of their studies, as the Industrial School is located in the middle of one of the company's branches.

In the company-driven vocational education program, interactions between the company and the training program are strongly reflected in the content of the training and teaching methods. The interviews revealed that changes and developments taking place in business activities are quickly translated to teaching content and practices: "As soon as (new products and technologies) are released, the school tries to get them as well. The school gets the latest information easily" (N3). The close connection between the company and the training program enables a smooth flow of information as well as rapid, timely, and flexible responses to the changes in working life and new competence needs: "At times it seems that the students know more about (new) things than the local engineers" (N3). At its best, the company-driven vocational education and training program is able to respond to the needs for change and is able to keep pace with the times more successfully than are conventional educational establishments.

The training program consists of theoretical studies at the Industrial School and practical work in KONE's own installation and maintenance premises. About 70% of the training is carried out as on-the-job training. Our case study showed that theoretical courses and on-the-job training are in dialogue with each other and alternate with each other in close cycles. The modular structure of studies combines theoretical studies and practical training effectively. In the best case, during the on-the-job-training periods, students get to apply the theoretical knowledge they acquire and also to become part of the operating culture of the company: "In this way, the students are involved in the day-to-day work at a very early stage as well" (N12). Practical training at the company's own facilities best enables participation in genuine, diverse, and responsible work, and students do not have to remain content with doing only the simplest, routine, or mundane tasks: "In on-the-job training I was given a lot of responsibility. I was given my own designated maintenance area, and I started doing elevator maintenance there" (N5). After half a year of studies, the students begin to work independently and at the same time prepare for their competence-based qualification, which is completed over the last six months of their studies.

In the Industrial School, the interconnection between education and working life is also constructed by teaching and guidance practices. Most teaching is provided by a handful of main instructors. More specific subject matters, such as "how HR works here in KONE" (N11) are taught by specialists in those areas. Teachers do not have pedagogical qualifications, as is generally the case in education and training that takes place in the workplace. Instead, in KONE, the teachers have strong substantive knowledge and pedagogical know-how that they acquire through experience.

Mentorship is provided by more experienced employees and is an important part of the training program. Each student is assigned a mentor with whom they work during the on-the-job training process and familiarize themselves with a wide range of tasks. Each student receives support and guidance from their mentor. However, the interviews brought up the fact that the success of mentoring depends largely on the mentor's commitment and willingness to guide their younger colleagues. Problems may occur if the appointed mentor is not dedicated to the program:

> I was allowed to go with the flow, nobody really cared too much, and no one asked me how things were . . . Then I went to another mentor, and things were different. The new mentor had things under control, and gave me clear instructions on what my role was, when my work career really begins, and what I needed to have learned by that time.
> (N1)

In recent years, the Industrial School has made efforts to develop mentorship by paying more attention to the choice of suitable and committed mentors and training them toward performing their duties: "The aim now is to educate mentors and superiors so that learning will be the top priority, not some production factor" (N3).

Developing Working Life Competencies

Earlier research showed that vocational education and training often produces very professional and industry-specific skills and, therefore, does not provide individuals with enough tools to adapt to rapid changes in their working lives (Hampf and Woessmann, 2017). Earlier studies have also revealed that in regard to learning in the workplace, specialized companies may not be able to support the development of a sufficiently broad range of working life skills (Baartman and Bruijn, 2011; Hampf and Woessmann, 2017; Hanushek et al., 2017). For example, students may be given simple routine tasks that do not help them acquire multifaceted skills. Researchers have also addressed the challenges related to the transferability of learning to other workplaces (Jørgensen, 2015). In our case study, we examined whether the company-driven vocational education prepares participants for the rapidly changing and technologically driven working life by supporting the development of necessary and transferable skills and competencies.

Our case study showed that a company-driven vocational education and training program is able to support the development of both field-specific skills and general working life skills. The interviewees revealed that the field-specific skills are basic skills necessary to work as an elevator engineer or as a maintenance engineer at KONE, such as technical skills and other skills that are needed in the field. For example, a deep technological understanding and a broad understanding of the entire professional field are particularly important. They create a good foundation for career advancement, not only in KONE but in other companies as well. The interviewees brought up the fact that even though employees usually stay at KONE for many years, the skills acquired in the elevator engineering training program are also transferable to other organizations in the same field. For example, one of the interviewees has been able to take advantage of the skills and understanding of the elevator industry in another company, to which he transferred soon after graduating. Overall, the training organized by KONE is appreciated widely and those who complete the elevator engineering training program go on to become employees that are desired by other companies in the same sector: "Other companies have been asking a bit about whether KONE trains anymore, since no workers are coming to them from here" (N3).

In addition to profession-specific skills, professionals working in the elevator and escalator industry need to have a wide range of general working life skills and competencies. These both relate to general changes that take place in working life, with a particular focus on changes in the elevator sector and the company's business operations, such as the digitalization of work. The data revealed that the changes in the field and the company's business operations are quickly transferred into and reflected in the contents and goals of the training. One of the key changes in KONE's business operations is that the customer-centered perspective has gradually become a key part of all work and is being brought to the heart of the company's operations: "Business is no longer merely preparing elevators but it is built on the whole service package and the customer experience" (N11).

Nowadays, KONE is strategically defined as a service company where the product itself may consist of steel, metal, and electronics, and the package of the services attached; it is the services that are produced for customers, and thus, the services become the key value provider, not the steel or metal in the product. Elevator engineers have significant roles to play as company representatives while operating as service providers for their clients. Therefore, preparing students to carry out high-quality customer work and developing service-expertise has also taken a central place in the training: "When talking of work, it always comes down to the customers. This was constantly emphasized throughout the training" (N9). Elevator engineers must be able to communicate "proactively with customers" (N4), as opposed to the past practice of working "unnoticed in the stairway" (N4).

Another example of general working life skills heavily emphasized in the training comprises internationality and language skills. The global company's official language is English, and work environments are also becoming increasingly international. Therefore, high-quality English-language teaching, which prepares students well for their working life, is an important part of the training. The importance of good language skills continues to grow, as work environments become increasingly international: "The role of English now is, of course, pretty important. Most of the instructions used in the job are in English, so you have to speak English pretty often" (N9).

The rapid upgrading of technology and the digitalization of work are omnipresent in the elevator engineers' profession. Changes, developments, and trends in the future cannot be predicted entirely, so company employees must have the ability and willingness to continuously update and extend their skills and competencies as well as to flexibly adapt to new types of operating models. On the other hand, although digitalization is a general trend, for example, some of the devices that are currently in use are very old. Therefore, elevator and maintenance engineers have to be able to work simultaneously with both old and rapidly developing technology and modern operating models. Our case study revealed that the firm knowledge base gained in the training helped employees to cope with these changes and to respond to new types of professional challenges with flexibility: "When the fundamentals of the profession are in place, changes are much easier to take on board" (N4).

Conclusions

Research addressing the impact of technology in both economics and in social sciences at large emphasizes the pervasive impact of technology in working life in several ways. The impact is not necessarily direct and is more often indirect, changing both the ways in which the work gets performed and the contents of the work itself (see, e.g., Brynjolfsson and McAfee, 2015). Technological development poses a wide range of challenges to individuals, educational institutions, and workplaces, and, most of all, to the relationship between education and working life. There is a need to strengthen the interactions between these two contexts and to rethink and transform the ways in which employees' competencies are cultivated over lifetimes in the face of accelerating change (Billett and

Henderson, 2011; Harteis et al., 2014; Hytönen, 2016; Susskind and Susskind, 2015).

Keeping education relevant in a technology-driven society requires responsive and flexible education for future professionals that can accommodate the needs of corporations in local and global environments. As mentioned at the beginning of the chapter, in these circumstances, it is of the utmost importance to examine, discuss, and consider the roles and responsibilities of individuals, educational institutions, companies, and working life (Kwiek, 2009). A closer and more strategic cooperation and new kinds of efforts to bridge and combine expertise, knowledge, and practice between education and business are needed to respond to future competence and capability needs. Here, increasing investment and involvement is necessary from the companies' side.

In this chapter, we focused on examining the ability of vocational education and training to take account of the new challenges posed by changes in working life. We introduced an educational design called a company-driven vocational education and training program. It is a good example of an educational model that is organized at the interface of education and industry and is administered in close partnership with a company. In our case study of KONE Elevators Ltd. (Hytönen and Kovalainen, 2018), we examined whether this educational design is able to support the development of multifaceted individual competencies that will be necessary for future working life and how the interconnections between education and working life are constructed in a sustainable manner.

The Finnish example shows that a company-driven vocational education and training program has many strengths. These relate especially to the close connection between the company and education, the company's commitment to students, and its ability to provide students with versatile and transferable competencies. The close connections enable the training to react to rapidly changing conditions in working life quickly and flexibly. The content and priorities of education can be developed without delay as new needs arise, such as those that result from developments in technology. It is particularly important that the training provides students with a genuine link to their working life and engages them early on in the company and its practices, providing effective and versatile learning environments. Strong interconnections between education and working life, support from experienced professionals, and the possibility of gaining experience on conducting varied and genuine duties have been emphasized to promote learning and the application and transfer of knowledge to other contexts (e.g., Davids et al., 2017; Jónasson, 2016).

As there is a need to strengthen the interface between education and working life at all levels of education, one significant question is how to ensure that companies commit themselves to sharing educational responsibility with educational institutions (Jørgensen, 2015). Upgrading skill formation according to the companies' purposes and needs has become highly important. Given that importance, an increasingly urgent task for all societies that face the challenges of rapid technological change and globalization is to work with the corporations. As the Finnish example shows, by organizing its own professional training, KONE was able to train a skilled workforce that would otherwise not be sufficiently equipped to engage in a specialized field. Through training, it can anticipate the availability of skilled employees in the future and effectively guarantee sound operating conditions. The aim is that through career guidance, in-house training, further training, and professional development, the students become committed and long-term employees who are highly competent to engage in many kinds of tasks. The results show that, at best, companies are able to create a genuine connection between training and working life, and to provide students with multifaceted learning possibilities and experiences.

It is obvious that some institutional requirements must be met in order for a company-driven vocational education and training program to be successful. In the Finnish case, funding provided by the state to specialized vocational institutions is of the utmost importance for KONE to maintain its own training system. The context of our study was a highly specialized professional field for which general vocational education did not provide skilled labor. KONE is a stable, global company with growth potential and is able to evaluate its employee needs far enough into the future. Its need for new employees has been significant enough to make it economically feasible to maintain its training institute.

Overall, our case study shows that a company-driven vocational education and training program that is provided with adequate resources enables educating employees in flexible ways and paves the way for individuals to build sustainable careers. There are elements of a company-driven vocational education and training program that are central to the broader applicability of the educational design (Hytönen and Kovalainen, 2018). These are related to its content, structure, and flexibility. The content elements refer to the close relationship between the educational content of the training and the business operations of the company. The content elements ensure the best knowledge in the practices of educating students in the Industrial School. The structural elements refer to the ways of organizing and implementing the training program. The program guarantees jobs in the company for graduates and also enables them to find work outside the company. The modular structure of the training effectively combines knowledge-based studies with practical training that circulate in close cycles. The flexibility elements refer to features that make the training model agile and adaptable to changes taking place in the company, its business activities, and the operational environment as well, more broadly, in work and in working life. In the future, it will be important to study how these elements of the company-driven vocational education program might be applied to other fields and areas of education.

Education has a significant role to play in affecting the working life skills of individuals and in influencing the way in which they develop before they enter the labor market. In Europe, the hybrid models of vocational education and training form a central part of the education system. The hybrid models of education have an increasing role to play in higher and further education as well. The upskilling trend in hiring practices of firms shows that more graduates with high cognitive skills and education are hired in the spirit of "Industrie 4.0" and smart factories (Baethge and Wolter, 2015; Doussard and Schrock, 2015). More research on how the platform economy can best draw results from the education system is necessary to deal with the prevailing situation, where national boundaries no longer restrict production in many cases. One of the plausible outcomes, unless the education systems remain stale, is that in the wake of the global platform economy, the upskilling of the national labor force will continue in its path of general development toward knowledge-based skills and the reduction of craft skills. In the course of this development, the vocational education and training system will only upscale and keep up with the accelerating change if it is renewed and supported by corporations and the state alike, as the Finnish case shows. In the course of this development, rapid technological renewal is one of the feeds that a collaborative interface can bring into the educational system.

This chapter discussed new educational needs and pressures, and proposed strengthening interfaces between education and working life. We introduced an educational design called a company-driven vocational education and training program, and used a global company, KONE Elevators Ltd., as the subject of our case study. We have examined whether the educational design organized in close partnership with the industry is able to support the development of individual competencies that will be necessary for future working life, and how these interconnections between education and working life are constructed in a sustainable manner. Our results support the stated assumptions. Based on literature on technological change, on the pace of educational institutional changes, and on our case study, we state that more profound interactions and partnerships between educational institutions and working life can provide a possible solution to meeting future educational challenges.

References

Autor, D., Levy, F. and Murnane, R. (2003). The Skill Content of Recent Technological Change: An Empirical Exploration. *Quarterly Journal of Economics*, 118(4), pp. 1279–333.

Baartman, L. K. and De Bruijn, E. (2011). Integrating Knowledge, Skills and Attitudes: Conceptualizing Learning Processes Towards Vocational Competence. *Educational Research Review*, 6(2), pp. 125–134.

Baethge, M. and Wolter, A. J. (2015). The German Skill Formation Model in Transition: From Dual System of VET to Higher Education? *Journal for Labour Market Research*, 48(2), pp. 97–112.

Berner, B. (2010). Crossing Boundaries and Maintaining Differences Between School and Industry: Forms of Boundary-Work in Swedish Vocational Education. *Journal of Education and Work*, 23(1), pp. 27–42.

Billett, S. (2008). Realising the Educational Worth of Integrating Work Experiences in Higher Education. *Studies in Higher Education*, 34(7), pp. 827–843.

Billett, S. and Henderson, A. (2011). *Developing Learning Professionals*. London: Springer.

Brynjolfsson, E. and McAfee, A. (2015). Will Humans Go the Way of Horses? Labor in the Second Machine Age. *Foreign Affairs*, 94(4), pp. 8–14.

Busemeyer, M. R. and Trampusch, C. (2012). The Comparative Political Economy of Collective Skill Formation. In: M. R. Busemeyer and C. Trampusch, eds., *The Political Economy of Collective Skill Formation*. Oxford: Oxford University Press, pp. 3–38.

Carlile, P. R. (2004). Transferring, Translating, and Transforming: An Integrative Framework for Managing Knowledge Across Boundaries. *Organization Science*, 15(5), pp. 555–568.

Costley, C. and Lester, S. (2012). Work-Based Doctorates: Professional Extension at the Highest Levels. *Studies in Higher Education*, 37(3), pp. 257–269.

Davids, A. I. R., Van den Bossche, P., Gijbels, D. and Garrido, M. F. (2017). The Impact of Individual, Educational, and Workplace Factors on the Transfer of School-Based Learning into the Workplace. *Vocations and Learning*, 10(3), pp. 275–306.

Davies, A., Fidler, D. and Gorbis, M. (2011). *Future Work Skills 2020*. Phoenix: Institute for the Future for the University of Phoenix Research Institute.

Doussard, M. and Schrock, G. (2015). Uneven Decline: Linking Historical Patterns and Processes of Industrial Restructuring to Future Growth Trajectories. *Cambridge Journal of Regions, Economy and Society*, 8(2), pp. 149–165.

Edwards, A. (2010). *Being an Expert Professional Practitioner*. London: Springer.

Endedijk, M. D. and Bronkhorst, L. H. (2014). Students' Learning Activities Within and Between the Context of Education and Work. *Vocations and Learning*, 7(3), pp. 289–311.

Facer, K. (2011). Taking the 21st Century Seriously: Young People, Education and Socio-Technical Futures. *Oxford Review of Education*, 38(1), pp. 97–113.

Freeman, C. and Soete, L. (1997). *The Economics of Industrial Innovation*. Cambridge: MIT Press.

Forster, A. G., Bol, T. and van de Werfhorst, H. G. (2016). Vocational Education and Employment Over the Life Cycle. *Sociological Science*, 3, pp. 473–494.

Frølich, N., Wendt, K., Reymert, I., Tellmann, S. M., Elken, M., Kyvik, S., Vabø, A. and Larsen, E. H. (2018). *Academic Career Structures in Europe: Perspectives from Norway, Denmark, Sweden, Finland, the Netherlands, Austria and the UK*. Oslo: Nordic Institute for Studies in Innovation, Research and Education NIFU.

Fürstenau, B., Pilz, M. and Gonon, P. (2014). The Dual System of Vocational Education and Training in Germany—What Can Be Learnt About Education for (Other) Professions. In: S. Billett, C. Harteis and H. Gruber, eds., *International*

Handbook of Research in Professional and Practice-Based Learning: Springer International Handbooks of Education. Dordrecht: Springer, pp. 427–460.

Graf, L. (2013). *The Hybridization of Vocational Training and Higher Education in Austria, Germany and Switzerland*. Budrich: Opladen.

Hakkarainen, K., Palonen, T., Paavola, S. and Lehtinen, E. (2004). *Communities of Networked Expertise: Professional and Educational Perspectives*, Sitra's Publication series, Publication no. 257. Oxford: Elsevier.

Hämäläinen, R., De Wever, B., Nissinen, K. and Cincinnato, S. (2019). What Makes the Difference—PIAAC as a Resource for Understanding the Problem-Solving Skills of Europe's Higher-Education Adults. *Computers and Education*, 129, pp. 27–36. https://doi.org/10.1016/j.compedu.2018.10.013

Hampf, F. and Woessmann, L. (2017). Vocational vs. General Education and Employment Over the LIFE Cycle: New Evidence from PIAAC. *CESifo Economic Studies*, 63(3), pp. 255–269.

Hanushek, E. A., Schwerdt, G., Woessmann, L. and Zhang, L. (2017). General Education, Vocational Education, and Labor-Market Outcomes Over the Life-Cycle. *Journal of Human Resources*, 52, pp. 48–87.

Harteis, C., Rausch, A. and Seifried, J. (ed.) (2014). *Discourses on Professional Learning: On the Boundary Between Learning and Working*. Dordrecht: Springer.

Hytönen, K. (2016). *Bridging Academic and Working Life Expertise in Continuing Professional Education: A Social Network Perspective*. Annales Universitatis Turkuensis, ser. B, tom. 424. Turku: University of Turku.

Hytönen, K. and Kovalainen, A. (2018). Boundaries Between Education and Working Life in Vocational Education Organized by a Company. A Case Study KONE Elevators Ltd. *Ammattikasvatuksen aikakauskirja*, 1, pp. 26–43.

Hytönen, K., Palonen, T., Lehtinen, E. and Hakkarainen, K. (2016). Between Two Advisors: Interconnecting Academic and Workplace Settings in an Emerging Field. *Vocations and Learning*, 9(3), pp. 333–359. doi: 10.1007/s12186-016-9156-5

Johnson, L., Adams Becker, S., Cummins, M., Estrada, V., Freeman, A. and Hall, C. (2016). *NMC Horizon Report: 2016 Higher Education Edition*. Austin, TX: The New Media Consortium.

Jónasson, J. T. (2016). Educational Change Inertia and Potential Futures. *European Journal of Futures Research*, 4(1), p. 7.

Jørgensen, C. H. (2015). Challenges for Work-Based Learning in Vocational Education and Training in the Nordic Countries. In: S. Bohlinger, U. Haake, C. H. Jørgensen, H. Toiviainen and A. Wallo, eds., *Working and Learning in Times of Uncertainty: Research on the Education and Learning of Adults*. Rotterdam: Sense Publishers, pp. 159–171.

Kaplan, A. (2011). *Reinventing Professional Services*. Hoboken, NJ: John Wiley and Sons.

Kenney, M., Rouvinen, P. and Zysman, J. (2015). The Digital Disruption and Its Societal Impacts. *Journal of Industry, Competition and Trade*, 15(1), pp. 1–4.

Kenney, M. and Zysman, J. (2016). The Rise of the Platform Economy. *Issues in Science and Technology*, 32(3), pp. 61–69.

Kessels, J. and Kwakman, K. (2007). Interface: Establishing Knowledge Networks Between Higher Vocational Education and Business. *Higher Education*, 54(5), pp. 689–703.

Knorr Cetina, K. and Reichmann, W. (2015). Professional Epistemic Cultures. In: I. Langemeyer, M. Fischer and M. Pfadenhauer, eds., *Epistemic and Learning Cultures*. Weinheim, Basel: Beltz Verlag, pp. 18–33.

Kunttu, L., Huttu, E. and Neuvo, Y. (2018). How Doctoral Students and Graduates Can Facilitate Boundary Spanning Between Academia and Industry. *Technology Innovation Management Review*, 8(6), pp. 49–54.

Kwiek, M. (2009). The Changing Attractiveness of European Higher Education in the Next Decade: Current Developments, Future Challenges and Major Policy Issues. *European Educational Research Journal*, 8(2), pp. 218–235.

Lamb, S., Jackson, J. and Rumberger, R. (2015). *ISCY Technical Paper: Measuring 21st Century Skills in ISCY*. Technical Report. Melbourne: Victoria University, Centre for International Research on Educational Systems.

Larson, M. (2013). *The Rise of Professionalism*. New Brunswick: Transaction Publishers.

Mikkonen, S., Pylväs, L., Rintala, H. P., Nokelainen, P. J. K. and Postareff, L. (2017). Guiding the Workplace Learning in Vocational Education and Training: A Literature Review. *Empirical Research in Vocational Education and Training*, 9(1), p. 9.

Nerland, M. (2012). Professions as Knowledge Cultures. In: K. Jensen, L. C. Lahn and M. Nerland, eds., *Professional Learning in the Knowledge Society* (pp. 27–48). Rotterdam: Sense Publishers.

Ohlsson, S. (2011). *Deep Learning: How the Mind Overrides Experience*. New York: Cambridge University Press.

Pajarinen, M. and Rouvinen, P. (2014). *Computerization Threatens One Third of Finnish Employment*. Helsinki: Brief-ETLA.

Palonen, T., Boshuizen, H. P. and Lehtinen, E. (2014). How Expertise Is Created in Emerging Professional Fields. In: T. Halttunen, M. Koivisto and S. Billett, eds., *Promoting, Assessing, Recognizing and Certifying Lifelong Learning*. Dordrecht: Springer, pp. 131–149.

Poortman, C. L., Reenalda, M., Nijhoff, W. J. and Nieuwenhuis, L. F. M. (2014). Workplace Learning in Dual Higher Professional Education. *Vocations and Learning*, 7(2), pp. 176–190.

Pullen, C. and Clifton, J. (2016). *England's Apprentices: Assessing the New System*. London: Institute of Public Policy Research. Available at: www.ippr.org/files/publications/pdf/Englands_apprenticeships_Aug%202016.pdf. [Accessed 16 January 2019].

Redecker, C., Leis, M., Leendertse, M., Punie, Y., Gijsbers, G., Kirschner, P., Stoyanov, S. and Hoogveld, B. (2010). *The Future of Learning: New Ways to Learn New Skills for Future Jobs: Results from an Online Expert Consultation*. Luxemburg: Publications office of the European Union.

Roxå, T., Mårtensson, K. and Alveteg, M. (2011). Understanding and Influencing Teaching and Learning Cultures at University: A Network Approach. *Higher Education*, 62(1), pp. 99–111.

Seppänen, L., Hasu, M., Käpykangas, S. and Poutanen, S. (2018). On-Demand Work in Platform Economy: Implications for Sustainable Development. *Paper Presented at the 20th Congress of International Ergonomics Association*, Italy, August 2018.

Siivonen, P. (2016). Becoming an Educable Lifelong Learning Subject: Adult Graduates' Transitions in Education and Working Life. *International Journal of Lifelong Education*, 35(1), pp. 36–50.

Sundararajan, A. (2016). *The Sharing Economy. The End of Employment and the Rise of Crowd-Based Capitalism*. Cambridge, MA: The MIT Press.

Susskind, R. and Susskind, D. (2015). *The Future of Professions: How Technology Will Transform the Work of Human Experts*. Oxford: Oxford University Press.

Talwar, R. and Hancock, T. (2010). *The Shape of Jobs to Come: Possible New Careers Emerging from Advances in Science and Technology (2010-2030)*. London: Fast Future Research.

Vallas, S. P. and Hill, A. L. (2018). Reconfiguring Worker Subjectivity: Career Advice Literature and the "Branding" of the Worker's Self. *Sociological Forum*, 33(2), pp. 287–309.

Vallas, S. P. and Kovalainen, A. (2019). Introduction: Taking Stock of the Digital Revolution. In: S. P. Vallas and A. Kovalainen, eds., *Work and Labor in the Digital Age*. Bingley: Emerald Publishing.

Vest, C. M. (2008). Context and Challenge for Twenty-First Century Engineering Education. *Journal of Engineering Education*, 97(3), pp. 235–236.

5 Digital Disruption in the Making

Digitalization of Finnish Employment Agencies

Aija Leiponen and Annu Kotiranta

Introduction: Digital Versus Traditional Recruitment

The digitalization of service industries can be an unsettling process that requires significant risk taking (Kane et al., 2015; Zysman et al., 2011). There are many examples of industries for which this transformation has proven turbulent, marked by mass exits of firms and an influx of new types of service providers. For example, during the first wave of internet-based commerce, travel agencies initially resisted digitalization, insisting on their traditional business models of customers personally visiting "bricks and mortar" offices to select flights and travel packages held only by agencies through limited access to the airfare booking systems. However, after airfare information became widely accessible through companies such as ITA Software, physical travel agencies lost their source of market power and, over a few years, lost much of their business to online travel agencies such as Orbitz, Expedia, and subsequently Kayak (Singh and Hess, 2017; Crowston and Myers, 2004).[1] The digital transformation of an industry is thus a tremendous managerial challenge for existing firms.

The current process of digitalization deeply influences the structure and operation of services (Chanias et al., 2019). With increased computing power, network bandwidth, cheap storage, and the rapid improvement of office software, service operations can be digitized to a high degree (Cusumano, 2010). In addition, machine learning and other "intelligent" technologies promise to digitize and automate much of the repetitive service interaction, at least in relatively stable and frequent activities. However, as described in the literature on disruptive innovation (Adner, 2002; Christensen and Rosenbloom, 1995), traditional service providers often have a hard time perceiving and acting upon the threats—and opportunities—of technological change. This is particularly true when the new way of doing business would require fundamentally redesigning the existing business model or when there is a substantial gap of technological skills and capabilities between the old and new models (Rogers, 2010). In the context of digitalization, there is likely a need for both new technological competencies and new organization forms (Bresnahan et al., 2002).

Employment agencies are typically small service firms that seek to match potential employees with potential employers. This is often done on a temporary basis, whereby a candidate usually works part time. When an employer has a temporary staffing need to substitute for an absent employee (e.g., due to family or sick leave), they contact the agency for potential candidates that are qualified and suitable for the job. Temporary employees may be employed for hours, days, weeks, or even months. The employment agency uses information about the employer and candidates to find the best available match. Many employment agencies also provide placement services; that is, they help employers recruit talented and skilled candidates for permanent positions. According to information from Adecco, the world's largest employment service provider, generalist workforce staffing (permanent or temporary) generates the most revenues and profit. However, specialist staffing has the highest profit margins (The Adecco Group, 2018, p. 6).

Leading providers in the employment service industry are well aware of ongoing technological changes. Among the workforce megatrends affecting the company's future opportunities and competitive challenges, Adecco describes flexible work and the gig economy; skill imbalances; automation, AI, and machine learning; and digitization, big data, and analytics (The Adecco Group, 2018, p. 10). The company is thus explicitly considering structural changes to labor markets and the nature of work as described by Kovalainen et al. in Chapter 2 of this book. As a response, Adecco is upgrading its technological infrastructure and launching a suite of digital platforms and solutions, including a mobile end-to-end platform for temporary staff recruitment developed in partnership with Infosys and the acquisition of Vettery, an online talent marketplace. The company intends to be well positioned to exploit these megatrends that might lead to market growth but also to significant consolidation because of the growing technological barriers to market entry and the economies of scale that ensue (The Adecco Group, 2018; Kovalainen et al. in Chapter 2 of this book). Similarly, leading Finnish companies, such as Barona and Eilakaisla, are developing digital recruitment tools and systems to address innovation opportunities (Barona, 2019; Eilakaisla, 2019).

The focus of this chapter is on Finnish native employment service providers that are traditionally small and have less technological savvy and fewer resources than companies such as Adecco. Although it is well understood that market disruption is difficult for such traditional firms, we know little about the strategic behaviors of firms anticipating digital transformation. As such, we explore what small and traditional service providers perceive prior to major market changes and how they prepare for competition against digital challengers. We survey the threats or opportunities brought on by digitalization and the preparedness of small Finnish service providers to address them. We also characterize the conceptualization by business leaders of the required strategic change when digitalization seems imminent but its nature uncertain.

Conceptual Background: Opportunities to Create Digital Platforms in Employment Services

Whereas digitalization tends to shift tasks from humans to computers, its paradox is that it requires human capital. While it is relatively simple to outsource existing business activities to a digital service provider, it is much more challenging to build digital business processes within the company. Investments in skills, technologies, and new organizational practices are required. Such organizational complementarities became evident from the early days of digital transformation (Bresnahan et al., 2002).

More recently, the availability of high connectivity and speed, and cheap storage, has enabled new organizational forms of digital business. First, cloud computing has transformed the cost structure of digital business operations, changing the traditionally large fixed cost of computing to a much lower variable cost under the Software-as-a-Service model, with a high degree of flexibility and little to no capacity constraint (Etro, 2009). Service startups can now more easily enter new markets due to their lesser need for capital, and they can quickly scale using outsourced computing resources. Such benefits of cloud computing can provide substantial competitive advantages to firms that are able to exploit these technologies and systems.

Second, the rise of digital platforms has provided a template for business models that orchestrate interactions in a system of exchange. Digital platforms are multisided markets where a large number of potentially diverse parties can digitally interact with their counterparts over a technical system by using standardized interfaces and transaction formats. All digital markets and communication services can be viewed through this theoretical lens. The rapidly advancing theoretical and empirical research on platform markets has highlighted the complex interactions and strategies of launching, growing, and competing on digital platforms (Spulber, 2019; Thomas et al., 2014).

The early economic research on platforms highlighted the need to balance demand on the different sides of the market through pricing and integration strategies (Weyl, 2010; Hagiu, 2009; Armstrong, 2006; Rochet and Tirole, 2006). When platform users care not only about the service they receive, but also about the number of counterparts they can trade or interact with—in other words, when there are network effects—the size of the platform market will influence users' benefits from it (Katz and Shapiro, 1985). Importantly, when there are such "cross-side" network effects (Parker and Van Alstyne, 2005), it will be challenging for the market to achieve critical mass. Without critical mass, that is, a sufficient number of parties to interact with, new users may not perceive the net benefits of the platform as positive and thus may not join it. Furthermore, when all platform users perceive the lack of existing counterparts on the opposite side of the platform to harm the viability of the platform, it is difficult to attract enough participants on any side. This is known as the chicken-and-egg problem (Caillaud and Jullien, 2003). Success begets success and failure begets failure across the different sides of the platform. The platform innovator must therefore engage and grow multiple sides of the platform in a synchronized fashion (Evans, 2011).

However, after digital platforms achieve critical mass, they may scale much more quickly and efficiently than physical marketplaces. As a result, platforms such as Apple's App Store, Amazon, or Google as an advertising platform have grown massively and taken over large market shares. By 2019, Amazon commanded almost half of all "e-tailing" (online retail) in the United States (CSA, 2019). It now sells almost 50 percent all books in the United States and 89 percent of all e-books (Bloomberg, 2019). Google has performed similarly in the digital advertising market, with a 38 percent market share (GeekWire, 2019). Together with Facebook (22 percent market share), Google is dominant in digital advertising. Therefore, while it is difficult to build and grow digital platforms, if successful, they can lead to the significant and relatively rapid disruption of the established order in the industry they enter. With the growth experienced by leading digital platforms, there is growing concern about their implications for competition. However, scholarly research on the competitive and regulatory aspects of platforms is only beginning (Evans and Schmalensee, 2014).

Thus, given the technological and organizational innovations of cloud computing and digital platform markets, employment agencies have clear opportunities for innovation, but their capacities to exploit such opportunities may be insufficient. We consider two primary reasons for this development. First, firms may lack complementary assets, such as skills and practices that allow firms to profit from digital platform innovations. Second, the significant market uncertainty (Chesbrough, 2003), compounded with the lack of digital capabilities, may render firms unable to even perceive innovation opportunities in a timely manner and, if perceived, reluctant to invest in them because of their limited slack resources for risk taking. Particularly, firms may be attached to existing value propositions and their ways of conducting business with existing clients (Christensen and Rosenbloom, 1995). Creating new value propositions for new client types can thus present too many innovation challenges at once. Therefore, this pilot study investigates (1) what types of digital capabilities firms have and (2) how they perceive digital innovation opportunities that may quickly "disrupt" their industry.

Empirical Setting: Finnish Employment Services Industry

We explore the degree to which employment agencies are prepared to initiate digitalization and actively or reactively respond to technological and competitive challenges. Specifically, we focus on private employment agencies because they appear to be at the cusp of a digital transformation and benefit from significant innovation opportunities, yet much of the industry is characterized by a low utilization of digital technologies and reliance on human communication and decision-making. Informed by the extant research on digital transformation and platform competition, we explore the digital investments of employment agencies, their concerns and constraints in adopting digital practices or creating new digital services, and their perceptions of and responses to the potential entry of digital platforms in their industry.

Recruitment and temporary employment services are essentially matching services (Roth and Peranson, 1999), where temporary employees are matched with employees for short-duration "gigs" and longer-term employees are selected by the specific needs of recruiting companies, usually at upper salaried levels rather than for entry-level positions. Both activities rely on information on employees' skills and abilities and the needs of employers, usually utilizing long-standing industry knowledge regarding how to match the two sets. Currently, this matching is done largely based on "small" data and human decision-making—heuristics and psychological evaluations through interviews. There is thus an opportunity for firms to collect more data and use them to build sophisticated machine-learning models that, over time, might exceed the human capacity to predict successful matches (Hoffman et al., 2018).

By 2016, a few Finnish companies had started to develop automated matching platforms. When this topic was discussed at the annual event of the Finnish industry association (Private Employment Agencies Association, PEAA), it attracted significant interest and created trepidation among the company representatives, as digital transformation was viewed as much as an opportunity as a threat. The discussions revolved around the possibility that some large (foreign) software service company might begin to offer such matching services purely based on data and technological capabilities, thus "disrupting" the industry. Concerns that small and low-tech Finnish companies might not be able to respond to such a competitive challenge were raised. As such, this chapter attempts to systematically describe how small-scale service providers view digital disruption before it happens, and how they anticipate responding to it. In a follow-up study, we plan to revisit the study participants to assess whether and how digitalization ultimately affected competitive market conditions.

Following a discussion with the board of the industry association, we decided to launch a small-scale pilot survey to assess the readiness of Finnish employment service companies to address digital innovation opportunities, as well as their perception of the likely evolution of the industry. We utilized a "survey experiment" methodology by asking respondents to consider one of two possible competitive threats: an automated matching platform launched by a large domestic company versus an automated matching platform launched by a US technology firm.

The survey was sent out to PEAA member companies in June 2017, followed by a reminder in August 2017. Altogether, 188 email links were shared with the companies and 43 responses were received, yielding a response rate of 23 percent. Finally, the survey data were enriched with companies' demographic and financial information retrieved from Statistics Finland. Despite the relatively low response rate, the respondents reflect reasonably well the structure of the industry. However, larger companies were more available to answer than smaller companies and the average number of employees among the survey respondents was 236, while the corresponding figure among non-respondents was 74. The pronounced share of large companies must thus be kept in mind when interpreting the survey results. As a result, our sample companies represent 46 percent of all employees working in the target companies.

Survey Sample

PEAA members belong to industry class 78 (employment activities), with subclasses 781 (employment placement), 782 (temporary employment agency), and 783 (other human resource provision). While many of the surveyed member companies conduct both placement and temporary employment services, their primary industry class is set as temporary employment agency (782). Overall, this industry is expanding. The number of companies increased by 6 percent between 2013 and 2016, whereas revenues and the total number of employees grew by 26 percent over the same period – please see Figure 5.1 (StatisticsFinland, 2018). The even growth of employees and revenues implies that productivity in terms of revenue per employee remained constant despite firm growth; that is, there are limited economies of scale within the traditional business model, and growth was achieved by adding new tasks for new employees. This suggests that, over the study period, the industry was largely dependent on human services, and there were probably significant opportunities to digitalize tasks.

About one-third of respondent firms belonged to a larger consolidated corporation and 13 percent were part of a franchising group. Belonging to either type of a group seemed to decrease firms' decision power on development projects and investments in general. This suggests that the survey responses reflect not only the choices of respondent firms, but also those of their principals and the consolidated corporation or franchising

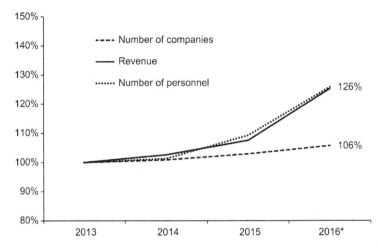

Figure 5.1 Number of Firms, Total Revenue, and Total Employment in the Employment Placement Agencies, Industry (TOL08, class 78200) for 2013–2016; Indexed, Year 2013 = 100%

group. Altogether, our sample firms mediated 36,100 temporary employees, totaling 13,600 person-years in 2016.

How Does Digitalization Proceed in Small Service Firms? Descriptive Analysis of the Survey Dataset

We were particularly interested in how employment service companies prepared for digitalization through the adoption of digital skills and practices. Figure 5.2 presents the numbers and shares of employees focused on digitalization by firm size. Most companies had not even meaningfully begun digitalization. In terms of digitalization inputs, an average employment agency employed only 0.5 persons focused on digitalization, such as a programmer, system developer, or analyst. The median is zero: at least half of companies had no human resources allocated to digitalization. However, in some larger companies, digitalization teams consisted of more than 10 employees. While large companies have more employees working on digitalization in absolute terms, in relative terms, smaller companies with 10–50 employees invest more in this area. Similar trends apply to monetary investments: large companies invest more in absolute terms but, relative to revenues, smaller companies invest more. However, the smallest firms (up to 10 employees) made no digitalization investments at all. Additionally, digitalization investments seem complementary: companies investing in human resources also invest more in monetary terms.[2] Similarly for outsourcing: companies that spend a

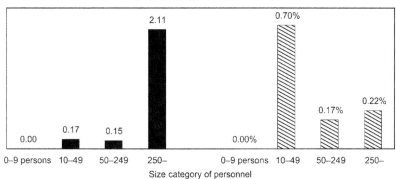

Figure 5.2 Employees Working on Digitalization in 2016 on Average Per Company and as a Proportion of Total Personnel by Size Category of Personnel

Data source: Survey data and Statistics Finland's company registration information, 2015 (StatisticsFinland, 2019).

larger share of their revenues on outsourcing IT services also have more in-house personnel related to digitalization or IT. This suggests digitalization inputs are mutually complementary and cannot be completely outsourced as the successful outsourcing of digital services appears to also necessitate in-house know-how.

The digitalization of general administrative processes in employment services is similar compared to other small Finnish service firms. Figure 5.3 displays the degrees of digitalization by business function. Typically, digital practices have been adopted in core administration: payroll and accounts payable and receivable are around 75 percent digitalized. However, this has little to do with preparedness for the digitalization of more strategic, core service activities. When looking at the core functions of employment agencies, such as sales and communication with clients, the share of digitalization drops significantly. Even lower is the utilization of data in decision-making, as per Figure 5.4. Data analyses inform strategic decisions such as investments and the establishment of new offices the least, whereas recurring business decisions such as recruiting and pricing are more likely to be based on data and analyses. Surprisingly, even temporary employee compensation decisions are based primarily on human decision-making as opposed to data about past wages and performance. It thus seems that small service firms are in the very early stages of adopting data-driven decision-making and business practices.

Next, we present baseline information on surveyed companies' views on market opportunities and competitive challenges. We also inquire

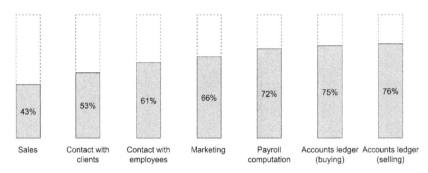

Figure 5.3 To What Degree Has Your Company Digitalized or Automated the Following Functions (0–100%)?

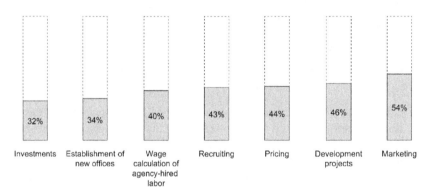

Figure 5.4 To What Degree Are the Following Decisions Based on Digital Data and Data Analysis (0–100%)?

about factors that might hinder the firms' abilities to address these opportunities or challenges. These questions, featured in Table 5.1, provide a view into the "business as usual" competition that the surveyed employment agencies experience.

All questions could be answered on a scale from 1 to 4, where 1 means "not at all," 2 "a little," 3 "somewhat," and 4 "significantly." New customers and general market growth were seen as the most likely new market opportunities (score of 3.3 out of 4). Additionally, new market niches (2.8/4) and launching new services (2.6/4) were identified as possible growth paths. However, growth via digital platforms and digital services were considered less likely (2.2/4). The least likely growth path was entry onto global markets (1.3/4), which suggests that most domestic companies are not interested in broadening their operating environment beyond the Finnish market, despite competing multinational firms in Finland.

Table 5.1 Companies' Expectations on the Following Year's Market Opportunities, Competition Challenges, and Factors Hindering Competition Strategies (Scale 1–4, Where 1 = Not at All, 2 = Little, 3 = Somewhat, 4 = Significantly)

What kind of market opportunities do you expect your company to utilize within the following 12 months? (Scale 1–4)		What kind of competition challenges does your company expect within the following 12 months? (Scale 1–4)		Which factors hinder your competition strategies with respect to the previously evaluated strategies? (Scale 1–4)	
New clients	3.3	Toughened competition on the availability of workforce	3.6	Lack of digital know-how (incl. automation)	2.3
Growth of markets	3.3	Competitors' new digital service innovations	2.6	Clients are not interested in innovations	2.3
New niches	2.8	Competitors' new digital (internet-based) platforms	2.6	Legislation concerning personal data	2.1
Launching of new services	2.6	Competitors' new service innovations	2.4	Lack of other skills or know-how	2.0
Launching of new digital platforms	2.2	Competitors' mergers or acquisitions	2.3	Lack of innovative ideas	1.9
Launching of new, purely digital services	2.2	Market entry of new foreign companies	2.1	Lack of managerial skills	1.8
Growth via acquisition or merger	1.8	Market entry of new domestic companies	1.9	Lack of funding	1.7
Entry to foreign markets	1.3	Slow market growth	1.8		

The most significant competitive challenge appears to be labor market competition for employees to place. Next, service innovations and new platforms are seen as somewhat challenging competitive issues. Interestingly, respondents tend to consider the threat of rivals' new digital platforms or services as more important than they view their own opportunities to create them. This is perhaps explained by the top factors hampering the adoption of these new strategies—lack of digital skills and clients that appreciate innovations. On the other hand, funding does not appear to be a constraining factor, nor the lack of ideas or managerial competence.

These data, together with the previous questions, create an interesting observation: on one hand, there are resources and opportunities to react, as on average, nothing seems to be hindering competition strategies significantly; but on the other hand, few investments have been made in digitalization, which is considered a major competition challenge in the near future.

The Impact of Digital Disruption: A Survey Experiment

In the final part of the survey, the respondents were asked to consider their responses to a new competitor in the market. Half of respondents were presented with scenario 1 and the other half with scenario 2. This exercise was intended to isolate the impacts of the different sources of disruption and how financial and human resources might moderate the response.

> Scenario 1: A large **domestic company** launches a digital matching ser-vice (automated recruiting service). What is your company's strate-gic reaction?
>
> Scenario 2: A **US-based technology company** enters the Finnish employment agency market and launches a digital matching service (automated recruiting service). What is your company's strategic reaction?

The firms were asked to predict the likelihood of their reactions by using a scale from 1 to 4, where 1 = impossible, 2 = unlikely, 3 = likely, and 4 = very likely. Altogether, the likelihood of eight different reactions were evaluated, as shown in Figure 5.5.

On average, the entry of a digital matching service was not considered a significant threat that required strategic action. In view of the previous analyses, this may be due to the lack of know-how or the fact that the scenario did not seem that threatening. There are few statistically signifi-cant differences between the reactions to scenarios 1 and 2, except in one respect: if the digital matching service is launched by a domestic competi-tor, the likelihood of forming research and development collaboration is higher than in the case of a new US-based digital competitor.[3] Mean-while, we found a weakly significant difference between the responses on accelerating the development of service innovations currently underway. If the competitive threat is from a US-based technology company, Finnish employment agencies are more likely to respond with innovation.

Within both scenarios, the least likely option is selling the company. This is interesting, considering the industry is undergoing significant con-solidation due to anticipated changes in the operating environment, for example, the integration of private and public employment services.

Next, the scenarios remained unchanged, but the respondents were informed they would receive substantial new funding within the follow-ing six months and were asked how likely they consider the different options now. Interestingly, funding does not seem to be a major obstacle

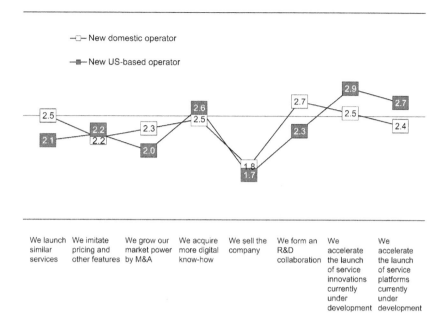

Figure 5.5 A Large Domestic/US-Based Company Enters the Market and Launches a Digital Matching Service (Automated Recruiting Service); What Is Your Company's Strategic Reaction? (Scale 1–4, 1 = Impossible, 2 = Unlikely, 3 = Likely, 4 = Very Likely)

for strategic development, and these results were insignificant: additional funding had minimal effects on the likelihood of strategic action. If anything, companies seek to acquire more digital know-how, especially if the new competitor is a US-based company (presumably with greater technological capabilities). We thus find no evidence that digitalization is constrained by financial resources.

In the final set of questions, another possible bottleneck was removed: the basic scenario remained the same, but the respondents were informed that they succeeded in recruiting a top-notch digital developer with a highly skilled team. Now, the likelihood of strategic action significantly increases, particularly in scenario 2, where the competitive threat is from a US-based technology firm. Specifically, the likelihood of copying and launching a similar service, forming a research and development collaboration, and accelerating the development of service platforms currently under construction were substantially and statistically significantly[4] increased compared to basic scenario 2.

Firms operating in scenario 1, where a domestic competitor launched a new platform, were more moderate in their responses, and only the likelihood of accelerating the development of service platforms currently under construction increased statistically significantly[5] compared to the basic scenario.

In our final analyses, we explored the strategic reactions by firm types. The scenario questions combined with demographic and financial information on the respondent firms allowed us to identify the factors behind their strategies. We combined the responses to scenarios 1 and 2 into one dataset and formed three equally large groups based on how likely the company saw itself reacting to a new digital competitor in the market. The groups were labelled as follows:

- *Forerunners* include companies that consider it more likely to react to the new market competitor.
- *Reactors* include companies that remain in the middle—typically the average probability of reacting is the arithmetic mean between "possible" and "likely."
- *Passives* include companies that are not likely to react to changes in the operating environment.

When the information on the likelihood of reacting to the new service platform in the market was combined with background information, forerunner companies were on average larger, had a greater number of digital experts, and their monetary investments in digital technology were larger than those of the other two groups. They were thus significantly better prepared for the potential technological upheaval.

As before, the sampled firms did not consider the lack of financial resources to be a particularly significant bottleneck for new competitive strategies. By contrast, especially among the more passive firms, acquiring a highly skilled digital development team significantly increased the probability of strategic action across almost all given options. Figure 5.6 illustrates the strategic responses of forerunners and passives, under both the basic and digital team scenarios. Among the forerunners, the marginal reactions to the digital development team were less pronounced. Interestingly, a top-notch digital development team was perceived to increase the likelihood of developing digital innovation and platforms, but to decrease the likelihood of traditional strategic actions such as pricing and mergers/acquisitions to attain increased market power. Altogether, a substantial enhancement of in-house digital capabilities would likely propel competitive laggards into innovative action but has a significantly lower impact on the market leaders, who were more likely to already be cultivating such teams.

Finally, we conducted a principal component analysis to explore the correlation structure of key variables. As item non-response was a challenge, we considered only a small set of variables on firm size, age, digital employees, degree of digitalization of payroll and sales; degree of

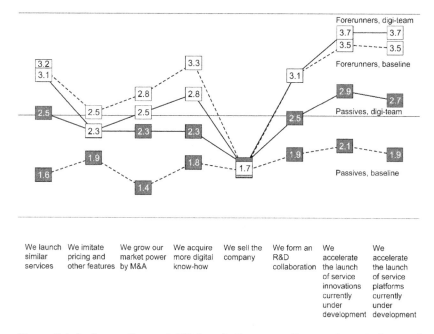

Figure 5.6 A Large Domestic/US-Based Company Enters the Market and Launches a Digital Matching Service (Automated Recruiting Service), *and* Your Company Is Able to Recruit a High-Level Digital Developer and a Development Team; What Is Your Company's Strategic Reaction? (Scale 1–4, 1 = Impossible, 2 = Unlikely, 3 = Likely, 4 = Very Likely)

digitalization of recruitment of temporary employees and marketing; and responses to the first scenario. The principal component solution is provided in the Appendix to this chapter.

These analyses reinforce the idea that firm size, age, and existing digital skills influence the degree of digitalization and the responses to the threat of digital competition. The profile that explains the greatest share of the total variance, the "digital innovators," corresponds to larger firms with existing digital employees, who would strongly respond to competitive challenges under the presented scenario but were not particularly focused on digitalizing all business operations. No other profiles responded as strongly to the potential entry of an automated matching platform. Instead, small and young firms represented a "selective digitalization" strategy, whereby they had digitalized some of their operations (e.g., payroll and temp employee recruitment) but had limited, if any, in-house digital competencies and would likely respond to the competitive challenge of the matching platform by seeking to acquire more competencies.

In contrast, older and larger firms not focused on innovation tended to have in-house digital competencies but primarily viewed digitalization through business operations, not innovation and platform development. Finally, a group of young firms that possess some digital competencies and activities viewed themselves as capable of responding to a potential platform creation in the industry through imitation.

This analysis highlights that firm size, age, and existing resources influence how a firm perceives digital innovation opportunities. Specifically, more mature firms are more likely to view digitalization as an operational efficiency issue and to focus on adopting digital technologies for different business functions. By contrast, very young firms may be "born digital" in some business areas but may be particularly constrained by the availability and cost of digital competencies in their digital innovation strategies. The presence of digital competencies depends on a firm's existing scale and enables a more proactive stance in exploiting digital opportunities.

Conclusions

We conducted an exploratory survey experiment to develop a methodology and draw inferences on how firms anticipate and react to a likely digital transformation of their respective industries. We studied the technological and competitive strategies of Finnish employment service firms to assess their digital preparedness and current levels of digital business processes and data-driven decision-making. Although this industry is ready for digital platform creation by one or more industry parties, the mainly small and medium-sized firms in the industry have done relatively little to address such innovation opportunities.

Our findings suggest that the relative lack of technological innovation was due not to financial constraints, but rather to the limited demand from existing clients and limited digital competencies. Companies operating in this industry thus appeared focused on the needs of their existing customers in terms of service development activities. For most firms, innovating new ways of conducting business with new customers over digital platforms did not emerge within the set of feasible strategies. Only a subset of larger firms that already had digital capabilities were able to perceive this strategy as viable. Other large firms appeared to focus on the digitalization of their operations but not on digital innovation, whereas smaller and younger firms were more likely to focus on digital competence acquisition. Nevertheless, in our survey experiment, a high-powered digital development team had a strong impact on digital innovation responses, particularly for firms who were otherwise passive in the digital competition.

While current clients' lack of interest for digital solutions to their employment and placement needs might be a real issue for employment service providers, their reactions are typical of digital disruption. That is, such disruptive innovations are often initially commercialized in relatively small or emerging niche markets, where margins are low and clients small and not wealthy. An example is the commercialization of open source software (OSS). OSS operating system Linux originated in academia in the early 1990s and was initially adopted among engineering students, scientific labs, and university spinoffs. Large corporations saw no need for these systems because they were perceived as cumbersome, unreliable, and riddled with legal risks. However, over time, the availability of Linux skills increased, and a consulting industry emerged to sell services to install and maintain OSS, making mainstream adoption more palatable. By 2017, Linux was the most common operating system for servers, supercomputers, and mobile devices (through Android), also rapidly growing in personal computing through the Linux-based Chromium OS used in the inexpensive Chromebook laptops. Thus, the disruption of the computing industry by open source operating systems lasted over 20 years but eventually took over most of the global device base. However, initially enterprise clients of software companies were reluctant to switch to OSS.

In our assessment, the industry-level development of digital competencies for data-driven operations, development of platforms and new software-based services, and deep analytics to inform strategic decision-making, will be critical in the digital transformation. Considering that all service industries are likely to compete for the same general-purpose capabilities, competition for IT talent will be tough and may delay transition for many existing companies, making them vulnerable to attacks by the agglomerations of existing technological know-how. As such, this might create opportunities for new entrants to build new temporary employment markets for either domestic or foreign technology leaders that already possess such technological capabilities. As a result, small, purely human resource-based boutiques may have a difficult time keeping up or may be pushed into narrow niche markets.

The digital transition of domestic, low-tech service markets is highly uncertain. How quickly should existing service providers invest and develop new competencies? Our advice is to monitor new entrants' technological practices. For example, startups may adopt and adjust digital technologies and practices from related industries and have different technological foundations. For example, our survey data suggest the latest cohorts of employment service firms may be more advanced than their more mature counterparts in digitalizing core business functions. Young and growth-oriented firms may also be more adept at imitating best practices and technologies, driving up their market shares and competing with older and more rigid rivals. Beginning development when market shares have already started to shift will be too late, and laggards are likely to run out of funds before they catch up.

Whether new entrants or startup companies are in the position to build major digital platform markets in this industry remains to be seen. It is well known that driving the adoption of digital platforms requires a lot of resources, meaning larger and better-resourced firms are more likely to withstand such major competitive challenges. Although the timing of technological transitions is impossible to predict, it seems inevitable that a much greater degree of digitalization of employment services will emerge because digital operations and platforms can eradicate substantial costs and inefficiencies and rapidly scale innovative business models. Digital technologies are "general purpose" in nature, such as electricity, and history suggests all industries will be transformed by such technologies; the only question is how soon. In our estimation, the question is "when" rather than "whether," and firms should prepare accordingly. Ultimately, employment agencies will likely blur boundaries with other work platforms, as discussed by Kenney et al. in Chapter 1 in this book.

Notes

1 See also Andal-Ancion et al. (2003).
2 Positive statistically pairwise correlation and positive statistically significant partial correlation (OLS) when the number of employees has been controlled for a 95 percent confidence level.
3 Statistically significant two-sided t-test with unequal variances, 90 percent confidence level.
4 Statistically significant two-sided t-test with unequal variances, 90 percent confidence level.
5 Statistically significant two-sided t-test with unequal variances, 90 percent confidence level.

References

The Adecco Group. (2018). Making the Future Work for Everyone: Full 2018 Annual Report. Available at: https://ar.adeccogroup.com/downloads.html [Accessed 8 June 2019].
Adner, R. (2002). When Are Technologies Disruptive? A Demand-Based View of the Emergence of Competition. *Strategic Management Journal*, 23(8), pp. 667–688.
Andal-Ancion, A., Cartwright, P. A. and Yip, G. S. (2003). The Digital Transformation of Traditional Business. *MIT Sloan Management Review*. Available at: https://sloanreview.mit.edu/article/the-digital-transformation-of-traditional-business/ [Accessed 7 May 2019].
Armstrong, M. (2006), Competition in Two-Sided Markets. *The RAND Journal of Economics*, 37(3), pp. 669–691.
Barona. (2019). Future in the Making. Available at: https://barona.fi/en/barona/ [Accessed 7 May 2019].
Bloomberg. (2019). The Enormous Numbers Behind Amazon's Market Reach. Available at: www.bloomberg.com/graphics/2019-amazon-reach-across-markets/ [Accessed 9 April 2019].

Bresnahan, T. F., Brynjolfsson, E. and Hitt, L. M. (2002). Information Technology, Workplace Organization, and the Demand for Skilled Labor: Firm-Level Evidence. *The Quarterly Journal of Economics*, 117(1), pp. 339–376.

Caillaud, B. and Jullien, B. (2003). Chicken & Egg: Competition Among Intermediation Service Providers. *The RAND Journal of Economics*, 34(2), pp. 309–328.

Chanias, S., Myers, M. D. and Hess, T. (2019). Digital Transformation Strategy Making in Pre-Digital Organizations: The Case of a Financial Services Provider. *The Journal of Strategic Information Systems*, 28(1), pp. 17–33.

Chesbrough, H. W. (2003) *Open Innovation: The New Imperative for Creating and Profiting from Technology*. Boston, MA: Harvard Business School Press.

Christensen, C. M. and Rosenbloom, R. S. (1995). Explaining the Attacker's Advantage: Technological Paradigms, Organizational Dynamics, and the Value Network. *Research Policy*, 24(2), pp. 233–257.

Crowston, K. and Myers, M. D. (2004). Information Technology and the Transformation of Industries: Three Research Perspectives. *The Journal of Strategic Information Systems*, 13(1), pp. 5–28.

CSA. (2019). eMarketer: Amazon to Capture 47% of All U.S. Online Sales in 2019. Available at: www.chainstoreage.com/technology/emarketer-amazon-to-capture-47-of-all-u-s-online-sales-in-2019/ [Accessed 8 May 2019].

Cusumano, M. A. (2010). Cloud Computing and SaaS as New Computing Platforms. *Communications of the ACM*, 53(4), pp. 27–29.

Eilakaisla. (2019). *Aikansa edelläkävijä*. Available at: www.eilakaisla.fi/eilakaisla/kaislan-tarina [Accessed 9 June 2019].

Etro, F. (2009). The Economic Impact of Cloud Computing on Business Creation, Employment and Output in Europe. An Application of the Endogenous Market Structures Approach to a GPT Innovation. *Review of Business and Economic Literature*, 54(2), pp. 179–208.

Evans, D. (2011). How Catalysts Ignite: The Economics of Platform-Based Start-Ups. In: A. Gawer, ed., *Platforms, Markets, and Innovation*. Cheltenham: Edward Elgar, pp. 99–130.

Evans, D. and Schmalensee, R. (2014). The Antitrust Analysis of Multisided Platform Businesses. In: R. D. Blair and D. D. Sokol, eds., *The Oxford Handbook of International Antitrust Economics 1*. Oxford: Oxford University Press, pp. 404–450.

GeekWire. (2019). Report: Amazon Takes More Digital Advertising Market Share From Google-Facebook Duopoly. Available at: www.geekwire.com/2019/report-shows-amazon-taking-digital-advertising-market-share-google-facebook-duopoly/ [Accessed 5 April 2019].

Hagiu, A. (2009). Two-Sided Platforms: Product Variety and Pricing Structures. *Journal of Economics and Management Strategy*, 18(4), pp. 1011–1043.

Hoffman, M., Kahn, L. B. and Li, D. (2018). Discretion in Hiring. *The Quarterly Journal of Economics*, 133(2), pp. 765–800.

Kane, G. C., Palmer, D., Phillips, A. N., Kiron, D. and Buckley, N. (2015). Strategy, Not Technology, Drives Digital Transformation. *MIT Sloan Management Review and Deloitte University Press*. Available at: https://sloanreview.mit.edu/projects/strategy-drives-digital-transformation/ [Accessed 7 April 2019].

Katz, M. L. and Shapiro, C. (1985). Network Externalities, Competition, and Compatibility. *American Economic Review*, 75(3), pp. 424–440.

Parker, G. and Van Alstyne, M. W. (2005). Two-Sided Network Effects: A Theory of Information Product Design. *Management Science*, 51(10), pp. 1494–1504.

Rochet, J-C. and Tirole, J. (2006). Two-Sided Markets: Where We Stand. *RAND Journal of Economics*, 37(3), pp. 645–666.

Rogers, E. M. (2010). *Diffusion of Innovations* (5th edition). New York: The Free Press.

Roth, A. E. and Peranson, E. (1999). The Redesign of the Matching Market for American Physicians: Some Engineering Aspects of Economic Design. *American Economic Review*, 89(4), pp. 748–780.

Singh, A. and Hess, T. (2017). How Chief Digital Officers Promote the Digital Transformation of Their Companies. *MIS Quarterly Executive*, 16(1), p. 1.

Spulber, D. F. (2019). The Economics of Markets and Platforms. *Journal of Economics & Management Strategy*, 28(1), pp. 159–172.

StatisticsFinland. (2018). Structural Business and Financial Statement Statistics. Available at: www.stat.fi/til/yrti/index_en.html [Accessed 9 April 2019].

StatisticsFinland. (2019). Business Register. Available at: www.stat.fi/tup/yritys-rekisteri/index_en.html [Accessed 15 April 2019].

Thomas, L. D. W., Autio, E. and Gann, D. M. (2014). Architectural Leverage: Putting Platforms in Context. *Academy of Management Perspectives*, 28(2), pp. 198–219.

Weyl, E. G. (2010). A Price Theory of Multi-Sided Platforms. *American Economic Review*, 100(4), pp. 1642–1672.

Zysman, J., Feldman, S., Murray, J., Nielsen, N. C. and Kushida, K. E. (2011). The New Challenge to Economic Governance: The Digital Transformation of Services. In: A. V. Anttiroiko, S. J. Bailey and P. Valkama, eds., *Innovation and the Public Sector*. Clifton: IOS Press, pp. 39–67. Available at: www.iospress.nl/book/innovations-in-public-governance/ [Accessed 3 June 2019].

Appendix

Table 5A.1 presents the first four components that jointly capture 69 percent of total variance and the fifth component that only adds 7 percent to the cumulative variance.

Table 5A.1 Principal Component Analysis of Digitalization

Variable	Component 1	Component 2	Component 3	Component 4
	Digital Innovators	Selective Digitalization	Digital Operation	Digital Imitation
Firm Age	0.0242	−0.3805	0.2673	−0.5196
Firm Sales Class	0.2081	−0.4842	0.2662	0.0531
Digital Employees	0.2043	−0.2467	0.2754	0.3109
Digitalization of Payroll	−0.0352	0.3423	0.4469	−0.0917
Digitalization of Sales	0.0285	−0.2345	0.1874	0.6576
Digitalization of Temp. Employee Recruitment	0.047	0.544	0.2585	0.1699
Digitalization of Marketing	0.0753	0.2194	0.5263	−0.116
Imitation Response	0.4088	0.0489	0.0075	0.1994
Competence Acquisition Response	0.4244	0.1774	−0.1959	0.0982
R&D Collaboration Response	0.3713	0.0978	−0.3623	−0.0219
Service Innovation Response	0.4561	−0.005	−0.0551	−0.2592
Platform Innovation Response	0.4596	0.0168	0.1746	−0.1742
Eigenvalue	3.4386	1.8558	1.6718	1.3435
Proportion of Variance	0.2866	0.1547	0.1393	0.1120

6 The Road to Productivity With Automatization

Dialogue Between the Experienced and Measured

Maija Vähämäki, Tero Kuusi, Maarit Laiho, and Martti Kulvik

Introduction: Adaptive Performance in the Digital Transformation

Productivity improvement is a key goal for companies and public sector organizations. Great hopes and expectations are placed, therefore, in introducing automatization into work processes through digital robotics that can produce outputs faster and more accurately than human workers. Investments in automatization can yield productivity increases in standardized work processes and, thereby, reduce personnel costs.

However, automatization introduces discontinuity points whenever it creates human-machine interfaces. When a digital robot cannot fully conduct the intended process, it requires *ad hoc* problem solving; non-trivial problems surfacing in more complex, non-standardized tasks are still beyond the reach of algorithms. In such hybrid human-machine service production, the process toward automatized work can be multilayered and more complex than the automatization technology. Human workers are at the center of service productions to be transformed, and robotics only gradually take over part of their workload and speed up workflows. The success of automatization still hinges on human workers' ability to adapt to the changing environment.

In this chapter, we focus on understanding the transition process by analyzing a single case of partial automatization in office work. We assess the productivity effects of partial automatization of office work and how employees adjust to digital change. We approach this by developing a fine-grained measurement instrument designed to evaluate productivity in the automatization environment.

In parallel, we look at the adaptation process through employees' eyes via focus group discussions. The human agency in a complex, digitizing service production environment faces endless updates and successive but typically incomplete automatization projects. This raises concerns about employees' abilities and motivation to adapt and, consequently, about the sustainability and true productivity impact of digital automatization.

Previous literature used the framework of adaptive performance to explain and understand individual behavior in changing and ambiguous work environments (Jundt et al., 2015). More specifically, Jundt et al. (2015, pp. 54–55) define adaptive performance as "task-performance-directed behaviors individuals enact in response to or anticipation of changes relevant to job-related tasks." The task-relevant changes include the method of working, the nature of work tasks, or the way effectiveness is measured. For this chapter, we consider adaptive performance to be a construct that indicates learning and individual adjustment to task-relevant changes caused by partial automatization of the work processes.

The identified antecedents to adaptive performance are manifold. Jundt et al. (2015) divides them into factors related to (1) persons and situations, and (2) motivation and knowledge. Within the former category, individual factors have caught most of the attention of prior studies, whereas contextual factors have been more or less neglected (Jundt et al., 2015). Because we strive to understand the diverse elements contributing to employee productivity, we conduct a parallel examination of both person- and situation-related factors. In line with Jundt et al., we believe that this kind of approach will yield a more versatile picture of how task-relevant changes affect productivity in complex social environments.

We carried out our multimethod research in a governmental organization, Palkeet (The Finnish Government Shared Services Centre for Finance and HR). Palkeet is the primary provider of payment and salary services for governmental offices. With 630 employees, Palkeet is a major developer of public administrative services and processes in the government sector. Digitalization, process automation, and the management of information systems are expected to have a significant positive effect on the organization's performance in the near future. Robotics development in Palkeet is trusted to experienced service production employees, thereby securing the correct transfer of work procedures to robots. Other employees are also encouraged to identify new targets for robotization.

There are a multitude of angles to the complex picture of working effectively in an organization that is going through constant technical and organizational changes. We elaborate on the challenge of measuring productivity by zooming in and out of a process of change (Nicolini, 2009). To zoom in, we apply our quantitative multilevel analysis framework and describe productivity variations across time and workgroups. Zooming out, in turn, is achieved by illustrating employees' meaning making of their changing work practices. In other words, we zoom in to study individual performance and zoom out to open up the context of their work. These two approaches are first presented separately, and their results are then set in discussion with each other. The approach generates a deep and multidimensional picture of the realities of an organization striving toward automatized work.

Research Design

The research consisted of a quantitative analysis to assess productivity and a qualitative study on the meaning making of working with digital robots. The qualitative and quantitative data collections were carried out in parallel subprojects by respective experts. Both studies were performed in the same organization in identical or similar working units that operate in public payment and salary services. The host organization contributed to data collection by providing HR data and arranging for two seminars on the reasoning and challenges of the digitalization process.

Our approach can be described as a dialectical mixed method: the two research groups interacted with strong collegial effort throughout the research process, from the design of the study, through data collection and seminars, up to the reporting phase. We also engaged the case organization's representatives in intensive dialogues.

Although the productivity-measuring task followed a typical quantitative research design and the qualitative task an opposite, more abductive reasoning, we were able to conduct a respectful dialogue between the divergent research paradigms (Shannon-Baker, 2016). Thus, the combination of two approaches produced an additional layer of knowledge.

Our measurement instrument is tuned for gaining detailed information on work productivity, whereas the qualitative analysis provides a contextual understanding and insights into working under constant procedural changes. The latter paradigm represents a worldview of many voices, whereas the former relies on measurable entities and produces hard data. We advocate here a view in which both bring important knowledge for understanding adaptive performance and for enabling both productive and sustainable work in practice.

Quantitative Research: Creating Novel Metrics of Work

Our quantitative study aims to numerically interpret the work performed in our case organization's automatized and digitalized service production. We apply a multifaceted productivity analysis that allows us to measure how human work adapts to the changing environment. We can thereby better understand the complementarities between automatization and labor productivity. The measured productivity is used to determine how different work characteristics affect production. Finally, because our quantitative data spans several years, it provides a sufficiently long and rich surveillance period to assess the implications of changes in work.

We quantify labor productivity as the total output relative to the labor input.[1] To measure output, we use task-level data and a novel analysis framework that quantifies productivity, as well as individual variances in the entire work process.

The analysis draws on data extracted from a variety of internal digital data banks of the organization. Data were collected from five operational units, with information on the volume of the provided individual services and used resources at a detailed level of aggregation. The core data consist of day-level observations of individual workers' total hours, the numbers of main administrative decisions and tasks, and other detailed outputs during the day. We characterize the tasks based on attributes, such as the dispatcher of the invoice and the form in which it was sent (e.g., digital or paper). These attributes are known to affect their average processing time.

The collected data also include health outcomes (a day- and employee-level variable indicating whether the employee was on sick leave) and survey-based readiness-to-change index observations. A high index value indicates that an employee's self-perceived attitudes toward work, available skills, and provided managerial support foster the successful transformation of work. The index data were collected once during the period of productivity measurements and analyzed to allow comparisons across employees. The index data were collected for a subsample of employees.

The data were originally collected by the organization and analyzed anonymously after all references to individual employees were removed. In total, the data involved roughly 160 employees and spanned four years (with gaps). The unit-specific number of tasks in the data varied from a few to over 100.

To obtain meaningful measurements, we overcame issues typical in a productivity analysis of automatized work inside organizations. The key problem was that the work process of payment and salary services includes multiple task entities, and there is no available data to make a societal valuation (price setting) of the various tasks. A valuation is, however, ultimately needed to measure the productivity of the organization.

To overcome this problem, we measured productivity using indices that aggregate the different outputs by weighting them with their measured costs. This is in accordance with the recent literature concerning the production of services such as those our case represents (Atkinson, 2005; Dunleavy and Carrera, 2013; OECD, 2015; Diewert, 2017; Dunleavy, 2017). The defined costs approximately reflect the relative valuation of the services in an organization's product offerings. Accordingly, we measure labor productivity by dividing the cost-weighted outputs by the employees' total working hours.[2]

We acknowledge that alternative methods are available for valuing service outputs in terms of their desirability (see, e.g., Diewert, 2017). The best option is through market price or purchaser valuations. In a market economy, prices provide a superior way of defining how valuable the production is for the users by communicating the amount of money that customers are willing to pay for outputs. However, this information is often not available in enough detail. Especially in the public sector, but also in many tasks of the private sector (e.g., administration, customer service, and R&D), outputs are not directly subjected to monetary valuation. Thus, it is necessary to resort to the second-best option; that is, to use the valuations of a producer's unit costs of production.[3]

We estimate administrative costs using an econometric approach—large-scale linear cost function estimations that measure the average resources spent on producing different services at a detailed level (see, e.g., Coelli et al., 2005). The Appendix at the end of this chapter presents the methodology in more detail.

In this respect, the recent digitalization has provided crucial assistance to the measurement of productivity in the area of service production: services are increasingly transactional, involving organizations with millions of interactions between citizens, enterprises, and other organizations (Dunleavy, 2017). The sheer amount of data allows us to make detailed characterizations of the outputs, costs, and quality. Accordingly, the measurement of productivity has become more mass-data-oriented.

In large datasets, econometric techniques provide benefits compared to a standard accounting approach. An econometric approach uses the full variation of the data to estimate the determinants of productivity, instead of relying on partial measurements or discretion. In addition to several other benefits, this reduces the measurements' cost and allows us to assess the estimates' uncertainty.

Qualitative Research: Opening Space for Diverse Voices From Within

Our working hypothesis for the qualitative study was that productivity should not be studied in isolation from its context, and that contextual understanding can be created only by listening to those living the change. The traditional theory of adapting to change by Lewin (1947), which consists of the three stages of unfreezing, moving, and refreezing, formed the grounding logic of a change process until the 1990s. Today, however, this logic is less applicable, as changes are constant and overlapping.

The radical move toward a processual understanding of change was initiated by Pettigrew (1985) and further developed by researchers such as Knights and Murray (1994), Bloor and Dawson (1994), and Alvesson and Willmott (1996). Dawson (2003) later took into account the complexity of change and reminded researchers and practitioners alike to keep in mind how change is shaped and reshaped over time, regardless of the rational corporate narrative (Dawson, 2003; Dawson and Buchanan, 2005; Buchanan and Dawson, 2007). He also underlined the importance of hearing the competing narratives living simultaneously within the organization when drawing conclusions of change (Dawson, 2003, p. 27).

To introduce depth and an essential understanding of working with robots in the context of constant changes, we facilitated focus group discussions with employees. Focus group discussions are organized social events with a group of people who have practical experience in the focal matter (Kitzinger, 1994; Goss and Leinbach, 1996; Eriksson and Kovalainen, 2008, pp. 173–209). They are used here to inform us about the measured processes and the changes, thereby supporting the interpretation of the quantitative data analysis (Castren et al., 2013). These discussions also illuminate local cultural practices and relationships (Rakow, 2011) and highlight the tacit voices of the organization (Smithson, 2000). As developmental processes in organizations are mostly initiated and planned by managers, employees' narratives can inform us of their implementation and success.

We organized six focus group discussions with 2–6 participants each, totaling 21 employees. These took place at two sites in the organization and lasted approximately 80 minutes each. They were recorded and later transcribed verbatim. Four participants were in managerial or leadership positions, three had been trained as automatization specialists, and 14 of the interviewed represented service production. We refer to this data as qualitative or interview data. We covered three main topics in the focus group discussions with employees: changes in their work, what steers their job, and the advantages and disadvantages they experience with work automatization. In addition, we asked about their expectations and concerns regarding their future work. The conversations were facilitated by two researchers, and the participants were encouraged to lead the talk in the directions they felt were of relevance.

The aim of the qualitative inquiry was to add depth and insight into the quantitative results by tracing employees' meaning making of their work changes. We particularly tried to find diverse aspects and voices, as the interviewees represented a variety of subgroups, ages, experience, and phases of the work process. As our qualitative inquiry aimed to complement the quantitative data and vice versa, it was more important to find variations between individuals than to look for generalizations. However, there are company-level understandings and professional identity-bound attitudes that are historically developed among coworkers. It is important to recognize these and to observe possible individual differences and concerns.

For the content analysis of the qualitative data, two researchers' individual analyses were compared and discussed in two rounds. From the first reading of the text, we summarized the main topics and traced employees' meaning making of their work changes. We also used our notes from the seminars and group discussions to ensure adequate contextual understanding. In the second phase, we reduced the multifaceted topics to the themes relevant to the research question and elaborated them further.

The quantitative and qualitative analyses' findings were discussed during the analyzing process. This was done to enable the two approaches to complement one another. There is always noise in the results, and by comparing the qualitative and quantitative understanding of the process in focus, we claim it is possible to construct a more credible and holistic picture of the challenges in digital automatization.

Including Our Case Company to the Dialectics: Joint Research Planning and Research Seminars

The study setup was developed as an incremental process together with our case organization, and our quantitative tool was tailored to meet the actual situation. The case organization also hosted two informative and discursive seminars onsite. They provided an important contextual understanding of the extent of the change process occurring within the automatization of work processes. At the same time, the open discussions with various actors from Palkeet contributed to transparency and overall ethical code of conduct of our study.

In the first seminar, our host highlighted the reasons for choosing between external and internal robotization development, the human resource and management problems they encountered, and their observations on learning new practices. We were thus able to check the compatibility of our research design with their current knowledge. In the second seminar, we discussed our project's preliminary results.

Results

In this section, we provide the main results from the case study. We first describe the effects of automatization on average tasks, then discuss the results of the interviews in terms of the adaptation of employees to the change, and finally use our productivity data to quantify the relationships between employee productivity and changes in work characteristics.

Automatization Makes Individual Tasks More Demanding

How much time an employee spends on an individual task provides a relevant measure of the task's general difficulty. Digitalization may change the characteristics of tasks through automatization and by providing new digital tools. Quantification of such a change yields insight both into understanding the automatization and quantifying its impact on productivity.

Our case example includes an operational unit for which we have data both before and after the onset of automatization. The unit involves dozens of employees who provide financial services, in which they process invoices and payments in cooperation with automatized and computerized work routines.

We differentiate between tasks based on attributes that are known to affect the substance and difficulty of the task. Examples include the dispatcher organization of the invoice and the form in which the invoice was sent (e.g., digital or paper). Our estimations show that the volume of individual tasks during a typical working day is relatively high. The individual tasks consume on average a couple of minutes, with a variability between different task classes spanning from less than a minute to some individual cases where the consumption exceeds one hour. Our detailed, task-level data allow us to make inferences on the difficulty of the tasks, as measured by their time use.

In our case example, the automatization routines range from preprocessing invoices to fully automatizing human tasks. Using the time estimates from prior to the automatization, we can study how it has affected time use. For example, if the digitalization affects existing tasks but does not completely omit them, the time estimates are likely to decrease. However, paradoxically, if routine tasks are fully automated and no longer involve labor, the time use estimates can increase.

We found that many of the estimated time consumptions for tasks increased after automatization was implemented. For the 12 most common tasks in the unit, the unweighted average increase in the time use per individual task was roughly 50%. Although other factors may affect the results, the change in the tasks is likely due to automatization.

An automatized task must be well defined by the programmer for a machine, which lacks flexibility or judgment, to be able to execute the task successfully (Acemoglu and Autor, 2011). Thus, automatization tends to eliminate simple routine tasks but also creates new, more complex, and time-consuming tasks (Acemoglu and Restrepo, 2018). The latter was indeed also exemplified in our case, as part of the workers developed into automatization planners and implementers.

Importantly, the aforementioned patterns have implications for the measurement of productivity. That is, the average labor productivity of a unit shows a declining tendency when the change in the tasks is not considered. As the average use of time increases and the number of produced tasks diminish, productivity estimates that do not take into account the underlying change result in underestimating labor productivity. The employees may be as productive as they were previously, but the nature of their work has changed (see also Chapter 8 by Saari et al. in this book). Instead, when the changes in tasks, as reflected in the increases of time use, are taken into account, the productivity decline decreases.

Regarding the overall productivity impact of automatization, our results show that the change in the structure of human work is one of automatization's key features. If increases in the difficulty of the remaining human tasks are not adequately considered, the overall productivity impact of automatization may seem vastly overestimated.

Employees Find the Flow of Changes Challenging

We now turn to the results of our focus-group interviews to further understand how the automatization and other changes have affected work. To illustrate these findings, we constructed two representative employee narratives of working with robots from the focus group discussions, as shown in Box 6.1. In the first, Mary's workday runs smoothly without any technical disturbances. In the second scenario, Mary's workday is a disaster, accumulating several complications she comes across with R12, one of the robots.

Box 6.1   Employee Perspective: Two Narratives of Working With Robots

Mary, a salary services administration assistant, enters the office early in the morning. She uses one password to open the entrance door and another to access the control system. She is a bit worried. Her newest teammate—salary robot R12—should have done its share of the salary payment process during the night. Mary's concern is twofold: (1) Is R12 able to handle the vast amount of data and complete its share of the process? (2) Did Mary complete her share correctly, such as saving the necessary files to the right folder using the correct file format and naming convention? Mary does not completely trust either the R12 or her own ability to remember every detail in the process. R12 is very helpful if all goes well, but when problems occur, it stops working without asking for help.

1. Mary opens her computer and signs in. Yes! She is delighted and relieved to find that everything is in order. R12 has done its job as expected. There is no error list in Mary's mailbox. She is enthusiastic because R12 has done the most routine and boring part of the process. Mary can continue the salary payment process right away, which is good because her most efficient working hours are early in the morning. Mary is confident that she will be able to finalize the salary payment process in time— even early—which allows some extra time to tackle any unexpected problems that may occur during the process.

    At the end of the day, Mary is pleased with her efficient and smooth work shift. Perhaps one day, robots will take over more of our routines! Then, she has an idea: there is at least one more manual matching task in the middle of the salary payment process that could be easily automated. She decides to contact Sarah, an automatization specialist, first

---

thing in the morning and suggest the new target for automatization, as encouraged by management. It would be enjoyable to collaborate with Sarah, whom she knows very well because they used to work together in the salary service unit. Mary leaves the office after a 7.5-hour workday, remembers to quickly complete a working hours report, and is ready for her leisure time.

2. Mary opens her computer and signs in. Oh no! R12 has crashed in the middle of the job! Were there too many exceptions to the rules it was programmed to follow? Mary starts to get stressed. How will she finalize everything in time? Now she has to manually start the matching process that R12 was supposed to do. This proves to be very time-consuming because the client has an extremely diverse personnel structure and, accordingly, various employment contracts. The pay criteria are numerous as well, causing significant extra work for Mary. Her work pressure is high because delayed salary payments are not permissible.

   Mary must use three monitors to complete the job. On one, she monitors the running process, and on the other two, she matches the payrolls. Mary has a brief lunch at noon and, upon returning to her work, finds that important information will not update from one data system to another. She calls the client to go over some details. She then asks her colleagues for help, and they try to solve the updating problem together. They also consult the service manager but are still unable to solve the problem. This means that Mary needs to contact system support, which usually requires an official service query (ticket). However, Mary does not have time to wait for a response. She must directly contact one of the system planners. Mary is relieved when she is able to reach Jake, who solves the problem in 10 minutes. Mary continues her work and is able to finalize everything in time. She decides to complete the working hours report the next day and hopes she remembers how much time she spent on each task. When she leaves the office after a 10-hour workday, she is exhausted. Work-related thoughts continue to occupy her mind after the workday, and she feels doubt and uncertainty. She questions why she could not solve the problem alone and whether the panic over keeping salary payment deadlines will ever end. She wonders if the robots will ever be able to take over the salary payment processes entirely.

These two narratives are representations of possible experiential spirals influencing the adaptation process identified from the data. These adaptation spirals are induced by interactions with the robotics, such as occasional technical disturbances (spiral 2) or positive learning experiences, which feed individual self-efficacy (spiral 1).

The interviews show that the reflections of change are twofold. Automatization and robotics change employee routines and bring learning possibilities, which might also offer professional development. However, the successive and constant changes make employees feel insecure and disconcerted. They are eager to learn new skills but feel stressed about the amount and pace of diverse reforms. Employees feel they do not have enough time to advance their skills to the level that allows the task performance to become routinized (faster).

Employees did not complain about the organization's efforts to support their learning and discussed solving occasional problems with coworkers. Based on such comments, we presume that formal and social support for learning is available, and that there are other reasons for their feelings of insecurity.

In this study, we focused on the changes caused and productivity achieved by robotics and automatization. However, in the group discussions, the talk turned toward all the experienced changes in employees' everyday work. It became evident that robots played a less important role than the stress associated with learning the technology rolling into procedural practices. Three kinds of change could be identified, which intermingled: technological (such as applications, systems, and robotics), procedural (such as handling a service order), and organizational. This is relevant when considering the effects of digital change, as it recognizes and allows us to focus attention on the context of individuals' adaptive performance.

To understand the flow of changes and variations in the individual adaptation spirals, we can follow the thinking of diverse actors on the scene. The *planner* of a specific change (such as a new account system launched by the IT department) sees the launching process as a clearly framed timeline and understands that the change takes time for the users to learn. *Automatization specialists* develop new robots to facilitate payment-handling procedures. With the new automated tasks, the organization saves employee time. Consequently, the *HR department* and *supervisors* can innovate new ways to use employee competencies and may change their job descriptions. The reorganization of the work processes is then easily followed by structural changes in the organization. However, it is important to learn how these changes appear from the employees' perspectives. They are living with diverse changes and are in a constant learning mode, which might not be easy to adapt to. This confirms earlier notions of the processual and multi-voiced nature of change (Dawson, 2003; Dawson and Buchanan, 2005; Buchanan and Dawson, 2007) and how important it is to understand the divergent viewpoints of those planning the change and those living with it in their daily work.

We noticed that learning and mastering the substance-related matters were inspiring for employees. They welcomed some new tasks, such as those referred to as "customer helping tasks" or solving tricky problems in their work. However, new tasks such as controlling the robots or learning technical tools and procedures were often neither valued nor considered motivating. However, these tasks are an integral part of digital advancement. Some employees who seemed highly skilled in content-related matters were insecure regarding learning and remembering technical details. This could be due to divergent ways of learning but also to the value given to diverse skills.

In previous literature, most work-related changes have been associated with high levels of strain. Stress caused by changes, in turn, has been found to inhibit adaptive performance (Schraub et al., 2011). Stress has also been shown to be negatively related to learning because of the memory impairment it causes (e.g., Vogel and Schwabe, 2016). This became obvious in our interviews, as employees' sense of self-efficacy was not restored until they believed they were adequately skilled at the new tasks, which helps foster a positive learning spiral. This is worth mentioning, as management appeared judgmental of slow adaptation rather than understanding of employee-learning stress.

Reconsidering the Productivity Effects of Changing Work

Next, we elaborate further on how different work characteristics and the changes affect labor productivity. Our analysis is motivated by our previous notion that digitalization alters employees' routines and challenges them to learn new tasks.

Based on our data, it is likely that the adaptation dynamics impact labor productivity, which is highly important in understanding the overall productivity implications of the transformation. This holds even in the case of automatization, as few occupations will be completely automated in the near or medium term, but, rather, only certain tasks will be automated, and people's jobs will be redefined (McKinsey, 2017).

In what follows, we study the implications of our task-level data and consider them possible explanations for the variations in employees' productivity in our case organization. The details of the analysis can be found in Box 6.2 and the Appendix. We stress that, in our data, the individual-level variation of productivity is high: on average, roughly 25% of the employees are at a statistically significant level above the mean in productivity, whereas 25% remain at a significant level below it.

Box 6.2 Work Characteristics and Productivity: The Econometric Approach

We subject the individual observations of productivity to an econometric analysis, with work and employee characteristics as explanatory variables. Let us first construct indicators of work characteristics and define the variable that measures the share of task k of person i in the amount of total work in period t, $sh_{kit} = \dfrac{\beta_k quantity_{kit}}{\sum_{k1}^{K} \beta_k quantity_{kit}}$:

- **Number of tasks:** We quantify the total number of tasks (different output classes) for which the individual has non-zero outputs in a given day.
- **Change of work index:** We analyze the share of new tasks compared to the previous day's tasks. To measure this, we sum the increases in the time-use shares of tasks relative to the previous day's observations: $Change\ of\ work_{it} = \sum_{k1}^{K} max(sh_{kit} - sh_{kit-1}, 0)$.
- **Unusual work index:** We measure the average absolute deviation of the current day's tasks from the average shares over time for individual i: $Unusual\ work_{it} = \dfrac{\sum_{k1}^{K} |sh_{kit} - sh_{ki}|}{Number\ of\ tasks_{it}}$.
- **Share of the main task:** We define the concentration of work by measuring the maximum time-use share of a single task during a day: $Concentration\ of\ work_{it} = max(sh_{kit})$.
- **Hours of work:** We collected the total hours of work devoted to the measured tasks.

First, we find that there is a negative correlation between a change in the tasks and an unusual combination. For instance, if the average deviation of the task shares is 10 percentage points from the usual, there is an associated approximate 1.4% fall in productivity. We also find a significant effect between the change of work and productivity. If 10% of the tasks are new compared to the previous day, there is an approximate 1.5% decrease in productivity.

The evidence on the effect of concentration and number of tasks is less clear. The share of the main task seems to be positively correlated with productivity but not statistically significant at the 5% confidence interval, and the correlation becomes negative in our robustness analysis. The number of tasks is highly positively correlated with productivity. When a person has one additional task, it increases productivity by over 15%. It is, however, worth noting that the direction of causation is not clear, and it could be that higher-productivity employees receive jobs that involve a high variation in the amount of tasks.

We also analyzed other work characteristics to see if our productivity measure is reasonable in its responses to variations. For example, we found that increasing the working day by 10% lowers productivity by only 0.9% compared to the personal average. However, the effect may be muted because the hours included are only ones that are recorded as those used for the tasks under the productivity measurement.

The quantitative results are consistent with our qualitative finding that the transformation challenges employees' former routines. We found that after controlling for the individual- and time-dependent factors, as well as reverse causality, the changes in the tasks either over time or relative to an employee's usual mixture of tasks tend to decrease productivity. Thus, our evidence suggests that not all employees may be able to advance their skills to the level that would allow the task performance to become routinized and faster in the changing environment.

We can draw a similar conclusion from our productivity measures' strong and positive correlation with survey-based readiness-for-change index values (see Figure 6.1 and the Appendix). A high index value indicates that an employee's self-perceived attitudes toward work, available skills, and provided managerial support foster the successful transformation of work. The positive correlation indicates that these factors, indeed, are associated with positive productivity outcomes. The correlation is based on a cross-section of personal average productivity and index values, and thus it is not possible to fully control for other employee-specific factors. Our findings underline that adaptive performance and its support are important for the success of the transformation.

Although we found a negative effect of unusual and changing task structures on productivity, we did not find the same result with the number of different tasks. At least in the current context, it appears that neither constraining the number of individual tasks nor concentrating on a single task leads to productivity improvements (see Box 6.2).

Coviello et al. (2015) and Friebel and Yilmaz (2016) find evidence of a negative effect on job performance from multitasking. Our results suggest that the negative effect may be related to adaptation and learning, although we also find that there may be some complementarities arising from working on interrelated tasks. This finding is positive, as it implies that with enough support and skills, it may be possible to achieve flexibility in handling a large variation of tasks without negatively affecting productivity. The result relates to studies of the optimal design of (real-time)

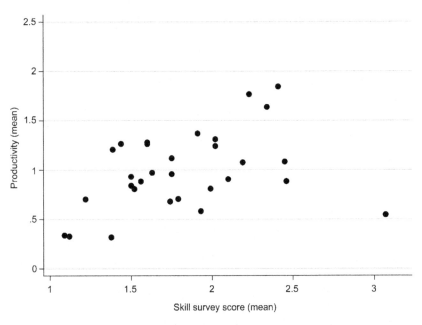

Figure 6.1 The Individual's Mean Productivity and the Corresponding Mean Score Concerning Readiness to Change

production systems (see, e.g., Park, 1996; Ichniowski et al., 1997; Chan, 2001; Chauhan, 2013; Ford, 2018).

Discussion and Conclusion

Digitalization has rapidly changed the organizational reality. Employee work is often accessed through a digital interface, which forces the worker to adapt to technological changes at an accelerating pace. Great hopes and expectations are put on the productivity-enhancing effects of the digitalization and automatization of work processes, but the progress is not always frictionless. Especially in hybrid human-machine service production, the process toward automatized work is multilayered and more complex than the automatization technology itself. Human workers are still at the center of service production, even if automatization and robotics take part of their workload and may speed up workflows.

To study the hybrid human-machine interactions in detail, we introduced a fine-grained and multilevel measuring instrument to zoom in to the micro-level of each employee and their accomplishments. Conversely, we zoomed out through rigorous qualitative interviews and analytics. The results revealed a complex pattern of changes that affect work and its productivity, and we found our integrative approach to adequately describe the changes.

We first found that as automatization was implemented for the easiest and most routine tasks, the workers were challenged with the remaining difficult and demanding jobs. This change became visible in the quantitative data as longer throughput times and, consequently, diminishing productivity. The data showed that productivity decreases the more a worker's tasks deviated from the normal routine. On the other hand, high scores in a questionnaire judging readiness to change was positively connected to individual productivity results.

Secondly, the qualitative analysis offered critical contextual and processual understanding. Consistent with our quantitative analysis, it showed how employees felt ambiguity and uncertainty due to the constant changes. Their discussion on changing work was as multilayered as the stream of organizational and technological changes, both minor and major. Workers strove for perfection but felt dissatisfaction, either due to unexpected technical disturbances or the emotional pressures of constant learning demands and the physical stressors of computerized work.

Our findings suggest that the symbiosis of humans and technology is still to some extent hazardous. That shakes the (much-hyped) rational picture of the growing productivity embedded in technological change. Therefore, organizations should take into account the entire situated context when they evaluate the results of their automatization processes.

A few lessons can be learned from this exercise. The findings exemplify how work changes put constant pressure on developing methods to monitor the resulting effects. Net effects on productivity can be assessed only by closely monitoring the effects of change and automatization. Reorganizing work necessitates a transparent and balanced monitoring system (Simons, 1994). The number and quality of outcomes, project monitoring systems, operating income reports by segment or business, cash flow statements, and variances are a few indicators that can be monitored. However, as added value in service production is, to date, dependent on human contribution, we must have insight into the dynamics of worker–task interactions.

Moreover, our results showed that productivity measurements are affected by changes other than those caused directly by one particular innovation. Stress affects the ability to learn, and in the midst of diverse changes, some employees were not able to achieve a routine speed of working. Indeed, the development of monitoring tools should keep pace with the development of work in its situated context.

The intensive data analysis cooperation between the qualitative and quantitative researchers rendered us sensitive to weak signals that might otherwise have remained unidentified in our datasets. The open discussions with representatives from Palkeet not only added to our understanding of the case, but it also helped us to follow the imperative guidelines of transparent codes of conduct (Kauhanen et al., 2012; Castren et al., 2013; Kotiranta et al., 2016). By combining the information gained from management, the lived experiences discussed in the focus groups, and the results from quantitative and qualitative data analyses, we formed novel insights about working in a world of automatization and constant digital change.

Our results indicate the importance of managerial support to help workers adapt to change. The ability to imbibe new logics inherent in next-generation user interfaces, accommodate digital robotics (automatization) into work processes, and trust in surrendering decision-making power to algorithms are becoming critical assets of a productive staff. Although a growing share of traditional work is being taken over by fast data processing, statistics show that the effects of the information era on overall productivity are still unclear—a phenomenon often referred to as the productivity paradox (see, e.g., Brynjolfsson et al., 2017) or the human factor (see, e.g., Vicente, 2006).

Overall, our results suggest that the hybrid-like service production by humans and machines combined introduces challenges within work, productivity, and the assessment of returns on investment in automatization. To fully harness the potential of new technology, successful digitalization projects require not only a vision of a new way to organize processes, but also the necessary support and time to learn, adapt, and monitor. It may involve both individual- and organizational-level support, consistent with substantial micro-level evidence on the organizational innovations that the successful adaptation of technology requires (see, e.g., Bresnahan et al., 2002; Brynjolfsson et al., 2017). If enough support is given, organizations can be efficient in providing the functional flexibility that the digital era demands.

References

Acemoglu, D. and Autor, D. (2011). Skills, Tasks and Technologies: Implications for Employment and Earnings. *Handbook of Labor Economics*, 4, pp. 1043–1171.

Acemoglu, D. and Restrepo, P. (2018). The Race Between Machine and Man: Implications of Technology for Growth, Factor Shares and Employment. *American Economic Review*, 108(6), pp. 1488–1542.

Alvesson, M. and Willmott, H. (1996). *Making Sense of Management: A Critical Introduction*. London and Thousand Oaks, CA: Sage Publications.

Atkinson, L. (2005). *Atkinson Review: Measurement of Government Output and Productivity for the National Accounts, Final Report*. Basingstoke, UK: Palgrave Macmillan.

Bloor, G. and Dawson, P. (1994). Understanding Professional Culture in Organizational Context. *Organization Studies*, 15, pp. 275–295.

Bresnahan, T. F., Brynjolfsson, E. and Hitt, L. M. (2002). Information Technology, Workplace Organization, and the Demand for Skilled Labor: Firm-Level Evidence. *The Quarterly Journal of Economics*, 117(1), pp. 339–376.

Brynjolfsson, E., Rock, D. and Syverson, C. (2017). Artificial Intelligence and the Modern Productivity Paradox: A Clash of Expectations and Statistics. *NBER Working Paper No. 24001.*

Buchanan, D. and Dawson, P. (2007). Discourse and Audience: Organizational Change as Multi-Story Process. *Journal of Management Studies*, 44(5), pp. 669–686.

Castren, L., Kauhanen, A., Kulvik, M., Kulvik-Laine, S., Lonnqvist, A., Maijanen, S., . . . Zhan, Y. (2013). *ICT ja palvelut. Näkökulmia tuottavuuden kehittämiseen (ICT and Services: Insights Into Productivity Enhancement)* (in Finnish). Helsinki: Etla.

Chan, F. T. S. (2001). The Effects of Routing Flexibility on a Flexible Manufacturing System. *International Journal of Computer Integrated Manufacturing*, 14(5), pp. 431–445.

Chauhan, A. K. (2013). Performance Evaluation of Flexible System of Integrated Manufacturing. *VSRD International Journal of Mechanical, Civil, Automobile and Production Engineering*, 3(3), pp. 71–76.

Coelli, T. J., Prasada Rao, D. S., O'Donnell, C. J. and Battese, G. E. (2005). *An Introduction to Efficiency and Productivity Analysis* (2nd edition). New York: Springer.

Coviello, D., Ichino, A. and Persico, N. (2015). The Inefficiency of Worker Time Use. *Journal of the European Economic Association*, 13, pp. 906–947. doi: 10.1111/jeea.1212

Dawson, P. (2003). *Reshaping Change: A Processual Perspective.* London: Routledge.

Dawson, P. and Buchanan, D. (2005). The Way It Really Happened: Competing Narratives in the Political Process of Technological Change. *Human Relations*, 58(7), pp. 845–865.

Diewert, W. E. (2017). Productivity Measurement in the Public Sector: Theory and Practice. *Discussion Paper 17–01, Vancouver School of Economics.* Vancouver: University of British Columbia. Available at: http://econ.sites.olt. ubc.ca/files/2017/02/pdf_paper_erwin-diewert-17-01-TheoryandPractice.pdf [Accessed 7 April 2019].

Dunleavy, P. (2017). Public Sector Productivity: Measurement Challenges, Performance Information and Prospects for Improvement. *OECD Journal on Budgeting*, 17(1), pp. 1–28.

Dunleavy, P. and Carrera, L. (2013). *Growing the Productivity of Public Services.* Cheltenham, UK: Edward Elgar Publishing.

Eriksson, P. and Kovalainen, A. (2008). *Qualitative Methods in Business Research.* London: Sage Publications.

Ford, M. (2018). Standards-Driven, Digital Design Flow for Industry 4.0. Accelerating Tech—Insights From the Smarter Factory. *DESIGN007 Magazine*, April 2019, pp. 16–19.

Friebel, G. and Yilmaz, L. (2016). Flexibility, Specialization and Individual Productivity: Evidence From Call Center Data. Available at: https://ssrn.com/abstract=2916042 or http://dx.doi.org/10.2139/ssrn.2916042 [Accessed 19 April 2019].

Goss, J. and Leinbach, T. (1996). Focus Groups as Alternative Research Practice. *Area*, 28(2), pp. 115–123.

Ichniowski, C., Shaw, K. and Prennushi, G. (1997). The Effects of Human Resource Management Practices on Productivity: A Study of Steel Finishing Lines. *American Economic Review*, 87(3), pp. 291–313.

Jundt, D. K., Shoss, M. K. and Huang, J. L. (2015). Individual Adaptive Performance in Organizations: A Review. *Journal of Organizational Behaviour*, 36, pp. 53–71.

Kauhanen, A., Kulvik, M., Kulvik, S., Maijanen, S., Martikainen, O. and Ranta, P. (2012). ICT:n lupaukset ja karikot terveydenhuollossa (Promises and Pitfalls of IT in Healthcare) (in Finnish). In: M. Lehti, P. Rouvinen and P. Ylä-Anttila, eds., *Suuri hämmennys: Työ ja tuotanto digitaalisessa murroksessa (The Great Confusion: Labour and Production in the Digital Rupture)* (in Finnish). Helsinki: Taloustieto Oy (Etla B254).

Kitzinger, J. (1994). The Methodology of Focus Groups: The Importance of Interaction Between Research Participants. *Sociology of Health*, 16(1), pp. 103–121.

Knights, D. and Murray, F. (1994). *Managers Divided: Organization Politics and Information Technology Management*. Hoboken, NJ: John Wiley & Sons.

Kotiranta, A., Kulvik, M., Maijanen, S. and Seppälä, T. (2016). *Behind the Scenes of Operation Theatres* (in Finnish). Helsinki: The Research Institute of the Finnish Economy (ETLA B271). Available at: http://pub.etla.fi/ETLA-B271.pdf [Accessed 19 April 2019].

Lewin, K. (1947). Frontiers in Group Dynamics: Concept, Method and Reality in Social Science, Social Equilibria and Social Change. *Human Relations*, 2, pp. 143–153.

McKinsey. (2017). *A Future That Works: Automatization, Employment, and Productivity*. New York: McKinsey Global Institute.

Nicolini, D. (2009). Zooming in and Out: Studying Practices by Switching Theoretical Lenses and Trailing Connections. *Organization Studies*, 30(12), pp. 1391–1418.

OECD. (2015). *OECD Compendium of Productivity Indicators 2015*. Paris: OECD Publishing. dx.doi.org/10.1787/pdtvy-2015-en

Park, K. S. (1996). Economic Growth and Multiskilled Workers in Manufacturing. *Journal of Labor Economics*, 14(2), pp. 254–285.

Pettigrew, A. (1985). *Awakening Giant: Continuity and Change in ICI*. Oxford: Basil Blackwell.

Rakow, L. F. (2011). Commentary: Interviews and Focus Groups as Critical and Cultural Methods. *Journalism & Mass Communication Quarterly*, 88(2), pp. 416–428.

Schraub, E. M., Stegmaier, R. and Sonntag, K. (2011). The Effect of Change on Adaptive Performance: Does Expressive Suppression Moderate the Indirect Effect of Strain? *Journal of Change Management*, 11(1), pp. 21–44.

Shannon-Baker, P. (2016). Making Paradigms Meaningful in Mixed Methods Research. *Journal of Mixed Methods Research*, 10(4), pp. 319–334.

Simons, R. (1994). How New Top Managers Use Control Systems as Levers of Strategic Renewal. *Strategic Management Journal*, 15, pp. 169–189. doi: 10.1002/smj.4250150301

Smithson, J. (2000). Using and Analysing Focus Groups: Limitations and Possibilities. *International Journal of Social Research Methodology*, 3(2), pp. 103–119.

Vicente, K. J. (2006). *The Human Factor: Revolutionizing the Way People Live with Technology.* New York: Routledge.

Vogel, S. and Schwabe, L. (2016). Learning and Memory Under Stress: Implications for the Classroom. *NPJ Science of Learning*, 1, Article number 16011. Available at: www.nature.com/articles/npjscilearn201611 [Accessed 19 April 2019].

Appendix
Details of the Productivity Analysis

Measurement of Productivity

The average labor productivity of the organization can be measured as the cost-weighted sum of outputs relative to the number of hours:[4]

$$\frac{\sum_{k=1}^{n} \beta_k quantity_k}{Hours}$$

where the outputs are indexed as $k = 1, \ldots, n$, and β_k denotes their cost weights. This measure also provides a straightforward comparison between employees. That is, it shows how much time an employee uses to provide a certain set of outputs, compared to the average time spent on a similar set of outputs.

To estimate the productivity with data, we use a statistical model that determines the total hours of employee i in period t:

$$Hours_{it} = \sum_{k=1}^{n} \beta_k quantity_{kit} + \sum_{i=1}^{I} \alpha_i I_{it} + \epsilon_{it}.$$

where kit denotes the corresponding output k. If the subscript is only i or ki (without t), it refers to the average over time.

We use the model to estimate the multipliers β_k, which are the average times spent on the production of output k conditional on producing the other outputs and after considering the individual-specific effects on the use of time, α_i. The indicator variable I_{it} receives a value of 1 if the observation belongs to person/unit i. The sum of the multipliers is set to zero, $\sum_{i=1}^{I} \alpha_i = 0$, in which case all time spent on work is divided between the different outputs. The model is solved using the constrained ordinary least squares (OLS) method. The key and standard identifying assumption is that the employee/unit-specific means of the error terms ϵ_{it}

are zero. The heteroscedasticity-robust standard errors for the estimates are used.

The model is simple, yet it can be powerful because the multiplier α_i directly defines the productivity of the employee. It can be shown that the average labor productivity of i relative to the comparable average ($= 1$) is

$$Labor\ productivity_i = \frac{\sum_{k=1}^{n} \beta_k quantity_{kit}}{Hours_i} = 1 - \frac{\alpha_i}{Hours_i}.\ ^5$$

The advantage of this approach is that, for a given set of core outputs, we can estimate the weights of the different outputs and the labor productivity simultaneously. By so doing, we obtain the respective uncertainties associated with each estimate of the relative labor productivity. Thus, by means of empirical testing, we can estimate both productivities, as well as the quality of the estimate: the model can validate or invalidate itself based on the amount and quality of the available data.

More generally, it is possible to assess the performance of an organization over time or compare individual working days by considering the individual error terms or their averages. For example, the average labor productivity of the organization in relation to the whole period's average ($= 1$) is

$$Labor\ productivity_t = \frac{\sum_{k=1}^{n} \beta_k quantity_{kt}}{Hours_t} = 1 - \frac{\epsilon_t}{Hours_t}.$$

The estimates based on a simple OLS method can provide further information about the roots of the productivity (gaps). After the model is estimated, the variation of productivity can be studied by subjecting the estimated error terms ϵ_{it} and individual productivities to further statistical analysis in the second stage. There are econometric methods such as the Stochastic frontier analysis or data envelopment analysis that directly estimate the efficient cost frontiers and productivity lapses. However, although they provide interesting avenues for further research, for instance, by allowing the decomposition of output growth into technological and efficiency components, we argue that our easy-to-solve linear estimator strikes a reasonable balance between solvability and the level of detail in the case of our large-scale cost functions that may involve over 100 separate tasks. Moreover, due to the frontier estimation, the estimated error terms are complexly correlated, which provides additional challenges for the second-stage estimations.

Estimation of the average time use is only one approach to solving the weights. If data are limited on some outputs, one can fix the multipliers based on cost accounting data or expert opinions. This approach is also applicable when the outputs are complex or the volume or its variation is low. Furthermore, the estimations can be conducted separately for several resources if, for example, detailed decomposition of the working hours is available. If the organization produces the outputs with varying amounts of inputs (intermediate goods or capital), and capturing this variation is essential to the measurement of productivity, they can be inserted into the equation on the right-hand side. In that case, the left-hand side variable is the total costs, whereas the right-hand side also provides the average mixture of different resources in the production.

In the current application, the production function is linear. This implies that the marginal cost of one extra unit of output remains constant; that is, providing three times more output takes three times more time. The linearity has several useful properties. First, it provides a natural benchmark to assess the average resource use. Also, on many occasions, one might be interested in estimating the elasticity of substitution between the production of different units. That is, transforming production from one good to another may not always be as frictionless as the basic model implies. Thus, we analyze the robustness of our results for alternative functional forms but find that the linearity is not a restrictive assumption.

A few other aspects of the estimations are worth discussing. First, in all quantitative cost estimations, it is necessary to ensure that the direction of causality is from the changes of outputs toward the costs. If the model instead features reverse causality, that may cause bias in the cost estimates. Typically, this problem arises in estimates that involve operational units, such as firms, which may choose their mixture of outputs as a result of cost changes. Furthermore, unmeasured factors may affect both the mixture of outputs and the costs, thus creating omitted variable bias. There are methodological options such as the instrumental variables method that can help alleviate this problem. We believe that in our framework, the selection and omitted variable bias is likely to have little effect, as the variation of tasks at the individual level is typically supplied by exogenously determined job queues. Although difficult tasks are sometimes transferred to more experienced workers, this does not appear to bias our results. Nevertheless, we have employed the standard practice of using the previous day's task observations as instruments. They are likely be correlated with the current day's tasks, but less likely to be correlated with the day-specific factors that could generate a reverse causality problem.

Second, a practical problem of our linear model is that the cost estimates can be negative. A negative value does not have a reasonable interpretation in the current context, as it implies that conducting a particular task would incur a penalty when productivity is measured. The problem typically arises from collinearity between the output variables or mismeasurement in cases in which there are only a few observations of the output production. To avoid this problem, the productivity estimations were based only on models that have positive cost estimates. If a negative estimate appeared, all productivity observations that included these outputs were discarded and the estimations were repeated until the productivity measurement involved only tasks that have positive cost estimates (i.e., the estimated coefficients of all tasks are positive in the cost function). This means we focus on the well-defined productivity observations, but we found few that were problematic.

Although we acknowledge there are estimators available that guarantee the positivity of the cost coefficients (such as the non-negative least squares), we again find that using the linear least squares estimator—while controlling for problematic tasks—strikes a reasonable balance between the feasibility of the estimations and a loss of detail due to the omission of some problematic data observations.

Econometric Analysis of the Work Characteristics

We now discuss the details of the (linear) econometric modeling of the relationship between work characteristics and productivity. We investigate alternative work and employee characteristics that could cause a variation of productivity, and, thus, we focus here on labor productivity rather than on total-factor productivity, which isolates the impact of differences in the use of productive capital, such as work-space characteristics or tools. As the comparisons are made within units, in which the employees should have access to similar productive capital, it is unlikely to cause the variation.

In the baseline model ("Baseline") in Table 6.1, we estimate the effect of the work characteristics on a subset of observations considered to be well defined. In particular, we only include employees that have more than 30 daily observations to ensure their usual work is well characterized. Second, we abstract from short working days (less than three hours of work).

The results of the robustness analysis on alternative specifications can be found in Table 6.1. First, we consider the instrumental variable estimation to control for reverse causality ("Instrumental variable"). In particular, we use the previous day's observations of work characteristics as instruments and maintain the same modeling setup. Second, we remove the restrictions on the length of the day and the minimum number of employee-level observations ("No data restrictions"). Third, we test whether our results stem from the linear cost function assumption. As a benchmark, it is justifiable to use the linear cost function because these are processing tasks that are separately administered in the organization. It is possible, however, that the processing work may be related, especially when it involves the same dispatcher. In these cases, complementarities could arise. To control for complementarities and possible increasing returns to scale, we use an alternative cost function in which the costs are allowed to be quadratic functions of the number of similarly classified tasks (i.e., same dispatcher), whereas the cross terms of the

Table 6.1 Results of the Econometric Modeling of the Relationship Between Work Characteristics and Productivity

Variable	Specifications:				
	Baseline	No day effects	No data restrictions	Quadratic cost function	Instrumental variable
Unusual work (t)	-0.135**	-0.133**	-0.173**	-0.184***	-0.153*
Change of work (t-1 to t)	-0.145*	-0.160*°	-0.145*	-0.184***	-0.634**
Concentration of work (t)	0.167	0.170*	0.334**	-0.275***	-0.545*
Number of tasks (t)	0.166***	0.170***	0.207***	0.136***	0.113***
Hours (t)	-0.090***	-0.091***	-0.226***	-0.105***	-0.046
Weekdays:					
Monday	–	–	–	–	–
Tuesday	0	–	0	0	–
Wednesday	0.248***	–	0.142***	0.197***	0.100***
Thursday	0.172***	–	0.145***	0.129***	0.006
Friday	0.114***	–	0.121***	0.111***	0
Number of observations	8038	8038	11522	8926	5112
Number of employees	83	83	150	83	82
R-squared	0.239	0.229	0.107	0.178	–

Notes: The table reports covariances of the corresponding variables and productivity (with mean normalized to 1) for various specifications (columns). For unusual work, change of work, and concentration of work, the coefficient provides the percentage change in productivity (relative to the data mean) when there is a 0.01 percentage-point change in the corresponding explanatory variable. The remaining variables show the effect of one more task and one extra hour of daily work on productivity (%/100 relative to the mean productivity). We control for individual-, week-, and year-specific fixed effects. In all except the "No day effects" specification, we also consider day-specific fixed effects. Confidence levels: *p < .05; **p < .01; ***p < .001.

different tasks (i.e., different dispatchers) are set at zero ("Quadratic cost function"). Finally, there appears to be some daily variation in productivity. We repeat the procedure with and without the day-level controls to check how sensitive our results are to daily variations ("No day effects").

As a conclusion of the robustness analysis, we find that the results remain qualitatively similar. The most prominent difference is that when the quadratic specification is used, the effect of the concentration of work becomes significantly negative. Our interpretation of this result is that there are some beneficial complementarities in processing similar tasks together. After taking this into account, the remaining effect of concentration on productivity is moderately negative.

Finally, it is worth noting that the quality of the productivity estimates differs widely between employees. In most cases, employees produce well-documented outputs and the productivity estimates are rather sharp, as indicated by small confidence intervals. Unsurprisingly, the productivity estimates are the most precise when there are many task performance observations. From the practical usefulness perspective of the productivity measurement, this is important, as the estimations work best to capture the key tasks of the unit. However, when the work involves tasks that are seldom performed, the estimation errors increase, and, consequently, the method implies that strong conclusions should not be made concerning the unit operations in that respect. We note, however, that although this should be kept in mind when using productivity data in management, this issue is taken into account when assessing the robustness of the econometric analysis results.

Notes

1 An alternative way is to define the total-factor productivity, that is, the productivity growth using accounting data, not only for labor but also for the uses of intermediate goods and services, as well as capital. Our analysis focuses mainly on the productivity observations of individual workers within production units, in which case it is relatively safe to assume that the workers operate under similar conditions in their use of capital, intermediate goods, and services.

2 Our approach treats quality as stable over time, unless there is clear evidence of a decline in quality or a quality lapse.

3 Ultimately, the idea of using cost weights arises from the notion that relative prices reflect—at least in an ideal situation—the market prices of the outputs. If there are competitive markets with no economies of scope and constant returns to scale in production, the first and second-best options are roughly equivalent; in other words, the purchaser's price will be approximately equal to the long-run marginal cost of producing one unit of the commodity (Diewert, 2017).

4 Alternatively, the hours can be replaced with an index that measures the amount of all inputs including capital, in which case the multi-factor productivity is quantified.

5 The result follows when both sides of the equation are divided by the average hours of person i and then averaged. Generally, it holds that and, therefore, the average of i in the model is: *Here is the space for equation 1. Please copy equation 1 from the original word document.* and because the average of the error term over *t* is *equation 2* the result follows.

7 The Digitalization of Migrants' Labor Market Integration Services

Boosting or Hindering Social Inclusion?

Satu Aaltonen

Introduction

This chapter critically investigates the parallel implementation of public e-government and integration policies in the intriguing Finnish context, where internet access is among the highest in the world and substantial immigration is relatively new. At worst, when these two policies collide in the process of executing them, and the provision of digital and other competences are overlooked, instead of improved equality—a value shared by both strategies—digital stratification and reinforced patterns of social exclusion increase (Ragnedda and Muschert, 2013; Ragnedda, 2017; Lloyd et al., 2013).

The rise in the number of migrants and asylum seekers in Europe calls for a more thorough examination of the receiving countries' integration mechanisms. Public services play an essential role in integration, particularly in welfare states; they are offered increasingly online due to the interweaving approaches of digitalization and austerity (Dunleavy and Margetts, 2010). However, users' needs do not necessarily match up with their ability to access digital and public services. To effectively benefit from digital resources, in addition to the internet and instrumental skills (to operate hardware and software), informational and strategic competencies to achieve one's goals are required (van Dijk and Hacker, 2003). Besides digital capacities, attention has been paid to language skills (Brazier and Harvey, 2017; Kaufmann, 2018), information (Lloyd et al., 2013), and administrative literacy (Grönlund et al., 2007) in terms of enabling the successful use of e-government services. Those who have entered new societies and linguistic regions especially lack these skills.

In a contextualized manner, this chapter describes everyday scenarios in which migrants encounter a hybrid of the so-called information and welfare societies. Considering the situations of these migrants, who aim to integrate into the labor market, this chapter illustrates the role played by the resources required to access public e-services and the deficiencies preventing their use. Previous studies on the digital divide and e-government have called for a more multifaceted understanding of the users of digital services (Grönlund et al., 2007; Lindblom and Räsänen, 2017; Helbig et al., 2009), the circumstances surrounding individual actions, and a recognition of structural and cultural embeddedness (Bürkner, 2012). This chapter contributes to that call.

The chapter starts by introducing some unwanted consequences of e-government: the digital divide and increased social exclusion. Next, the reader becomes familiar with Finnish migration and integration practices, in addition to the sources of the data and the methods used. The findings outline general observations of e-services' role in assisting migrants, followed by an in-depth case study of a Somali homemaker and her struggles with the service system. Her narrative, as told by a non-governmental organization (NGO) worker, shows how complex the service landscape appears to someone who is new to the culture and overwhelmed by the difficulties of everyday life. Solutions are offered by street-level service providers. The conclusion draws the main points of the chapter together and mentions both policy and academic implications.

The Digital Divide, Social Exclusion, and E-Government

Studies have revealed disparities related to accessing information and communications technology (ICT) both among countries and between social groups within them, as well as among those who engage in public life through digital means and those who do not (Helbig et al., 2009; Yu, 2006; Norris, 2001). There are mixed findings regarding the magnitude and direction of these discrepancies (Yu, 2006). The division between the "haves" and "have-nots" tends to strengthen existing inequality and stratification (Lindblom and Räsänen, 2017; Zillien and Marr, 2013), but the rift is declining due to the relatively lower prices of equipment and network access. As the access gap shrinks between and within countries, the focus has shifted to variations of usage patterns within unique segments of the population (van Deursen and van Dijk, 2014; Lindblom and Räsänen, 2017).

Digital exclusion, which has deepened social exclusion, can be caused by differences in motivation and attitudes toward using ICT, as well as shortcomings in terms of access and skills (Helsper, 2012; van Dijk, 2013). Digital and social exclusion (as well as inclusion) mutually reinforce each other in the economic, cultural, social, and personal spheres of people's lives (Helsper, 2012); they can even come to be passed down through the generations (Witte and Mannon, 2010). Several kinds of resources influence the quantity and quality of ICT use; these include income, employment and education, gender, ethnicity, generation, social ties, lifestyle, personality, and psychological and physical health (Witte and Mannon, 2010; Helsper, 2012; van Deursen and van Dijk, 2014).

This list is certainly not comprehensive, but points out that many other resources (besides access to ICT, motivation, and skills) are needed to benefit from the internet, whose organization and content is often designed by—and for—"the included" instead of "the excluded" (Witte and Mannon, 2010; Lin, 2004).

The inclusiveness of e-government is also socio-culturally embedded. Basic requirements for it include online access, the determination to use e-services, and the ability to operate a computer or smartphone, but these do not guarantee that one receives services such as unemployment or housing benefits (Cestnik and Kern, 2014; Lloyd et al., 2013; Brazier and Harvey, 2017). Based on people's resources, their situations, and reference groups, individuals have different perceived and "objective" needs as well as capabilities and opportunities to meet them through digital services (Selwyn, 2004; DiMaggio and Garip, 2012; Zillien and Marr, 2013; Lindblom and Räsänen, 2017). Digital exclusion is thus linked to information and social inequalities that existed long before the rise of the information society (Yu, 2006).

Attempts to identify barriers between digital competencies and the ability to fully exploit e-services have introduced the concepts of administrative literacy (Grönlund et al., 2007) and information disjuncture (Lloyd et al., 2013). Administrative literacy refers to

> the ability to navigate bureaucracy which includes having a good idea of how society's institutions work, the terminology involved and hence being better able to know where to go to find the forms, procedures, contact information etc. necessary, and indeed understand the information once found and being able to act upon it.
> (Grönlund et al., 2007, p. 217)

Lloyd et al. (2013, p. 122) use the term "information disjuncture" to illustrate the same sense of newness to the service system. They note that "individuals new to . . . information landscapes . . . find that their previous information practices may no longer be adequate or appropriate." Both Grönlund et al. and Lloyd et al. discuss a similar phenomenon whereby one has to know one's way around the service system, including what to look for and where to search.

Language skills become essential when operating online in a foreign tongue. If one has difficulty understanding the language used, e-services are not the best option (Aspinall, 2007; Brazier and Harvey, 2017). When e-services replace civil servants, inevitable changes take place. Many face-to-face aspects are removed, often unintentionally (Grönlund et al., 2007.) This complicates service use for migrants with limited proficiency since they find text more difficult to comprehend than oral and visual information. In a face-to-face interaction, one can ask for clarification and the service provider can give alternative explanations, which are not usually possible in e-services (Lloyd et al., 2013). The newly arrived, who may not have local contacts (or access to professional translators) to translate official texts for them, are in a weak position (Lloyd et al., 2013; Alam and Imran, 2015; Kaufmann, 2018). While non-native speakers have problems when using e-services, high language proficiency does not always avoid mistakes in information retrieval (Brazier and Harvey, 2017); this suggests that problems using e-services are not entirely language based.

The Context of Integration: Finland

The data for this study come from Finland, a forerunner in the use of information technology and digitalization development in the early 2000s (Castells and Himanen, 2002). In 2018, it was among the top five European countries in terms of internet access (94% of households) and e-government interaction with public authorities (83% of individuals over the past 12 months) (Eurostat Database, 2019). According to the latest United Nations E-Government Survey, in 2018, Finland ranked first on the e-participation index and sixth on the e-government development index. In addition, there is a strong political will to further digitalize public services, which the Finnish government announced as a key project for its 2015–2019 term (Government Programme, 2015).

Finland offers a very interesting arena for studying the adoption of e-services by migrants since considerable immigration is relatively recent, with the total number of first- and second-generation immigrants growing from 37,600 in 1990 to 384,000 in 2017. Overall, Finland has 5.5 million inhabitants. Although immigration has risen, first- and second-generation immigrants still constitute only 6% of the population. (Statistics Finland, 2019). There was a notable expansion in the number of asylum seekers in 2015 with more than 32,000 applications, almost 10 times more than in 2014. After this peak, this figure fell to approximately 5,500 people. Most asylum seekers in 2015 came from Iraq (63%) and Afghanistan (16%) (Wahlbeck, 2018). Due to a general trend of increasing migration and the spike in asylum seekers in 2015, criticism of the integration service system and its effectiveness has risen (OECD, 2018; Ala-Kauhaluoma et al., 2018).

The Act on the Promotion of Immigrant Integration (1386/2010) views integration as a two-way process between immigrants and the host society; its scope includes matters of culture, language, society, and economic wellbeing. The law emphasizes multiculturalism, but the implementation has elements of assimilation (Vuori, 2015; Saukkonen, 2013). Finnish integration policy—as well as the whole welfare system—highlights labor market integration (Kettunen, 2011). In line with many other European countries (Gebhardt, 2016), Finland has a state-led civic integration program (CIP) that targets only third country migrants currently in the labor force. Local authorities (such as cities and munici-palities) are responsible for providing services to individuals outside the workforce. This has made it easier to enter integration training if one is unemployed than if one is a student, homemaker, pensioner, or for some other reason outside the labor force (OECD, 2018). In addition, the organization and funding of local integration services are often project-based, thereby giving these services a weak institutional position (Vuori, 2015; Martikainen et al., 2012).

For those who enter integration training and for whom a personal inte-gration plan is arranged, the integration period usually lasts three years. For a newcomer, a social worker is a key person who helps the migrant to navigate the service system, provides psycho-social support, and fos-ters trust between the migrant and society (Vuori, 2015). According to Vuori (2015, p. 398, translation by S.A.), fitting real-life problems into the logistics of service organizations can lead to a situation where "soci-ety can be pictured as one big bureaucratic machine." After the integra-tion period (and right away for those not in the integration program), migrants are on their own in terms of using general services, and lan-guage problems become more prevalent (Vuori, 2015).

Methodology

The data of this chapter are derived from eight interviews with public service providers and project workers from NGOs that provide labor market integration services to immigrants. The interviews were mainly conducted face-to-face and lasted between 45 and 90 minutes; the aver-age time was 65 minutes. Of the interviewees' employers, two are semi-public business support groups and four are NGOs. One interviewee works for a public employment service and one for an integration project coordinated by an educational institution.

The interviewees were selected because they are experts on migrants' labor market integration. In line with Meuser and Nagel (2009), the interviews were carried out in a flexible, non-bureaucratic way, where the interviewer guided the discussion from one theme to another. The inter-viewees were encouraged to give examples and to generate narrations. This was done in order to make their knowledge visible. Experts are sel-dom conscious of the knowledge they possess since it is often contextual, procedural by nature, and non-explicit (Meuser and Nagel, 2009).

Digitalization of services was not the main topic, but all interviewees were asked about their experiences and opinions. They evaluated their clients' ability to use digital services, as well as the pros and cons of digi-talization from the angle of their clients, who either face difficulties enter-ing the labor market or wish to become self-employed. It is important to emphasize that the interviewees' recollections do not necessary reflect the experiences and preferences of migrants; they spoke based on their roles as service providers and as representatives of their respective entities (whether public or non-governmental). On the other hand, service providers have encountered a large number of migrants and have thus been able to form a comprehensive perspective on the benefits and disadvantages of newly arrived and self-employed immigrants using e-government services. Their views may also reflect some general taken-for-granted perceptions of the usefulness of e-services for this target group.

Qualitative content analysis (Eriksson and Kovalainen, 2015) was used to analyze the interviews. First, extracted segments of text (that mention e-services, digital applications, platforms, and migrants' service preferences) were separated from the data and coded based on themes appearing in them. Hence, the coding was mostly data-driven instead of theory-driven. The aim was to identify topics that the service providers pointed out as relevant for migrants' service usage.

Contextualized expert knowledge is apparent in the case of a Somali homemaker, which will be described later. In this chapter, her narrative is presented verbatim to ensure the "thickness" of the description (Geertz, 2008). What is meant by "thickness" is "verisimilitude" (Denzin, 1989, p. 83), which illuminates the multifaceted nature and complexity of situations in which public services are used. A "thick" description allows for a glimpse into how social networks—as well as the surrounding society's wider socio-economic and political-institutional environments—are reflected in the ways that opportunities are perceived, rational thinking is bounded, and sensemaking takes place within individual circumstances (Szkudlarek and Wu, 2018; Tolciu, 2011; Kloosterman et al., 1999; Jones et al., 2014).

Findings

Migrants and E-Government: General Findings

Social welfare is an essential component of a Nordic welfare state like Finland. To fully benefit from it, certain skills are required to navigate the information landscape since information processes are an integral part— the backbone, one might say—of public service provision (Lloyd et al., 2013). One interviewee commented that migrants cannot truly integrate into Finnish society if they cannot use e-services:

> You cannot be a full member of [Finnish] society . . . unless you have the basic skills [needed for] using e-services. It is one of the basic things.
>
> (H9, NGO)

Another interviewee believes that Finns and migrants struggle similarly with this challenge. Both groups have people who are capable—and incapable—of using e-government services. She views the digital divide as being more prevalent between the younger and older generations:

> I suppose, its [the digitalization of services] effects [on migrants] are pretty much the same among Finns. For some it makes things easier; for some it makes things more difficult. The younger generation is more accustomed to using e-services—like us—but the older [generation is] not.
>
> (H2, NGO)

The importance of digital, language, and information literacy competencies in using e-services is evident. Digital skills vary among migrants, as they do among other sectors of the population. Service providers assert that the use of digital devices is more common among younger people; hence, they are more digitally savvy. However, being able to employ entertainment apps and services does not guarantee access to e-services.

> We have many young customers, especially young men who started to work right after elementary school. They know their way around social media, mobile [phones] and computers, but if they start filling out digital forms—as one would to register a company—they cannot do it. If you have a foreign background, if you do not have good Finnish language [proficiency], you can't cope.
>
> (H1, Business support organization)

An official from the public employment service sees using email as no problem among integration service users, who are newcomers to the labor market integration program. This could indicate that access to computers and networks is not a serious hindrance to e-government, but a potential problem lies deeper in a bundle of several simultaneous shortcomings (for example, in areas such as digital, language, and governance literacy skills). The solution to this stumbling block was to provide a one-stop shop where customers could call with integration and labor market-related questions.

> Integration services has its own e-mail inbox where we get a lot of questions and messages from our customers. They have learned to use it quite well . . . if you call these national phone numbers, they can forward us a message and ask us to call back.
>
> (H4, The public employment service)

A lack of language skills is an extra obstacle to surviving in the world of e-services, as the previous quote testifies. Official forms and websites are mainly in Finnish and Swedish, the country's official languages. Basic information on services and providers is available in other languages, mainly English. For those without English skills, this does not help much.

> [O]f course, [everything] is in Finnish and Swedish . . . There is some information in English as well. Of course they visit our websites and can search for information, look for jobs, courses etc.
>
> (H4, The public employment service)

Adequate proficiency in Finnish or Swedish does not guarantee that migrants will be able to use e-services since they are often provided in so-called officialese, which is unnecessarily complex, abstract, and formal. Difficult phrases and governmental concepts are easier for clients to understand if they have good administrative literacy (Grönlund et al., 2007), to which an NGO worker referred when discussing tacit knowledge of Finnish culture:

> We teach them to run errands, but only when [they] don't have enough language skills . . . There is a lot of tacit knowledge about the culture. I do understand [that] it is really difficult to perceive in the beginning. [. . .] They don't have enough language skills to read them . . . because officialese, or the "language" of Kela [Finland's Social Insurance Institution] is difficult for Finns as well.
>
> (H6, NGO)

The information landscape (Lloyd et al., 2013) of Finnish public services is quite complex; a lot of information is available, and there are many service providers. This is partly what Vuori (2015) means when describing the Finnish service system as a "big bureaucratic machine." When using digital services, clients are more on their own than when receiving a service face-to-face. This may cause problems when unfamiliarity, together with the complexity of the service system, makes it difficult to understand what services are offered and where. The internet is full of all kinds of information, which makes it hard to assess what is relevant and current.

> [T]here is a lot of information online, but it is difficult to find the right and essential information . . . That may be . . . why many people want personal guidance.
>
> (H7, Business support organization)

Unfamiliarity with Finnish integration services and the rapid increase in their demand after 2015 caused an ongoing transformation and expanded service offerings. Even professionals have difficulty keeping up with the changes.

> [W]e are in the know [regarding] where our customers should be, where they should go, when they should go, what each invitation for interviewing means. Now responsibilities [for] employment, for example, [are divided between two authorities and they have different practices] . . . therefore . . . support services are needed.
>
> (H3, NGO)

In sum, the general findings verify obstacles that migrants face when using e-services, as identified in the literature. The challenges examined here include a shortage of digital and language skills, as well as a lack of knowledge of Finnish culture and the service system. Prior studies have often analyzed these elements separately, but the interviews convincingly demonstrate that they are intertwined into different kinds of bundles, with unique relevance to each migrant's situation.

A Migrant Navigating the Service System: The Case of Astur

The previous section reviewed potential hurdles between the goals of migrant integration and e-government policies and their realization in Finland. The story of Astur (an alias), a Somali homemaker, illuminates the multifaceted essence and problems of situations in which public services are used. Astur does not use e-services herself, which is critical here. E-government studies are often biased toward studying those who use the services, instead of trying to understand the reasons for not using them (Distel, 2018).

Astur often has a hard time comprehending the letters she receives from public agencies such as those related to healthcare, education, or job training. Her narrative was told by an NGO worker who has helped her several times to survive the "service jungle." The worker was not specifically asked to tell it. However, based on her expertise (Meuser and Nagel, 2009), she found it relevant to demonstrate everyday scenarios that she encounters on the job, and to give the researcher some perspective on the phenomena under study.

Astur is an unemployed homemaker and a single migrant parent with a "challenging" son and limited Finnish skills. Each of these characteristics is associated with a disadvantaged position even on its own, but here, they are accumulated. In connection to the aforementioned traits, Astur and her son also use several public services: healthcare, social care, schooling, employment, and housing. Her case shows how the functional and informational separateness of different services obligates the service user to be the coordinator of appointments and the middleman, forwarding information from one agency to the next.

Box 7.1   Astur's Story

We have a really good example here, [it may be] good or bad . . . this does not even entail all the difficulties that she has encountered . . . once when she came over, she had received "a letter requesting an explanation" from the job center because she had quit a language course. She [i.e., Astur] receives invitations on a regular basis from the job center to enroll in language courses. This was Finnish for nursing workers. She had attended this course in September, but then [quit]. This needed to be explained.

So, I started to write. I called the job center. They told me right away that this was not all. She had missed another course as well. Well, I asked her about it. She had gotten an invitation after she left the first course. It was a course on Finnish for metal workers. She did not go since she did not even understand that she was supposed to go. The metal workers' language course . . . started in October, just a couple of days ago. When they understood in the job center that this person was sitting next to me, they gave me permission to act on her behalf. They told me that this would lead to a new "letter requesting an explanation." But this one would need to be written first.

I told the officer on the other end that we have a situation where her son is "challenging." He only goes to school for two hours a day . . . because no afternoon activities are organized for him since no assistant [can] be with him . . . Some sort of childhood development thing . . . the diagnosis was only recently discovered. At the time, I only knew that he was going to [the name of a local school] and one usually has to have severe problems to attend there. [The explanation ended up being:] "OK, we'll write that the son is challenging and that he has a note from his teacher that he cannot manage alone and needs someone around." This explanation is basically okay for the job center. But then they realized that since this was the situation, the mother could not be searching for a full-time job (if she needed to be home with her son) and was therefore not entitled to an unemployment allowance. I said, "Let's sort this out."

At that point I found out she had started to take sick leave at the end of September due to her rheumatism, or suspected rheumatism. She showed me a note and said it was the certificate of sick leave. I took a look at the paper and told her, "No, this is not a certificate of sick leave; this is an invitation to a dentist from a university hospital." I took an even closer look and realized this was not for her but for her son. The mother said, "This is not important. We have already been to the dentist to remove tartar from his teeth." But this appointment was for an operation that included anesthesia. Therefore, I suspected it was relevant. So I called the hospital, and they told me it was vital for the mother and son to go there. The dentist had already contacted the child welfare inspector and issued a child welfare notification. I strongly emphasized to the mother the importance of going to the dentist with her son and wrote down the new date.

She passed me another letter from the university hospital. No, this was not the sick leave certificate either, which she would need for the job center. This was something else. But the date had also passed. "Have you been there?" I asked. "No," she said, "it is also postponed." We have a worker here who has handled a lot of things with the hospital, so she called the hospital and a private doctor, then again the hospital, then another ward, then a physiotherapist and so on. Six calls altogether. At the end, she had written down all the appointment times and places, which she gave to the mother.

In the afternoon, she actually came back with the sick leave certificate, a copy of which was attached to the letter to the job center. I gave her the original back and asked her not to lose it since she may need it for somewhere else. Then we applied for the sickness benefit, which took another two hours. Then it was done. Then we settled the afternoon care for the son. Now he has a place for the afternoons and the mother has more time. But the mother is in such a loop . . .

Astur's story illustrates how problems accumulate when one has trouble with the language and understanding how the service system is organized in the host country. When hardships from several parts of life occur simultaneously, coping becomes increasingly difficult. Astur did not know that she could not quit a language course appointed to her by the job center without permission. Due to that, she got a letter requesting an explanation. She understood that she had to respond to this letter in order to avoid losing her benefits, but alone, she was not able to do that. Since she did not realize that every action (like an invitation to a course) is a separate administrative deed and needs a response, she did not think she would need to explain why she did not attend the language course for metal workers; assigning the same person to a language course for nursing and metal workers seems quite arbitrary.

Astur's language difficulties became apparent when her son received an invitation to the dentist. She misunderstood it to be a certificate of sick leave for herself. Failing to bring her son to the dentist at the correct time had already caused more trouble. Language and administrative literacy issues are also intertwined. Since Astur and her son have several health problems, they are offered many kinds of specialized help. The terms for each specialization are difficult to understand, even for a native speaker, but for a person who has not lived and grown up in a similar service system, navigation is nearly impossible.

The benefits of having a service counselor guide clients through the service system are unquestionable. Healthcare service providers have online appointment systems, and job centers have personalized websites where one can send secure messages and fill out forms online. Yet when a person does not comprehend what is expected and what online services should be used and when, the usefulness of e-services is limited.

Suggested Solutions From the Field

It is possible to identify several potential solutions to the current e-government system's shortcomings based on the comments of the integration professionals. The importance of face-to-face, personalized services was emphasized in all interviews as they can overcome some of the problems caused by a shortage of digital and language skills, as well as a lack of administrative literacy. It was also highlighted that in face-to-face interactions, migrants tend to speak about other concerns as well. This opens up opportunities to spot service needs and guide them to other relevant services.

> And especially, the migrants, they want that personal advising. [. . .] Sometimes I make a list of what our work entails. One part is giving business advice, [while another part] is [a] kind of psychotherapy and family therapy . . . Quite often we'll go through [their] whole life situation, especially with migrants. Many [migrants] who come here say they have not discussed [it] with anyone else.
>
> (H1, Business support organization)

There is an evident need for a support person who is able to create a long-lasting, trust-based relationship with clients and who can teach them how to navigate the local information and service landscape. The emotional aspect of face-to-face interactions also emerged in the interviews. The interviewees pointed out that interactions between people have intrinsic value.

An obvious way to ensure that migrants' needs are better met is to involve them in the development of services. The business advisor (H1) brought this up as well:

> [I]f we talk about migrants, they don't really understand what to write . . . There is this kind of . . . I am really critical now, but it

seems that these national . . . Enterprise Finland and Suomi.fi services are developed in some ministry and they do not ask for input from clients or business services.

(H1, Business support organization)

Incorporating user-centered design methods into public e-service development may help to overcome bias toward the preferences and logic of "common" people (Witte and Mannon, 2010) and to increase the inclusiveness of e-government.

Conclusion

This study identified three problems that need to be solved before e-government can be fully exploited: (1) the unknown medium of ICT, (2) a lack of language proficiency, and (3) unfamiliarity with the service system (i.e., a new information landscape). Previous studies have come to similar conclusions. However, the interviewees did not see the inability to use ICT as a major obstacle. More urgent issues underlie the lack of language skills, in addition to knowledge of the local culture and the service system (i.e., governance literacy).

The main novelty of this study lies in how it shows that these three factors are interconnected, and none of them affects the ability to utilize e-government in isolation from another one. Traditionally, these elements have been analyzed separately (Grönlund et al., 2007; Lloyd et al., 2013; Brazier et al., 2017). This chapter demonstrated how integration experts, who have long-standing experience working with newcomers, view these facets as interconnected in migrants' lives. A metaphor of eyes and lenses illustrates the situation. In order to fully utilize e-government, one must have all three lenses correctly ground in order to "see" clearly through all of them (see Figure 7.1).

Secondly, Astur's story makes visible how particular characteristics (such as social relationships, economic status, and gender) are intertwined

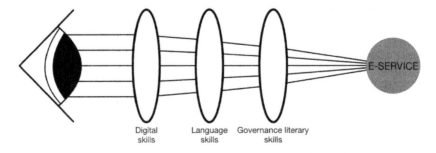

Figure 7.1 The Three Essential Skills Needed to Use E-Services

into different kinds of bundles, which have a bearing on one's willingness and capability to use e-government. Migrants constitute a very heterogeneous group; hence, their needs vary as well. Therefore, it is essential to make this multifaceted nature obvious, and to indicate how the role of e-services in individuals' lives is embedded in their social and structural circumstances. Digital technology is only one resource among many and cannot be utilized without other resources (Wessels, 2013; see also Zillien and Marr, 2013). Furthermore, the general context of one's life defines the possibilities and limitations of utilizing digital technology.

Being a migrant, a woman, unemployed, or a refugee does not dictate one's ability to utilize e-services alone. Intersectionality, which takes into account structural and cultural circumstances and overlapping inequalities (Choo and Ferree, 2010), is necessary in migration studies (Bürkner, 2012). Helbig et al. (2009) already called for making the intersections of certain elements (such as race, gender, age, and income) more prominent in examining people's usage preferences, resources, and abilities to use public e-services, but this call is still timely. Even if this chapter focuses on the integration process, the same difficulties in using e-government are present in other sections of the population as well.

The findings underscore the importance of face-to-face services, which are essential in fulfilling both informational and emotional needs (see Chapter 8 by Saari et al. in this book for a detailed analysis on the competencies needed by service advisors in the social and healthcare sectors). Service providers can mediate between the service system and migrants, in addition to acting as guides in the new service landscape, identifying and interpreting migrants' needs, and helping them to find relevant services. However, they are not merely mediators between institutions and online services; they also offer mental support, foster a sense of belonging, and sometimes even serve as "life coaches" as the case of Astur shows.

Despite the downsides of e-government, service providers also see its benefits. The general consensus is that one has to choose the medium of communication and service provision based on beneficiaries' particular needs. When developing services, the users' needs and preferences should be taken into account, and they should be involved in the development process, if possible. The relevance and usefulness of digitalizing services depend on the match between users' needs and resources, service providers' needs, and the features of e-services. Underprivileged individuals, who are often socially marginalized, have the highest odds of becoming excluded from e-government (Ragnedda and Muschert, 2013; Ragnedda, 2017; Lloyd et al., 2013). Active steps to prevent this are in order.

For researchers, the main takeaways from this chapter are the call to (a) pay more attention to migrants' combined ICT, language and governance literacy skills, and (b) utilize the analytical tools of intersectionality when investigating the reasons behind not using e-government within groups that have multiple, intersectional inequalities. The implications for policymakers are to (a) focus more on developing migrants' ICT, language, and governance literacy skills, (b) be on the lookout for potential dropouts from the information society across all sectors of the population, and (c) to ensure that the need for personalized resources is fulfilled in the future, either through face-to-face interactions or more developed digital services.

References

Ala-Kauhaluoma, M., Pitkänen, S., Ohtonen, J., Ramadan, F., Hautamäki, L., Vuorento, M. and Rinne, H. (2018). Monimenetelmäinen tutkimus kotouttamistoimenpiteiden toimivuudesta. *Eduskunnan tarkastusvaliokunnan julkaisu*, [online] 1. (Includes an English summary.) Available at: www.eduskunta.fi/FI/tietoaeduskunnasta/julkaisut/Documents/trvj_1 + 2018.pdf [Accessed 31 May 2019].

Alam, K. and Imran, S. (2015). The Digital Divide and Social Inclusion Among Refugee Migrants: A Case in Regional Australia. *Information Technology & People*, 28(2), pp. 344–365.

Aspinall, P. J. (2007). Language Ability: A Neglected Dimension in the Profiling of Populations and Health Service Users. *Health Education Journal*, 66(1), pp. 90–106.

Brazier, D. and Harvey, M. (2017, April). E-Government and the Digital Divide: A Study of English-as-a-Second-Language Users' Information Behaviour. In: *European Conference on Information Retrieval*. Cham, Switzerland: Springer, pp. 266–277.

Bürkner, H. J. (2012). Intersectionality: How Gender Studies Might Inspire the Analysis of Social Inequality Among Migrants. *Population, Space and Place*, 18(2), pp. 181–195.

Castells, M. and Himanen, P. (2002). *The Information Society and the Welfare State: The Finnish Model*. Oxford: Oxford University Press.

Cestnik, B. and Kern, A. (2014, May). Improving Responsiveness of Public Services in Housing by Monitoring Social Media Impact. In: *Conference for e-Democracy and Open Government*. Austria: Krems, p. 169.

Choo, H. Y. and Ferree, M. M. (2010). Practicing Intersectionality in Sociological Research: A Critical Analysis of Inclusions, Interactions, and Institutions in the Study of Inequalities. *Sociological Theory*, 28(2), pp. 129–149.

Denzin, N. (1989). *Interpretive Interactionism*. Newberry Park, CA: Sage Publications.

DiMaggio, P. and Garip, F. (2012). Network Effects and Social Inequality. *Annual Review of Sociology*, 38(1), pp. 93–118.

Distel, B. (2018). Bringing Light into the Shadows: A Qualitative Interview Study on Citizens' Non-Adoption of E-government. *The Electronic Journal of E-government*, 16(2), pp. 98–105.

Dunleavy, P. and Margetts, H. Z. (2010). The Second Wave of Digital Era Governance. In: *American Political Science Association Conference*. Washington, DC (Unpublished): LSE Research Online. Available at: http://eprints.lse.ac.uk/27684/1/The_second_wave_of_digital_era_governance_%28LSERO%29.pdf [Accessed 10 January 2019].

Eriksson, P. and Kovalainen, A. (2015). *Qualitative Methods in Business Research: A Practical Guide to Social Research*. Newcastle upon Tyne: Sage Publications.

Eurostat Database. (2019). *Eurostat Database.* [online] Available at: https://ec.europa.eu/eurostat/data/database [Accessed 10 January 2019].

Finlex. (2010). *Act on the Promotion of Immigrant Integration (1386/2010).* [online] Available at: www.finlex.fi/en/laki/kaannokset/2010/en20101386 [Accessed 3 April 2019].

Gebhardt, D. (2016). When the State Takes Over: Civic Integration Programmes and the Role of Cities in Immigrant Integration. *Journal of Ethnic and Migration Studies*, 42(5), pp. 742–758.

Geertz, C. (2008). Thick Description: Toward an Interpretive Theory of Culture. In: *The Cultural Geography Reader*. Abingdon, UK: Routledge, pp. 41–51.

Government Programme. (2015). *The Programme of the Finnish Government 2015–2019*. [online] Available at: https://valtioneuvosto.fi/en/sipila/government-programme [Accessed 26 April 2019].

Grönlund, Å., Hatakka, M. and Ask, A. (2007, September). Inclusion in the E-Service Society—Investigating Administrative Literacy Requirements for Using E-Services. In: *International Conference on Electronic Government*. Springer, Berlin: Springer, pp. 216–227.

Helbig, N., Gil-García, J. R. and Ferro, E. (2009). Understanding the Complexity of Electronic Government: Implications From the Digital Divide Literature. *Government Information Quarterly*, 26(1), pp. 89–97.

Helsper, E. J. (2012). A Corresponding Fields Model for the Links Between Social and Digital Exclusion. *Communication theory*, 22(4), pp. 403–426.

Jones, T., Ram, M., Edwards, P., Kiselinchev, A. and Muchenje, L. (2014). Mixed Embeddedness and New Migrant Enterprise in the UK. *Entrepreneurship & Regional Development*, 26(5–6), pp. 500–520.

Kaufmann, K. (2018). Navigating a New Life: Syrian Refugees and Their Smartphones in Vienna. *Information, Communication & Society*, 21(6), pp. 882–898.

Kettunen, P. (2011). The Sellers of Labour Power as Social Citizens: A Utopian Wage Work Society in the Nordic Visions of Welfare. In: H. Blomberg and N. Kildal, eds., *Workfare and Welfare State Legitimacy*. Helsinki: Nordic Centre of Excellence NordWel, pp. 16–45.

Kloosterman, R., Van Der Leun, J. and Rath, J. (1999). Mixed Embeddedness: (in)Formal Economic Activities and Immigrant Businesses in the Netherlands. *International Journal of Urban and Regional Research*, 23(2), pp. 252–266.

Lin, K. (2004). Sectors, Agents and Rationale: A Study of the Scandinavian Welfare States With Special Reference to the Welfare Society Model. *Acta Sociologica*, 47(2), pp. 141–157.

Lindblom, T. and Räsänen, P. (2017). Between Class and Status? Examining the Digital Divide in Finland, the United Kingdom, and Greece. *The Information Society*, 33(3), pp. 147–158.

Lloyd, A., Kennan, M. A., Thompson, K. M. and Qayyum, A. (2013). Connecting With New Information Landscapes: Information Literacy Practices of Refugees. *Journal of Documentation*, 69(1), pp. 121–144.

Martikainen, T., Valtonen, K. and Wahlbeck, Ö. (2012). The Social Integration of Immigrants in Finland. In: J. Frideres and J. Biles, eds., *International Perspectives: Integration and Inclusion*. Montreal, Quebec: McGill-Queen's University Press, pp. 127–146.

Meuser, M. and Nagel, U. (2009). The Expert Interview and Changes in Knowledge Production. In: A. Bogner, B. Lieg and W. Menz, eds., *Interviewing Experts*. Basingstoke, UK: Palgrave Macmillan, pp. 184–200.

Norris, P. (2001). *Digital Divide: Civic Engagement, Information Poverty, and the Internet Worldwide.* Cambridge, UK: Cambridge University Press.

OECD. (2018). *Working Together: Skills and Labour Market Integration of Immigrants and Their Children in Finland.* Paris: OECD Publishing.

Ragnedda, M. (2017). *The Third Digital Divide: A Weberian Approach to Digital Inequalities.* Abingdon, UK: Routledge.

Ragnedda, M. and Muschert, G. W. (eds.) (2013). *The Digital Divide: The Internet and Social Inequality in International Perspective.* Abingdon, UK: Routledge.

Saukkonen, P. (2013). *Erilaisuuksien suomi: vähemmistö-ja kotouttamispolitiikan vaihtoehdot.* Helsinki: Gaudeamus.

Selwyn, N. (2004). Reconsidering Political and Popular Understandings of the Digital Divide. *New Media & Society,* 6(3), pp. 341–362.

Statistics Finland. (2019). *Statistics Finland's StatFin Online Service.* [online] Available at: http://tilastokeskus.fi/tup/statfin/index_en.html [Accessed 15 January 2019].

Szkudlarek, B. and Wu, S. X. (2018). The Culturally Contingent Meaning of Entrepreneurship: Mixed Embeddedness and Co-Ethnic Ties. *Entrepreneurship & Regional Development,* 30(5–6), pp. 585–611.

Tolciu, A. (2011). Migrant Entrepreneurs and Social Capital: A Revised Perspective. *International Journal of Entrepreneurial Behavior & Research,* 17(4), pp. 409–427.

Van Deursen, A. J. and Van Dijk, J. A. (2014). The Digital Divide Shifts to Differences in Usage. *New Media & Society,* 16(3), pp. 507–526.

Van Dijk, J. A. G. M. (2013). A Theory of the Digital Divide. In: M. Ragnedda and G. W. Muschert, eds., *The Digital Divide: The Internet and Social Inequality in International Perspective.* Abingdon, UK: Routledge, pp. 36–51.

Van Dijk, J. A. G. M. and Hacker, K. (2003). The Digital Divide as a Complex and Dynamic Phenomenon. *The Information Society,* 19(4), pp. 315–326.

Vuori, J. (2015). Kotouttaminen Arjen Kansalaisuuden Rakentamisena. *Yhteiskuntapolitiikka,* 80(4), pp. 395–404.

Wahlbeck, Ö. (2018). To Share or Not to Share Responsibility? Finnish Refugee Policy and the Hesitant Support for a Common European Asylum System. *Journal of Immigrant & Refugee Studies,* 17(3), pp. 1–18.

Wessels, B. (2013). The Reproduction and Reconfiguration of Inequality: Differentiation and Class, Status and Power in the Dynamics of Digital Divides. In: M. Ragnedda and G. W. Muschert, eds., *The Digital Divide: The Internet and Social Inequality in International Perspective.* Abingdon, UK: Routledge, pp. 17–28.

Witte, J. C. and Mannon, S. E. (2010). *The Internet and Social Inequalities.* Abingdon, UK: Routledge.

Yu, L. (2006). Understanding Information Inequality: Making Sense of the Literature of the Information and Digital Divides. *Journal of Librarianship and Information Science,* 38(4), pp. 229–252.

Zillien, N. and Marr, M. (2013). The Digital Divide in Europe. In: M. Ragnedda and G. W. Muschert, eds., *The Digital Divide: The Internet and Social Inequality in International Perspective.* Abingdon, UK: Routledge, pp. 55–66.

Part IV

Theoretical Opportunities for Understanding New Emergent Phenomena in the Digital Platform Economy

8 Emergence of Agentic Professional Competence in the Digitalization of Social Services and Healthcare

Eveliina Saari, Mervi Hasu, Sari Käpykangas, and Anne Kovalainen

Introduction

The global shift from manufacturing economies to innovation-driven economies, where the emphasis is on services and value creation, demands reconsideration of how we understand work and how we conceptualize the competences and learning of employees. Technology optimists claim that digitalization and artificial intelligence may replace almost all the work tasks of professionals in the future (Sundararajan, 2016) We suggest that introducing agency to the concept of competence makes human capability and intentionality visible in the process and resists the intention of seeing professionals as only passively adapting to automation. Agency is seen here as an individual capacity to act and as a behavioral process, which is influenced by the social context of everyday work (Eteläpelto, 2017)—in other words, having an ability to affect collective change. If competence is seen as only individual-related phenomena and referring only to knowledge already acquired by the individual, work organizations may not realize how professionals change their work and themselves, continuously and voluntarily, when given opportunities to influence on organizational and technological development.

The empirical context of our study is public social and healthcare services that aim to benefit from digitalization. General policy hopes set by governments on the effects of digitalization are currently high; in health and social services the hope is that digital platforms will help make social and healthcare services paperless, more efficient, citizen-oriented, and integrated (European Commission, 2018; DigitalEurope, 2018). As key implementers of change in work organizations, public professionals in expert and leadership positions are expected to increase clients' autonomous agency while exercising control over increasing service needs and expenses, and, concurrently, act responsibly. Further, public sector professionals are expected to lead the implementation of new digital tools and platforms for professional and client use. In the implementation of digitalized services, agency of users—instead of employees—has been the core focus (Oborn and Barret, 2016). There is indeed a need to understand the service professional's agency as an active participator and contributor in technological change.

This chapter is structured as follows. First, we provide an overview of the ongoing change towards digitalized healthcare, which radically influences the relationship between professionals and citizens. Second, we provide an overview on how digitalization influences service professionals. Third, we sketch key theoretical approaches to conceptualize agentic professional competence for our combined framework. Fourth, we demonstrate our framework with a case study that unfolds an emerging profession—*service advisor*—in the customer interface domain, indicating how professionals may become proactive authors of their own working roles. Finally, we discuss the theoretical and practical implications.

Towards Digitalized and Platformized Co-Production of Healthcare

Social and healthcare service provisioning is experiencing intensive changes, which have consequences for work, such as job descriptions and competence requirements, as well as the collaboration and coordination of professional knowledge and work practices in organizations. Concerning work-related consequences, two contemporary trends may have the capacity to reshape healthcare delivery significantly in the coming decade (Oborn and Barret, 2016). The first trend is digital health and big-data science (in short, datafication of health and social care), and the second is increasing patient and citizen engagement through digital platforms (in short, platforms of health and care services). Both trends are strongly connected to the ideas of increasing citizen responsibility, as well as the co-production of information, usage and the mastery of one's own health data, and the digitalization of (self-) services.

These two trends also play a major role in ongoing social and health sector development in Nordic countries, especially Finland, where major reforms for integrating social and healthcare services have been implemented or will be executed over the next few years. The government has adopted strategies for implementing the digitalization of public services, as well as related information communications technology (ICT) re-tooling operations to help the standardization and integration of said services. The aim is for information systems and new e-services to support users and professionals (Ministry of Finance and the Ministry of Social Affairs and Health, 2018).

From the point of view of our case study, service advisors work in healthcare. The platform trend of digitalization is expected to be the most significant in framing the material and technological work environment of the studied employees in their local context (European Commission, 2018). From the platform perspective, health services rely on collaboration and coordination between multiple actors in an ecosystem. The roles, activities, and responsibilities of service users and professionals are changing from a one-directional means of knowledge transfer towards the co-production of knowledge and services. Patients are assumed to engage with their health and other care services in new ways, such as via digital platforms; social media; and by creating new forms of data, evidence, knowledge, and support that can offer value to diverse stakeholders (Oborn and Barret, 2016). These changes challenge traditional hierarchies, power relationships, and forms of professional collaboration, as well as entail a transformation of how responsibilities in knowledge production are delegated, how trust is constructed, and who has access to learning the new operations. Emerging new roles such as service advisors that enable citizens to navigate in the network of changing services are at the center of the platform trend in the public health sector.

Thus, concerns have arisen regarding citizens' ability to use and access digital services, as well as the changing work tasks of care professionals and new competence requirements (Hyppönen and Ilmarinen, 2016). Polarization of the population of citizens who have the resources to use digital services, and those who are not capable of using self-services through digital platforms, may increase. Digital services require not only digital skills for becoming a co-producer of the service; taking responsibility for one's own health is also needed. Hence, the change towards digitalized healthcare, surrounded by structural reforms, will not take place without the acceptance of professionals, guidance of the citizens, and systematic change management. Our empirical case study indicates that these challenges are currently becoming pervasive questions in healthcare.

Digitalization of Services and Its Impact on Professionals

How to integrate notions of agency with frameworks of professional learning and competence is an intriguing question between social and educational sciences (Goller and Paloniemi, 2017; Eteläpelto et al., 2013; Grant and Parker, 2009). Agency is seen here as an individual's capacity to act and as a behavioral process that can influence collective change (Eteläpelto, 2017). We searched for more dynamic definitions of professional competence development than only acquisition of new knowledge to cope with changing work tasks. Bringing agency to the fore underlines professionals' capability to transform work practices—individually and collectively.

While face-to-face human interaction has traditionally dominated service work, the digitalization of services changes it partly or entirely into a form of technology-mediated activity. As ICT-enabled service interfaces turn clients into operators of their own services, the role of employees may change and diminish (Rust and Huang, 2014). However, as the face-to-face servant role of service employees may seemingly fade away as the technological interface pushes them—into the background, back offices, and distant work—there may arise also new opportunities for new alliances and agencies and for the adoption of new roles and relationships.

In service work, especially in healthcare and social services, the agency of an employee is related to and dependent on clients' life situation and on employees' workload. This concerns all sectors; however, here, our case example stems from public services. The relationship between employees and clients has been studied in the public service context from the viewpoints of emotional labor (Hochschild, 2001). Face-to-face contact makes the emergence of empathy and emotions possible and thus influences the outcome of a service encounter; however, as shown in studies of emotional labor (e.g., Vallas, 2012), it also makes it more stressful. Emotional labor has become part and parcel of the relational work in services (see Hochschild, 1983, 2001).

Case studies to date have indicated that empowering and allowing employees to apply their tacit knowledge, customer know-how, and their own ideas to service innovations increases the preconditions and possibilities for development, improves services overall, and positively influences workers' wellbeing (Honkaniemi et al., 2015; Hasu et al., 2014). This is conditional on the ways that technologically driven work is organized. Although technology automatizes part of service work, new roles for workers are emerging. Bowen (2016) noted that the new roles mean that workers may become innovators of new services based on their deep experience with clients; they may become enablers, helping and training clients to use technology. In addition, the roles may include differentiators, who give a genuinely empathetic and personal face to the surface of the service; and coordinators, who handle integration between different tasks and building bridges between diverse offerings (Bowen, 2016).

However, many classifications, such as the one described, fail to provide firm ground for any determined relationship between technology and service work, and are often based on assumed immutable relations between the workers, technology, and the clients. Additionally, not all work is alike: the effects of gender (e.g., Poutanen and Kovalainen, 2017), age and class (e.g., Vallas and Hill, 2012), and, indeed, labor competition in general can all change the process of how technology and work exist together.

In at least the implementation phase of digital services, service workers' agency may depend on how quickly and smoothly customers are willing to adopt the role of co-producer of the service, and how well guided they are to increase the use of self-service aspects of ICT systems (Berger et al., 2016; Breit and Salomon, 2015). This is a crucial question as we design digital services for citizens who may not have the resources to acquire the technical devices, or the resources needed to learn how to use digital platforms.

Conceptualizing Professional Competence

Competence as Knowledge Creation and Mediated by Tool Use

In a rapidly changing society, work is increasingly focused on the creation of new artefacts and activities, and objects for consumption, such as new products, services, and work practices. By artefacts we refer to material tools and objects made by human beings. Therefore, there is a need for an approach that makes learning at work the focus, and which considers *learning as knowledge-creation*. This approach emphasizes the aspect of collective knowledge creation for developing shared objects of activity (Paavola et al., 2004). Several influential theories explain and give analytical guidance on how to capture this phenomenon: e.g., Nonaka and Takeuchi's model of knowledge creation (1995), Engeström's model of expansive learning (1987), and Bereiter's model of knowledge building (2002). Their criticism is that the Western epistemological tradition has valued knowledge as such, but not (1) how to create new knowledge (Nonaka and Takeuchi), (2) how to create changes in activity systems (Engeström) or (3) how to go beyond the current level of accomplishment and competence to adapt to the changing environments (Bereiter).

The focus of experts is not only to improve individuals' understanding but to work for developing new, culturally shared knowledge objects (Bereiter) or culturally and societally new practices (Engeström). This creation process is depicted as a cyclical, iterative, even ambiguous process that transforms existing ideas and practices. Also critical for human agency and learning are opportunities to participate in expansive tasks, in addition to obtaining access to information and knowledge about the wider infrastructures and system of services in which the tasks are embedded (Nerland and Jensen, 2014; Fuller and Unwin, 2010).

All three of these learning models bring a mediating element between the subject and object of learning. Taking this conceptual frame into practice, it is possible to relate the rather quick digitalization into agentic learning. Human agency requires conceptualizing digitalization related to the changing role of tools and the competence of tool use at work. Technologies are significant in these processes. By relating to advanced tools, individuals gain access to collective knowledge in the field of work and, concurrently, to instruments aimed at invoking and adapting such knowledge to the purposes of the situation at hand (Säljö, 2010). This analytical stance is in line with information systems research that recognizes that information technologies (IT) as tools are neither fixed or static nor completely adopted or rejected by users. Hence, attention should be given to how employees as users change technologies to attain new goals;

i.e., reinvent IT, and whether their reinvention pattern is performance-oriented (more adaptive and present) or mastery-oriented (more expansive and future-oriented; Nevo et al., 2016).

In sum, learning as a form of knowledge creation provides important aspects that can be used to analyze work as a form of co-creation and mediated by tool use in turbulent change. However, when the unit of analysis is focused on social interaction and collective problem-solving, the role of individual agency, or the development path of individual agents, is not prioritized or made visible in concrete analyses. In these transformational theories, the individual tends to be seen only in relation to the current situation, not from his or her lifelong perspective or professional identity as the developmental socio-cultural approaches usually do (Eteläpelto, 2017). The kind of embedded values and power asymmetries that determine agency are not dealt with in these approaches, either. Therefore, we strive to understand how the relationships and ability to become an active agent are framed by the institutional value-structures and power relationships.

The Awareness of Asymmetry of Power Relationships

In organizations and in actual work contexts, individuals might not have equal opportunities or resources to influence how problems are solved, nor concerning what technological devices are available for problem solving. The element of power asymmetries between people and in hierarchical relationships are not sufficiently addressed in the above learning models. In workplaces, employees are often aware of the official power relationships; however, unofficial power is often invisible and embedded in subject positions, relationships, and discourses, and these forms of power have a significant influence on how agency is constrained in the workplace (Eteläpelto et al., 2014).

Gender studies in care and feminist analyses of care work (e.g., Tronto, 2013; Lewis, 2010, 2002) have shown how power relationships are inscribed in hierarchical positions, across sexes, and in care recipient–care worker relationships. For example, the trend of digitalizing—e.g., homecare visits—can be interpreted as representing a more male-dominant medical model. Inequalities in paid and unpaid care work and in the workforce are deeply interrelated. According to a recent global report on care work (International Labour Office, 2018), persistent gender inequalities in households and the labor market are inextricably linked to care work divisions and organizing care. In the wake of the care crisis, the questions of who performs caring work, and who pays for it, are intertwined with the care providers' sex. The intersectionalities and multitudes of dependencies built into agency positions and agentic relations are often not included in the analyses of agency. By opening discussions to include the underlying power discrepancies and inequalities, we aim to link these to the current technological discourses anew, thus bringing greater materiality into the agency discussion.

Margaret Archer (2003) describes human agency as influenced by his or her social position defining his or her life-chances. The rationality in actions of an individual depends, according to Archer, on the many individual possibilities in his or her structures. As the human agent becomes aware of the interests he or she shares with other members of his or her class, he or she becomes a corporate agent who transforms society according to his or her ultimate concerns.

We need to understand how the institutional and organizational position of individual actors creates agency towards an opportunity to become a proactive agent of change or a mainly reactive adaptor to the institutional-level frame and its vision for the future. The exercise of agency is never a matter of free choice; rather, it is constrained by the power and the options—what is possible to do under certain circumstances (Eteläpelto et al., 2014). Thus, when analyzing professional agency, we should be sensitive to how the professional observes and feels his or her power to change routines and what kind of autonomy at work he or she has. On the other hand, in the context of workplace learning, agency is a force for change and resistance to structural power. The manifestations of professional agency are individuals' creative initiatives for developing existing work practices (Sawyer, 2012). In the following, we will address the concept of agency in greater detail.

Concepts of Agency and Organizational Authorship Contribute to Elucidating Competence

We now relate the concept of human agency to its socio-cultural or institutional environment. We discuss three approaches to agency in professional contexts: the approaches of Emirbayer and Mische (1998), representing a sociological classic text about human agency; the elaborations of professional agency by Eteläpelto et al. (2013, 2014); and Gorli et al. (2015), who presented the concept of organizational authorship.

According to Emirbayer and Mische (1998), all social action is a concrete synthesis, shaped and conditioned. This, on the one hand, consists of temporal-relational contexts of action and, on the other, comprises the dynamic element of agency itself. From an empirical sense, social action will never be completely determined or structured. Human agency may imaginatively distance itself from the received structures (Emirbayer and Mische, 1998).

Emirbayer and Mische (1998, p. 968) lean on elaborations of George Herbert Mead (1932) in their insights—that the concept of time is constituted through emergent events, which require human beings to refocus on the past and future. They see human consciousness as being constituted of the capacity to be both temporally and relationally in a variety of systems at once. What Mead calls, "the deliberative attitude" is interpreted concerning actors responding to changing environments who must continually reconstruct their view of the past to understand the emergent present, while controlling their responses in the arising future (Emirbayer and Mische, 1998, p. 969). This process is a fundamentally intersubjective process, including the ability to simultaneously hold one's own and another's viewpoint. They depict agency as a dialogical process, in which actors immersed in the temporal passage are engaged in collectively organized contexts of action (p. 974). In digitalizing healthcare, this may mean that the work community benefits from such an agent who helps others to foresee future services, after the learning of new tools has been acquired.

Eteläpelto et al. (2014, 2013) brings together the concepts of agency and professional identity. They argue that agency should be understood related to concrete aspects of professional identities and duties. Even within the same profession (e.g., teacher or nurse), professional agency can vary, leading to distinct versions of how to conduct the job tasks in question. Eteläpelto and colleagues state that professional agency should be analyzed both as an individual and as a collective phenomenon—strong individual agency does not guarantee that work practices will be transformed, and collective agency may be needed.

Eteläpelto et al. (2014, p. 62) name their approach a "subject-centered socio-cultural approach to professional agency." They list seven implications illustrating the role of agency as a change-maker: (1) professional agency is practiced when professional subjects or communities exert influence, make choices, and take stances in ways that affect their work and their professional identities; (2) it is exercised for certain purposes and with certain socio-cultural and material circumstances, which also constrain or provide resources; (3) it is closely intertwined with professional subjects' work-related identities consisting of their professional and ethical commitments, motivations, interests, and goals; (4) professionals' unique prior experiences and knowledge function as individual affordances and resources for the practice of professional agency at work; (5) individuals and social entities are analytically separate but mutually constitutive of each other; (6) professionals have discursive, practical, and natural relations to their work; and (7) professional agency is needed for developing one's work, for taking creative initiatives, for professional learning, and renegotiating identities in changing work practices. Competence as a concept seems to refer, in the authors' texts, to something that has already been acquired. We aim to involve (individual and collective) competence as a significant element of the practicing of professional agency. Therefore, we use the term "agentic professional competence."

Gorli et al. (2015) elaborated on the concept of organizational authorship to consider people as the authors of their work. Their approach derives from socio-cultural psychology and dialogical constructivists and provides methodological tools to examine the phenomenon empirically. Organizational authorship provides a theoretical framework for analyzing professionals' experiences as a meaningful, reflexive, and sustainable narration of their work. Authorship is a key aspect in constant interpretations of practices, the freedom of judgment, and even contributes to organizational goals. A person may become an author of his or her own work setting, when he or she plays an active role in the daily production, reproduction, and transformation of the work processes (Shotter and Cunliffe, 2003). The concept of authorship captures the idea of agency from the point of view of workers' actions and choices, which are simultaneously framed by the social context. They provide also a method to study the phenomena of authorship—the "instructions to the double" technique (Ivaldi et al., 2015). This provides a valid method for expressing interviewees' own choices and actions as a personal narrative in their own social context, instead of forcing them into researchers' predetermined themes and thus silencing their voice.

A Framework for Agentic Professional Competence in a Digitalized Care Work Environment

In the previous section we identified four important elements to include in the analysis to understand professional agency replacing the common-sense way to conceptualize competence as just something that exists purely inside everyone's mind, and which refers only to knowledge that has already been acquired. What is common to the previous approaches is the understanding of professional competence as a dynamic interaction between agency, the relationships, and the institutional and technological environment. The professional practitioner is confined by his or her institutional-material environment but, concurrently, may have an opportunity and capability to change or question these circumstances. We call this agentic professional competence. These elements have an impact on a professional's ability to become a proactive agent in the changing organizational and institutional context, embedded with an intense re-tooling phase of digitalization. We consider this in the following analyses.

Reflexivity and Temporal Orientation

Reflexivity is a method and means of questioning current practices. This provides a basis for future and deliberate action. Reflexivity is a link between work and learning that benefits both the worker and the organization. Practical reflexivity is encouraged in interview situations because it encourages social actors to see themselves as agents and authors of the organizations in which they live (Gorli et al., 2015).

In the analysis, we emphasized how the interviewee describes how he or she created his or her work practice reflecting his or her personal agency, and how he or she sees the ability and opportunities to create new practices for the future and influence the prevailing digitalization process. Temporal orientation refers to how actors may engage with patterns and repertoires from the past, project hypothetical pathways forward in time, and adjust their actions to the exigencies of emerging situations (Emirbayer and Mische, 1998).

Relationships With Other People

To obtain a realistic understanding of the work context, we should consider professionals' relationships with other people (both clients and other professionals), how are they formed and sustained, and what kind of feelings they contain. We examined what kinds of relationships professionals actively form, and how they influence their individual and collective agency or authorship (Saari et al., 2017; Gorli et al., 2015).

Sensitivity to Social Position and Power Asymmetries

We should be aware of the social position related to the institutional change that professionals are working from and how the organization supports or dismantles these positions and power asymmetries (Archer, 2003). From the interviews, we examined how autonomous agent professionals define their work tasks; what kinds of rules, standards, or procedures they follow in their work; and finally, how do the hierarchies or divisions of labor of their work organization function and influence their work.

Institutional, Material, and Technological Arrangements

We should identify "the institutional arrangements and the material artefacts" (Gorli et al., 2015, p. 22) at hand for the professional to reconstruct his or her authorship in the organization. This also refers to whether the professional has access to tools, and how she or he considers the technology and its current phase when solving present and future institutional problems. Opportunities for change may vary depending on the objective conditions of the organization and the implementation phase of the technology.

To conclude, agentic professional competence unfolds as a form of proactive, reflexive, relational, and collective knowledge creation, as well as agency, which is sensitive to power asymmetries and constrained and facilitated by the institutional-technological context.

Service Advisors as an Example of Professionals' Emerging Agentic Competence

The social and healthcare district is a national forerunner in organizing social and healthcare services in a new and novel way. Currently, the region is increasing its e-services and implementing a new digital strategy. The social and healthcare district is in the middle of constant implementation of new ICT systems and efforts to integrate social care and healthcare, highlighting the platform trend discussed earlier. The prevention of health problems and self-sufficiency of elderly populations at home are key elements of its core strategy. Owing to this strategic reorientation, multiple changes in the service system are ongoing (unpublished research materials, 2019).

The social and healthcare district is in a rural district in Finland. It is responsible for the entire (integrated) social care and healthcare in the region, involving a population of 132,000 people, a 450 M€ budget, and 4,600 employees. The challenges involve a rapidly aging population and low population density: in 2021 the estimated share of people aged older than 65 years in the peripheral areas of the region was 35–41%. Unemployment is relatively high in the region, and social and health problems tend to accumulate when unemployment is prolonged (unpublished research materials, 2019). The data concerning service advisors were collected in Autumn 2016. The data and methods are described in the Appendix at the end of this chapter.

Service Advisors as Guides for Citizens in Navigating Between Services

Service advisors are an example of how professionals may become proactive authors of their own working roles. Service advisors work as pioneers in social and healthcare districts to help citizens navigate between the different services. Because of the ongoing digitalization of the services, they have become the boundary-crossing personnel between ICT interfaces and citizens. When managers nominated service advisors to help citizens in the complex social and healthcare system, they were not aware of what these jobs would entail. Therefore, the starting point was that the professionals involved were free to construct their own job almost as they wished without a specific mandate or competency requirements demanded by the managers.

From the five service advisors interviewed, we distinguished three types of profiles based on their educational background, authorship, relationships, what kind of tools they used, and what kind of local context they worked in: (1) the proactive caretaker and co-creator, who takes care of the client comprehensively; (2) the sensitive service integrator and interlocutor, who collaborates smoothly with other professionals; and (3) the digital guide and snag solver, who uses digital systems and assists customers in their use.

The most vulnerable customers were served by a proactive caretaker and co-creator service advisor type, who was committed to each client until she or he got help. In turn, the sensitive service integrator and interlocutor worked with both vulnerable and active citizens in a mixed

Table 8.1 Analysis Framework and Operationalization for the Interviews

Analytical element to evaluate from the interviews	Operationalization
1. Reflexivity and temporal orientation	Describe how the role creates practices and has created his or her job practices. How does the agent reflect on the tasks? What kinds of rules or principles are followed or bent? Does the agency focus on routinely reflecting on the past? Does the agency focus on making sense of the present? Does the agency focus on strategically orienting to the future?
2. Relationships with other people	How much does the role involve facing clients or professionals face-to-face, on the phone, or via e-service? What kinds of problems are solved? How are contacts created and sustained with other services and professionals? What kinds of feelings and attitudes do the relationships contain? How are the relationships with clients/other professionals handled? Whose needs are fulfilled in the relationships?
3. Sensitivity to social position and power asymmetries	Does the individual represent a communicative, autonomous, or meta-reflexive type of agency? Does the individual question the prevailing institutional circumstances or adapt to the institutional environment? Is something hindering her or his actions? Does the individual mobilize others, or is she or he mobilized by someone or some domain? What kind of values does the individual talk about and represent?
4. Institutional, material, and technological arrangements	In what kind of physical context does the individual work? Describe the workspace; how are other services located? What kinds of tools are used during the day (e.g., papers/information communications/technology programs)? How enthusiastic or critical is this person about future technology?

role: social worker and service advising. Third, the digital guide and snag solver, was available as a service contact point when citizens, who were mainly capable of applying services by themselves, had questions or sought advice. In the following, we present the three variations based on our analysis framework (see Table 8.1).

The Proactive Caretaker and Co-Creator

This service advisor takes the highest responsibility for customers' well-being compared to the other types. One of the interviewees represented clearly this type of agentic professional competence (we refer to the types by "she," although one of the five service advisors was a man).

She works in the wellbeing center in a town-like district. She has a desk of her own but moves around the building during the day, depending on where help is needed or where she assumes customers need her. She has an educational background both from healthcare and social services. The nurses' background provides an understanding of the medical state of the customers, as she describes, "My nurse education is very good because sometimes I find out that the customer has too much medication. Sometimes, I myself reserve a doctor's appointment from the desk, and I refuse to go away before the appointment is reserved" (Interview 25). She has created new practices to find and handle outcast citizens. She is very devoted to her work and helping customers comprehensively—even fight against other professionals until she gets into another service. She reflects on her role and tasks and can compare them to those of others.

The caretaker acts very actively to find customers. She has created her job from scratch, by observing and "grabbing" clients from the reception desk, where she could foresee who would need service advising. As she explained, "I just went and collected (my clients) from the desk. I looked at the clients in the reception room and noted to the nurses that, 'that one looks like she could come to meet me after the doctor's appointment'" (Interview 24).

She actively searches for face-to-face service events with mainly disordered citizens or their relatives, who need several services quickly. Their digital skills are tenuous, and they may not know what kind of services are available or are reluctant to receive them. She also serves younger customers on the phone, but often invites them to face-to-face contact, "Most of the people who are my customers just are not capable enough. Younger ones with mental health problems or alcohol problems cannot. They do not have the computers or such; they might have prepaid telephone connection, which is valid only a week every now and then" (Interview 24).

She adjusts her way of talking to clients depending on their personality. She scans indirectly the lifestyle and circumstance of the client by chatting in a familiar, friendly way with him or her. She accompanies clients' opinions and is emphatic. The communication strategy of the caretaker is to ask indirect questions about his or her way of living, as she describes the way of talking with a customer, "So are you from this town originally? Do you have relatives here? What kind of work you have done? Do you have hobbies? What kinds of neighbors' you have? . . . Interviewer: And you make conclusions? Yes, I write down, and go on, it takes time but . . ." (Interview 24). She writes notes during the appointments to Post-it papers and writes reports as narratives into Effica, a patient record system. She prints out documents from the system and pastes her notes into them to remember the specific customer. She is not very ICT enthusiastic; however, she can cope with the health record systems.

The Sensitive Service Integrator and Interlocutor

Three interviewees fit this profile. She works in a wellbeing center, which provides extensive healthcare services in a multi-professional institutional environment. She has a room of her own near the reception desk of the wellbeing center. She moves around the corridors and meets other professionals in coffee breaks and at lunch. The door is knocked on all day long. She has a basic education in another human-related sector; however, she has also educated herself in social work. She works in collaboration with other professionals, and the customer flow comes through them. After a puzzling moment of realizing there are not any models or job descriptions on how to do the job, she enjoys the freedom to create her own personal one. She describes, "It is true that I have taken the power into my own hands in a way" (Interview 26).

Gradually, the other professionals, such as doctors, noticed the new emerging professional role in the wellbeing center and started to guide their patients to her and ask the advisor into their meetings. She seems to collaborate more with other professionals in the wellbeing center as compared to the caretaker service advisor. She does not have to search for clients, and there is not any talk about fighting for them.

Helping clients use digital interfaces seemed to play a minor role for the sensitive service integrator, although this was one of the original motives of the management to initiate the role. She decided to put most of her time into face-to-face service with the most vulnerable citizens, who are in crisis. This choice indicates her agentic professional competence. She creates a trustful space for clients to talk about their life and problems, listens very sensitively, and asks additional questions. By sensitively encountering the customers face-to-face, she treats customers as people with problems more so than the recipients of individual services. She has skills to empower the agency by listening and supporting him or her as an equal, not as a patient. She starts with a small talk, or asks clients about the reason for a doctor's appointment. Broader understanding of the customers' anxieties became helpful, and discussions often became therapeutic for the clients. She uses a social-work approach and methods: "A human being reveals his or her problem if one just gives space to talk . . . only one sentence may come, and I may latch onto it. So, one must be extremely present and recipient, about what he or she reveals" (Interview 26).

The person in question has gained a position in handling difficult cases among the professionals of the wellbeing center. Clients are directed from appointments with MDs and nurses to the service advisor. Other professionals are relieved because the service advisor saves their time, by having time to encounter the client and by knowing how to guide the client towards other services and how to write successful satisfactory statements for applications. She is invited to other professionals' meetings and has become a conflict resolver between professionals. She has ideas on developing services in a preventive future-oriented direction based on social work or previous education: "I have had permission from my supervisor to conduct motivating discussions" (Interview 28). She reflects the diverse tasks of the job in a finely tuned way. Her temporal orientation is mainly towards the present, trying to make sense of the change.

Digital Guide and Snag Solver

One interviewee represented this kind of agentic professional competence. The digital guide and snag solver worked at a contact point, which was a small building in the suburbs. She took care of local and acute social and healthcare needs. Her office was opposite the lobby and next to the nurses' room. She was educated in healthcare and adult social services. Her work history was in social services. She uses several ICT systems fluently and can guide clients in using them. She works two positions: two days a week as a service advisor and three days a week as a social worker. She seems to adapt easily to this hybrid advisory role.

Clients from the neighborhood actively enter or call the contact point. They are taken with and without appointments from the lobby as they arrive. She keeps the door open for enquirers, advises citizens in their welfare applications, and guides them to use the digital service-portal of the social and healthcare services. She has a positive attitude towards e-services. She has organized but reactive ways of working. The individual has the best digital skills compared to other types; however, she has a more reactive way of encountering the clients than do the other types: "When someone arrives here, I listen and evaluate what kind of help he or she needs; then, I decide what kind of help is needed—medical or social . . . then, we may print out his applications and I may fill it with the customer. I ask and write down" (Interview 27).

The person in question encourages clients to register on the digital portal:

> It is demanded that they register into the digital service portal, and then inform me by e-mail that he or she has registered. Then, I add the customer to the system and the access is available for him or her . . . I increasingly guide customers to use it; I even made handwritten instructions how to do it.
>
> (Interview 27)

Since she worked only two days a week as the contact point, there were enough enquirers. It seems they were served quite quickly or directed to the nurse as needed. She made occasional contact with other profession-als by phone. She was not actively connected to other service advisors. Multitasking was a natural part of her work duties. She wrote her notes concerning customers using electronic records. She used Excel, Effica, a healthcare patient data program, and Skype for Business daily.

Conclusions Related to Agentic Professional Competence

Concerning our theoretical argument of agency and relationships being important elements of competence, the framework brings forward how service advisors' own perceptions of who to help and how to help them were developed during their actions and interactions with clients and other professionals. All service advisors were acting autonomously when relating to their superiors, and they were free to modify their job tasks. In that sense, they *reflected* that they had power in their own hands. The three different variations of service advisors may thus be an outcome of professional agentic competence, which consists of a dynamic interaction between personal agency, relationships (including power relationships), and institutional and technological environment.

The analysis shortly presented here indicates that the agentic profes-sional competence of the service advisors is partly framed by their rela-tionships with other professionals and clients, which they also actively create and renew. The most vulnerable groups of citizens, with multiple needs for various services, were sometimes reached only via home vis-its after a hint from a relative or neighbor. Service advisors developed sensitive communication strategies for such clients (i.e., ways to under-stand their life circumstances or specific situations). This communica-tion seemed to be critical for understanding what kind of help the clients needed. Furthermore, in these cases, the service advisors acted as nego-tiators between the clients and the service providers. Recognition of this emerging agentic competence helps other professionals guide their own clients to talk with service advisors when in vulnerable situations.

Service advisors worked in an increasingly digitally dense environ-ment, in which they consistently made agentic choices—not only regard-ing the clients they serve, but also the ways that they help them, with what tools, and what digital systems they may be able to teach to their clients. They asserted power in these decisions. Helping customers use digital interfaces seemed to play a minor role in proactive caretakers' and sensitive service integrators' roles, whereas face-to-face service with the most vulnerable citizens took most of their time, and their own digital skills lagged.

Focusing on face-to-face client interactions increased their sensitivity in relation to digitalized services and their restrictions and possibilities. At the same time, face-to-face interactions developed their professional interpersonal skills. It was their own choice to focus on the clients and to help them cope with their problems, instead of straightforwardly guiding them to use, for example, digital interfaces; although the prevailing healthcare strategy paves the way towards self-service of the client in producing and monitoring his/her own health information and care paths. In that sense, the caretaker and interlocutor service advisor types partly question the future vision of the digital healthcare, indicating the power of professionals' agentic competence. However, in the contact point service advisors' case, the role became like a digital guide and snag solver, encouraging customers to use digital portals. This may be because of more active and capable clients coming to the contact points or better ICT skills among the service advisors. The capability of the service advisor to use digital devices and programs also seemed to influence how the service advisor modified her tasks.

Discussion

This chapter provided a theoretical framework, which defines professional competence as a dynamic interaction between agency, relationships, and the institutional and technological environment. We argue that, currently, competencies cannot be understood without understanding how they emerge in different institutional and technological circumstances— as an interplay involving professional proactivity, actions, reflexivity, and relationships. Competence is thus simultaneously something personal— derived from personal education and work history—and, concurrently, confined by the environment and enacted in work practices (Eteläpelto et al., 2013; Emirbayer and Mische, 1998). Professional competence has an undetermined and unpredictable element as it changes in accordance with the actions and agency of human beings. If we involve agency in the concept of competence, the work organization realizes that knowledge creation and competences are constructed not by educating individual professionals only, but by focusing on what kinds of structures, possibilities to participate to organizational and technological development, and rules that restrict personal autonomy influence opportunities of agentic professional competence to grow and flourish.

Through the empirical analysis of health and social care work, we demonstrated the agentic professional competence in the context of the digitalization and platformization of social services and healthcare. The field of healthcare and social care is currently in need of new professional roles, as the prevailing relationships between practitioners and patients are changing with the implementation of new technologies. We presented a service advisor as a new emerging profession manifesting three distinct types of agentic professional competence: (1) the proactive caretaker and co-creator, whose motivation is based on providing comprehensive support to customers in crisis; (2) the sensitive service integrator and interlocutor, who saves time from the other professionals in finding out the service needs of the disordered customers; and (3) the digital guide and snag solver, who uses fluently digital systems and assists capable customers in their use. Most of the service advisor types questioned the efficiency-oriented vision of social care and healthcare by focusing on face-to-face encounters, empathy, and care. The three variations are also an example of professionals' own power of agency and sensitivity to relationships.

The professional roles also reflect the fact that the ongoing implementation of digital technology in healthcare in our empirical case is just emerging, although hopes for a radical change in healthcare are developing (see Oborn and Barret, 2016). Service advisors trying to cope with clients' various problems and guiding them with how to use digital platforms is currently just a minor task. It seems that, during the hazy phase of digital and organizational change, it would be a wise strategy for top management to trust professionals' own agency at work.

The theoretical contribution of this chapter is that we identified four elements that are important to include in the analysis of professional agentic competence: (1) the reflexivity and temporal orientation of the professional, (2) relationships with other people, (3) sensitivity to the social position and the power asymmetries between professionals, and (4) institutional and material arrangements. Future research should longitudinally explore how agentic professional competence among various employee groups is enacted, supported, and modified as digitalization intensifies with automation, digital analytics, and algorithmically aided decision-making.

Our study made visible how the changing institutional circumstances create new professional positions, in which agency, reflexivity, and the capability and power to act become more relevant than the prior education or knowledge acquired by the professional. If agentic professional competence is understood as we suggest, the resilient, proactive, and intentional nature of human beings becomes more visible and valued. This kind of inclusion of agency in the concept of competence is particularly needed to oppose mechanistic claims that machines and digital platforms could replace almost all human work tasks in the future.

References

Archer, M. (2003). *Structure, Agency and the Internal Conversation*. Cambridge, UK: Cambridge University Press.

Bereiter, C. (2002). *Education and Mind in the Knowledge Age*. Hillsdale, NJ: Lawrence Erlbaum.

Berger, J. B., Hertzum, M. and Schreiber, T. (2016). Does Local Government Staff Perceive Digital Communication with Citizens as Improved Service? *Government Information Quarterly*, 33(2), pp. 258–269.

Bowen, D. E. (2016). The Changing Role of Employees in Service Theory and Practice: An Interdisciplinary View. *Human Resource Management Review*, 26(1), pp. 4–13.

Breit, E. and Salomon, R. (2015). Making the Technological Transition—Citizens' Encounters with Digital Pension Services. *Social Policy & Administration*, 49(3), pp. 299–315.

DigitalEurope. (2018). *Reflection Paper on Regulatory Frameworks for Digital Health Technologies in Europe*. Brussels: DigitalEurope.

Emirbayer, M. and Mische, A. (1998). What Is Agency? *The American Journal of Sociology*, 103(4), pp. 962–1023.

Engeström, Y. (1987). *Learning by Expanding*. Helsinki: Orienta-Konsultit.

Eteläpelto, A. (2017). Emerging Conceptualisations on Professional Agency and Learning. In: M. Goller and S. Paloniemi, eds., *Agency at Work: An Agentic Perspective on Professional Learning and Development: Professional and Practice-Based Learning*, 20. Dordrecht: Springer, pp. 183–201.

Eteläpelto, A., Vähäsantanen, K., Hökkä, P. and Paloniemi, S. (2013). What Is Agency? Conceptualizing Professional Agency at Work. *Educational Research Review*, 10(1), pp. 45–65.

Eteläpelto, A., Vähäsantanen, K., Hökkä, P. and Paloniemi, S. (2014). Identity and Agency in Professional Learning, In: S. Billett, C. Harteis and H. Gruber, eds., *International Handbook of Research in Professional and Practice-Based Learning*. Dordrecht: Springer, pp. 645–672.

European Commission. (2018). Transformation of Health and Care in the Digital Single Market. Available at: https://ec.europa.eu/digital-single-market/en/policies/ehealth [Accessed 21 June 2019].

Fuller, A. and Unwin, L. (2010). Knowledge Workers as the New Apprentices: The Influence of Organisational Autonomy, Goals and Values on the Nurturing of Expertise. *Vocations and Learning*, 3(3), pp. 203–222.

Goller, M. and Paloniemi, S. (2017). Agency at Work, Learning and Professional Development: An Introduction. In: M. Goller and S. Paloniemi, eds., *Agency at Work: An Agentic Perspective on Professional Learning and Development. Professional and Practice-based Learning*, 20. Dordrecht: Springer, pp. 1–14.

Gorli, M., Nicolini, D. and Scaratti, G. (2015). Reflexivity in Practice: Tools and Conditions for Developing Organizational Authorship. *Human Relations*, 68(8), pp. 347–375.

Grant, A. M. and Parker, S. H. (2009). Redesigning Work Design Theories: The Rise of Relational and Proactive Perspectives. *The Academy of Management Annals*, 3(1), pp. 317–375.

Hasu, M., Honkaniemi, L., Saari, E., Mattelmäki, T. and Koponen, L. (2014). Learning Employee-Driven Innovating: Towards Sustained Practice Through Multi-Method Evaluation. *Journal of Workplace Learning*, 26(5), pp. 310–330.

Hochschild, A. R. (1983). *The Managed Heart: Commercialization of Human Feeling*. Berkeley: University of California Press.

Hochschild, A. R. (2001). The Nanny Chain. *The American Prospect*, 11(4), pp. 32–36.

Honkaniemi, L., Lehtonen, M. H. and Hasu, M. (2015). Wellbeing and Innovativeness: Motivational Trigger Points for Mutual Enhancement. *European Journal of Training and Development*, 39(5), pp. 393–408.

Hyppönen, H. and Ilmarinen, K. (2016). Sosiaali—ja terveydenhuollon digitalisaatio [The digitalisation in social services and health care]. National Institute for Health and Welfare. Available at: www.julkari.fi/bitstream/

handle/10024/131301/URN_ISBN_978-952-302-739-8.pdf?sequence=1 [Accessed 12 January 2018].

International Labour Office. (2018). *World Employment and Social Outlook: Trends 2018*. Geneva: International Labour Office.

Ivaldi, S., Scaratti, G. and Nuti, G. (2015). The Practice of Evaluation as Evaluation of Practices. *Evaluation*, 21(4), pp. 497–512.

Lewis, J. (2002). Gender and Welfare State Change. *European Societies*, 4(4), pp. 331–357.

Lewis, J. (2010). Gender and the Development of Welfare Regimes. In: M. Gray and S. A. Webb, eds., *International Social Work*. Los Angeles: Sage Publications, pp. 305–322.

Mead, G. H. (1932). *The Philosophy of the Present*. LaSalle, IL: Open Court.

Ministry of Finance and the Ministry of Social Affairs and Health. (2018). Regional Government, Health and Social Services Reform. Available at: https://alueuudistus.fi/en/frontpage [Accessed 19 November 2018].

Nerland, M. and Jensen, K. (2014). Changing Cultures of Knowledge and Professional Learning, In: S. Billett, C. Harteis and H. Gruber, eds., *International Handbook of Research in Professional and Practice-Based Learning: International Handbooks of Education*. Dordrecht: Springer, pp. 611–640.

Nevo, S., Nevo, D. and Pinsonneault, A. (2016). A Temporally Situated Self-Agency Theory of Information Technology Reinvention. *MIS Quarterly*, 40(1), pp. 157–186.

Nonaka, I. and Takeuchi, H. (1995). *The Knowledge-Creating Company: How Japanese Companies Create the Dynamics of Innovation*. New York: Oxford University Press.

Oborn, E. and Barrett, S. K. (2016). Digital Health and Citizen Engagement: Changing the Face of Health Service Delivery. *Health Service Management Research*, 29(1–2), pp. 16–20.

Paavola, S., Lipponen, L. and Hakkarainen, K. (2004). Models of Innovative Knowledge Communities and Three Metaphors of Learning. *Review of Educational Research*, 74(4), pp. 557–276.

Poutanen, S. and Kovalainen, A. (2017). *Gender and Innovation in the New Economy: Women, Identity and Creative Work*. New York: Palgrave Macmillan.

Rust, R. T. and Huang, M. (2014). The Service Revolution and the Transformation of Marketing Science. *Marketing Science*. Available at: http://pubsonline.informs.org/doi/abs/10.1287/mksc.2013.0836 [Accessed 1 February 2017].

Saari, E., Käpykangas, S. and Hasu, M. (2017). *Sensitive Networked Professional— Service Advisors as Agents Between Citizens and Digitalized Services*. Paper presented to XXVII International RESER conference, Bilbao, September 7–9. Available at: www.reser.net/ [Accessed 11 May 2019].

Säljö, R. (2010). Digital Tools and Challenges to Institutional Traditions of Learning: Technologies, Social Memory and the Performative Nature of Learning. *Journal of Computer Assisted Learning*, 26(1), pp. 53–64.

Sawyer, K. (2012). Extending Sociocultural Theory to Group Creativity. *Vocations and Learning: Studies in Vocational and Professional Education*, 5(1), pp. 59–75.

Shotter, J. and Cunliffe, A. L. (2003). Managers as Practical Authors: Everyday Conversations for Action. In: D. Holman and R. Thorpe, eds., *Management and Language*. London: Sage Publications, pp. 15–37.

Sundararajan, A. (2016). *The Sharing Economy: The End of Employment and the Rise of Crowd-Based Capitalism*. Cambridge, MA: MIT Press.

Tronto, J. C. (2013). *Caring Democracy: Markets, Equality, and Justice*. New York: New York University Press.

Vallas, S. P. (2012). *Work: A Critique*. London and Malden, MA: Polity Press.

Vallas, S. P. and Hill, A. (2012). Conceptualizing Power in Organizations. In: D. Courpasson, D. Golsorkhi and J. J. Sallaz, eds., *Rethinking Power in Organizations, Institutions, and Markets*. Bingley, UK: Emerald, pp. 165–197.

Appendix

Data and Analysis Methods

The qualitative data on service advisors was gathered in three different phases in 2016. We interviewed five service advisors and ethnographically observed two service advisors by shadowing, discussing, listening, and chatting, in addition to informal and background materials. A feedback workshop, which was organized for employees and managers, concerning the everyday work of the service advisors was additionally used as a data source. All interviews and workshop discussions were audiorecorded and transcribed, and reflective memos were written. The ethnographic observations were written in a field report.

In the service advisor interviews, we applied the "instructions to the double" technique (Ivaldi et al., 2015). Professionals were requested to imagine having a double, who would take their place at work the next day. Their task was then to advise this person on "what to do" and "what not to do." They could review their routines by explaining their everyday actions and imagine a typical working day.

We sent the instructions by email about a week before the interview to help participants orientate themselves to the situation. In the interview, we supported the interviewee in a very informal way and encouraged open discussion. If interviewees could not start imagining the situation, we helped them by using questions and prompts: "Tell us about your background; how did you find this job?" "Tell us about your typical working day; what do you do first?" "What kinds of tools you use in your work?" "Whose help do you need during the day?"

9 Cultural Transition in the Sharing Economy

Introducing Platform Work With Activity Concepts

Laura Seppänen and Seppo Poutanen

Introduction

Are our existing theories and research approaches well equipped to grasp new societal phenomena? Platform work, or platform organizing in general, is a relatively new phenomenon which, despite overwhelming literature, is still undertheorized due to its complexity, rapid development, and ambiguous vocabulary. Platform work has raised mixed opinions as offering great business potential for companies (Parker et al., 2016) and improving workers' chances for flexible income (Anderson and Westberg, 2016), but also increasing uncertainty, risks, and even gendered or racialized exploitation of workers (de Stefano, 2016; van Doorn, 2017; Kenney et al., Chapter 1 in this book; Kovalainen et al., Chapter 2 in this book).

This chapter focuses, in a preliminary step, on applying an activity theoretical perspective to platform work with the aim of better understanding the essence and developmental potential of this new and assumedly increasing phenomenon. In particular, our interests lie in the activity concepts workers perform when concretely doing tasks or projects through platforms and how these practices may relate to ideas at the beginning of the platform economy. This examination suggests that despite the platform rhetoric of sharing and social cues replacing prices, workers largely follow a price-based market logic, and platform companies might benefit from enhancing mechanisms where the creation of knowledge and innovation, typical for networks, are enhanced.

In this chapter, we define platform work and briefly describe reasons for its emergence and essence, as depicted especially by Arun Sundararajan (2016) in his well-grounded book *The Sharing Economy: The End of Employment and the Rise of Crowd-Based Capitalism*. After presenting the notion of the activity concept, activity concepts of a so-called "adhocratic network," as theorized by Clay Spinuzzi (2015), are presented in the section "Clan, Hierarchy, Market and Network as Activity Concepts". We apply these concepts for empirically investigating sample data from interviews with Finnish freelancers working for Upwork, a platform mediating client-determined specialist online work. The data and methods are described in the section "Research Questions, Data, and Methods". The findings in the sections "How Does Upwork Function for Freelancers?" "What Are the Upwork Platform's Characteristics in Terms of Activity Concepts?" and "How Do Finnish Upworkers Enact Activity Concepts in Their Platform Work?" illustrate the functions and activity concept characteristics of Upwork and show how freelancers enact activity concepts in their work. This may also give readers an ethnographic insight into their activity. In the end, we discuss the findings and conclude that activity concepts can, in fact, be useful in understanding platform work, and it is worth going forward with this preliminary study. At the metalevel, this chapter aims to examine what kind of understanding can be gained from analyzing platform work through the notion of activity concepts.

Platform Work

Currently, different platforms are springing up quickly in Europe. In this chapter, we are interested in platform work, which can be defined as "a form of employment that uses an online platform to enable organizations or individuals to solve problems or to provide services in exchange for payment" (Eurofound, 2018). It is estimated that there are 173 labor platforms in Europe (Fabo et al., 2017). Eurofound (2018) offers a useful categorization of 10 types of platform work in the EU based on service and platform characteristics. Upwork, the empirical platform of this study, falls into the category of 'online client-determined specialist work,' in which projects are completed totally online, the workers' required skill level is relatively high, and the worker or freelancer is selected by the client by means of an offer.

A new activity concept is developed when a problem or need exists that cannot be solved in any other way (Virkkunen, 2007). In work activities organized through platforms, there are two needs that platform work could help solve: clients' need for getting time-bound tasks or projects done, and workers' need to turn their time and resources into income and skill, in a relatively flexible way. In the platform-based, sharing economy, new resources are incorporated into economic activities, services and products are crowdsourced, and contractors and workers may easily shift between roles. The technology of algorithmic management of organizing, along with the spread of ICT, makes platform work possible (Sundararajan, 2016).

Sundararajan (2016, p. 4) importantly contributes to our understanding of the emergence of platform organization as a commercial peer-to-peer exchange. He argues that the forms of exchange, commerce, and employment in the sharing economy are not new. "Today's digital technologies seem to be taking us back to familiar sharing behaviors, self-employment and community-based exchange that existed in the past [before the Industrial Revolution]" (Sundararajan, 2016, p. 5). However, the sharing with strangers and the scale of sharing are new. He considers "accessing assets without ownership" and "networks replacing hierarchies" as central features of the peer-to-peer sharing economy, where "new assets and services into markets . . . are used at levels closer to their full capacity" (Sundararajan, 2016, p. 27).

The mixture of peer-to-peer sharing in the context of capitalistic markets, or "crowd capitalism," is an appealing one and emphasizes not only the enabling power of digital technologies but also a trust-based community. Referring to Yochai Benkler (2004), Sundararajan (2016, p. 32) states that the sharing activities among peers resemble market-based interactions, with the difference being that "social cues and motivations replace prices as means to generate information and motivate action". Indeed, the rhetoric just stated expresses characteristics of networks and communities that are also present in Spinuzzi's (2015) research on activity concepts in modern non-salaried work, called "all-edge adhocratic networks".

Activity Concepts

Activity concept refers to a notion, idea, or logic according to which a certain entirety is built, functions, and develops. Its theoretical roots lie in the cultural-historical research approach of activity theory. Based on the works of Vygotsky (1978) and Leont'ev (1978), the notion of activity or production concept has been modified and applied by various activity theory scholars (Engeström and Sannino, 2012; Launis and Pihlaja, 2007; Seppänen, 2014; Virkkunen, 2007).

An activity concept includes both the relationship of exchange between producer and user and the relationship between use value and exchange value (Virkkunen, 2007). Use value means the benefit for the service users in their activities, and exchange value means the general value, mostly understood as money and price. Activity concepts resemble organizational cultures (Cameron and Quinn, 2006; Weick and Sutcliffe, 2007) in that they are not often verbally expressed, nor are people aware of them until they are challenged by changes or disruptions. As compared with organizational cultures, or somewhat similar institutional logics (Thornton et al., 2012), the notion of an activity concept may enrich insights into platform work in at least three ways:

1. An activity concept always *exists in the practice of work*, regardless of its degree of explicitness or articulation. In this sense, it differs from a business model or an organization concept, the latter defined by Heusinkveld et al. (2013, p. 9) as a more or less coherent prescriptive vision, including guidelines, which is known by a particular

label. As activity concepts live within work and collaboration, they are never totally fixed or stable. A concept crystallizes a culturally evolved idealization and generalization of a human experience, and its relevance is in constituting an important type of cultural mediator of human action (Virkkunen and Ristimäki, 2012).

2. Activity concepts inherently include the perspective and intentionality of the involved actors. This is theorized with the notion of object of activity, which means both a concrete and a mental thing to be constructed, and which gives motivation and meaning in practical activities (Engeström et al., 2003). The notion of an activity concept helps understand meaningfulness and wellbeing, particularly with respect to transformations at work (Launis and Pihlaja, 2007). Discussing and experimenting with activity concepts reveals an activity's changing quality (that is, the concept), which in turn has implications for reflection and learning on the one hand, and for branding and commodification on the other (Seppänen, 2014).

3. Activity concepts focus on and depict qualitative changes in forms of work activities, and because they are both given and created by humans, their investigation fundamentally advances developmental possibilities. One point of reference in the examination of activity concepts involves considering the societal and historical evolution of activities (Seppänen, 2017). The previous section included a brief description of the emergence of platform work. Historically formed contradictions such as clashes between activity concepts are developmentally interesting. The analysis of activity concepts strives to understand the dynamic nature of intentional individual and collective activities in their historical, socio-cultural, and material contexts. In this study, organizational forms of work, such as craft or clan, hierarchy, market, and network (Adler et al., 2008; Pihlaja, 2005; Spinuzzi, 2015), are used as points of reference.

Clan, Hierarchy, Market, and Network as Activity Concepts

In his studies of non-employer firms, coworking spaces, and a search engine optimization company, Spinuzzi (2015) examines how people realize their work with a kind of networking he calls "all edge adhocracy". In his book, he considers adhocracy to be a model of action of networks, just like bureaucracy is the model of action of hierarchies. It is a flexible, adaptable and informal form of organization (as to the roots of the concept "adhocracy", see, e.g., Mintzberg and McHugh, 1985). In the 1990s, institutional adhocracy was internal to an organization, layered on top of an organizational bureaucracy, without which adhocracy could not flourish. Adhocratic networks, in turn, are interorganizational, interdisciplinary by necessity, and voluntary. They rely on always-on, all-channel connections among specialists in open networks. Spinuzzi (2015) depicts adhocratic networks as a prominent and increasing feature of "new work" outside standard salaried employment.

Based on approaches of Boisot et al. (2001), Cameron and Quinn (2006), Engeström (2008), and others, Spinuzzi (2015, pp. 139–160) depicts adhocratic networks as consisting of four different kinds of configurations: clans, hierarchies, markets, and networks. These configurations are considered necessary ingredients to proceed with the work activities and their objects—however, their co-existence causes tensions that people creatively manage and solve as they work. As the configurations are similar to activity concepts and they share the same theoretical basis, we shall refer to them as "concepts" in this chapter.

In ideal terms, *clans* are high-trust, promoting the value of identity and interdependence of a group and achieving belonging. *Hierarchies* aim at control through authority and dependence. Work within the *market* concept is organized on the basis of competition among independent actors, and trust, based on price mechanisms, is low. Trust-based *network* concepts are used when open-ended, emergent objects are worked on and when outcomes of knowledge creation and innovation are needed.

It is of interest how Spinuzzi (2015) reformulates these concepts in terms of how the object, motive, and meaning of an activity is defined, and where it is defined (Figure 9.1).

If the object is defined in an open-ended or non-articulated way, actors have a lot of discretion in the activity. In clans and networks, the object

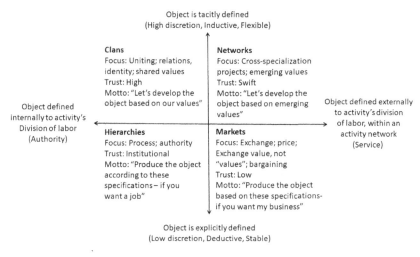

Figure 9.1 A Typology of Activity Concepts in Adhocratic Networks
Source: Spinuzzi (2015, p. 144).

is open-ended but in different ways. In clans, the making is embedded in the internal culture of teams; the outcome is often team identity and belonging. Networks deal with open-ended, complex objects such as problems to be solved, but the object is defined externally (see the horizontal dimension in Figure 9.1) across a network of different activities.

Hierarchies and markets, in turn, operate with explicitly defined objects, such as specifications to be filled. In hierarchies, objects may be mass-produced and controlled to reach outcomes such as quality, cost, and time. Hierarchical activities are defined internally in the organization and tend to be steady, predictable, and repeated. In a hierarchy, rules are developed and promulgated by an authority, and relationships among actors tend to be dependent (Spinuzzi, 2015, p. 147).

Markets are based on low-information, high-velocity transactions that tend to quicken the process of transforming the object, with no necessary permanent relations. "Markets allow individuals to meet their personal interests through free, flexible interactions, interactions that link them with trade partners who are otherwise unaffiliated with them" (Spinuzzi, 2015, p. 148). Rules are agreed in formal contracts and enforced via reciprocal self-regulation. In a pure market, trust between buyer and seller is low, since the market involves making exchanges between two otherwise unrelated activities that may interact for just a single transaction (Adler et al., 2008). This is often the case in online platform work.

Network relations are collaborative and interdependent, with high discretion and a high external focus, geographically dispersed and loosely coupled. Like markets, networks are flexible. They require continual communication because they are flat, spanning boundaries and connect many different types of actors. Since networks value equity among the participants, they rely on mutual adjustment similar to clans, but instead across boundaries and distances rather than internally.

Typically, network relations are longer-term, and the level of trust is stronger than that of the market concept. The focus is on the opportunities that might be inductively defined at the meeting point of separate activities. Networks work with objects that require various types of expertise and collaboration across specialties, and they are especially well positioned for producing innovative outcomes. Now, we turn to our empirical investigation on Finnish freelancers working for Upwork.

Research Questions, Data, and Methods

The analysis of platform work with the notion of activity concepts is operationalized through examining how workers on platforms act according to the four concepts explained in the previous section in their platform work. The research questions are thus:

1. How does the Upwork platform function for freelancers?

2. What are the Upwork platform's characteristics in terms of activity concepts?
3. How do Finnish Upworkers as freelancers enact activity concepts in their platform work?

Before answering the research questions, we briefly describe the data and methods used.

In December 2017, a survey was conducted of Upwork's freelancers who named Finland their place of residence (Pajarinen et al., 2018). In the still-ongoing research, six Finnish Upworkers were interviewed during June–August 2018. The interviewed freelancers were either native Finnish or Swedish speakers. Only two (about 33 percent) of them were students, while the percentage of students in the survey was 65 percent. They were the first interviewed, and thus their availability, rather than chosen criteria, led the sampling. Two of them were not currently active on Upwork, but they were able to describe their recent Upwork activity well and to illuminate reasons for leaving the platform. The six interviewees represent to approximately 5 percent of the survey respondents and 8.3 percent of those available for an interview. The interviewed Upworkers represent differing skills, interests, and task categories, and thus, the commonalities in the interview data enable us to depict preliminary findings to be examined later in detail.

The thematic interviews addressed the history and role of platform work in their lives, their Upwork projects, means of support, and possibilities for learning and career building. The interviews were mainly carried out via a telephone call and lasted 40–80 minutes. The main features of the six interviewed Upworkers are given in Table 9.1.

The data were transcribed and coded according to the contents using ATLAS.ti software. Later, the data episodes showing operationalized features of activity concepts (Spinuzzi, 2015, p. 40) were identified and categorized accordingly. A qualitative method, as described by Ruusuvuori et al. (2010) was used with the following criteria (see also Launis and Pihlaja, 2007):

- In the clan concept, the object is social identity formation, and the outcome of belonging is sought. This means paying attention to how interviewees strive for collective identities and belonging in their platform work.
- In the hierarchy concept, the object is control, achieved through authority and dependence. We search the interview data for indications of how Upworkers encounter hierarchical authority or control on Upwork, or how freelancers may gain authority in their platform activities.
- In the market concept, the object is flexibility and price exchange based on competition. This is operationalized by analyzing the ways

Table 9.1 Occupations, Activeness and Dependence on Upwork Income, and Experienced Success of the Six Interviewed Upworkers in Finland

Number	Category	Activeness in Upwork	Dependence on income through Upwork	Experienced success on Upwork
1	Graphic design, unemployed	Daily	No dependence	Very low
2	Conversion optimization	Almost daily	Strong dependence. Acts also as a client on Upwork	Very high
3	Translation, writing	Almost daily	Additional income for a student	Moderate
4	Programming	Not anymore	Partial dependence	Good
5	Translation	Regularly		Good
6	Graphic design	Not anymore	No	Good

in which freelancers construct their object of activity, get clients, and compete with other freelancers.

• In the network concept, the object is knowledge generation and innovation, and the outcome is to solve complex problems. We investigated this by examining how freelancers get support from the platform, what potential they have for exchange between freelancers, and how Upwork enables freelancers to expand their networks.

The findings presented in the later section "How Does Upwork Function for Freelancers?" are based on the interview data and information from Upwork's website. Sections "What Are the Upwork Platform's Characteristics in Terms of Activity Concepts?" and "How Do Finnish Upworkers Enact Activity Concepts in Their Platform Work?" discuss the freelancers' experiences as presented in the interviews and interpreted through the four concepts, and thus, they may differ from the factual services or mechanisms offered by Upwork. Data excerpts in these sections, as expressed by various interviewees, represent general ideas across all interview data.

How Does Upwork Function for Freelancers?

Upwork, the case example of this chapter, is the world's largest freelancing website targeting the demand and supply of high-skilled contingent work. It aims at creating economic and social value at a global scale by providing a trusted online workplace to connect, collaborate, and succeed (Upwork.com, 2019). Upwork's platform functioning from the point of project success has been studied elsewhere (Claussen et al., 2018), and Pajarinen et al. (2018) have specifically investigated the characteristics of Finnish Upworkers.

Upwork categorizes expert work to be exchanged into web, mobile, and software development; IT and networking; translation; and many other occupational or task domains. For freelancers, this means that they first need to have some skills within the Upwork categories to become registered as freelancers in Upwork and be able to get projects from customers. Freelancers need to have or develop several competencies to succeed (Excerpt 1).

Excerpt 1

INTERVIEWER 1: So, what is specifically needed for this kind of platform work, on Upwork and other platforms, so that you are able to do it?

FREELANCER 5: At least you need some kind of competence in some field that you can offer online to customers, who usually live abroad. It takes discipline to be able to manage your own use of time, so that everything gets done even if no one is supervising. You need to study how to price your work and things about your own competence area, and you need good online information search skills. And you have to be able to network with the people in your field, since Upwork does not offer a platform for this. [. . .] Of course, you also need to find out how taxes work as a freelancer and where you pay your taxes, if you don't live in your home country, and things like that. Upwork doesn't provide any information about this.

The first thing to do for a newcomer to the Upwork platform is to write a profile that is visible to everybody on the site. The profile is very influential when clients search for suitable freelancers for their projects. Besides the profile text, freelancers can market themselves by including keywords and portfolios about their skills and by completing relevant skill tests provided by Upwork free of charge. Freelancers also upload a photo of themselves, their desired hourly pay, and location in the profile (for detailed examples of such profiles, please see Upwork.com, 2019).

Upwork's platform is huge; there are all kinds of freelancers and clients on the site, and thus it is important to build trust. On Upwork, one of the ways to build trust is a *Job Success Score* (JSS) provided by the platform to a freelancer's profile. The JSS is based on the feedback the client provides on a project, but contracts without activity or excessive lack of feedback may lower the score (Upwork.com, 2019). If freelancers are successful in building a solid reputation with multiple clients and comply with Upwork's policies, then they may acquire *Top Rated* status, marked with a crown symbol. Upwork can also reward progressing freelancers with a *Rising Talent* patch. By clicking on the profile, clients may read about the freelancer's projects and related feedback. If a freelancer desires, Upwork shows the amount of money earned through this platform.

All elements in the profile are of utmost importance, as clients may use them to filter their search. According to our interviews, the JSS and Top Rated designation are highly influential in securing projects and being able to exert more influence on pricing. For freelancers, Upwork's reputation system is an in-built way of marketing: they may use their Upwork profile as a reliable CV both inside and outside the platform.

The clients first formulate their projects so that their execution can be evaluated and priced. Once clients post their offers on Upwork, freelancers can search for them using keywords. Alternatively, clients can send the offer to a selected group of freelancers, or even to only one. If a freelancer finds an interesting project, s/he may evaluate the client by examining how much money the client has spent on previous Upwork projects. A freelancer then sends a cover letter or bid to the client, and if interested, the client may contact the freelancer for possible negotiations.

The contract can be either fixed-price or based on an hourly rate. For fixed-price contracts, the client pays the amount at the start of the project to a payment system held by Upwork, and the freelancer receives the money after the project is deemed by the client to have been acceptably accomplished. In hourly rate projects, a certain sum of money is transferred from the client to the freelancer's Upwork account on a weekly or bi-weekly basis. Upwork charges service fees of 20, 10, or 5 percent, depending on the total amount they have billed with one particular client (Upwork.com, 2019).

Indeed, the great advantage of Upwork for freelancers is that it exists as an alternative opportunity for them. Upwork offers many benefits for freelancers, such as freedom and flexibility, ease of access to projects and to a well-functioning payment system, and a transparent rating scheme (Excerpt 2).

Excerpt 2

INTERVIEWER: What kinds of pros and cons do you see in this?

FREELANCER 3: It's an easy platform. I have kind of conflicted feelings: there are good things about it, but also plenty of cons. So if we start with the pros, I think that it is a pretty easy way to start marketing yourself. You don't need any massive marketing campaigns, so I think it's a good place to start when you don't have much experience, and you want to start building your career or gaining experience. I like how people leave feedback there and *everyone can see what kind of feedback others have received*, and the platform also rewards you if you do everything well. There are these patches that are kind of "honorable mentions". These kinds of things are really good. It's easy to find jobs, and all contracts and payments are completed through the platform, so it is easier, on the one hand.

The greatest disadvantage, according to our interviewees, is the proportion of the fees charged by Upwork. A 20 percent fee on all projects with new clients is heavy for Finnish Upworkers given the global competition on Upwork's platform. Although income is often very modest (Pajarinen et al., 2018), some Upworkers are able to get good or even excellent hourly pay. For Finnish freelancers, Upwork features as a good way for beginners to acquire experience, to increase client contacts, and to earn additional income. However, as experience and skills grow, highly skilled Upworkers may face limits in advancing their career and income (Excerpt 3).

Excerpt 3

INTERVIEWER: What kind of goals do you have for your work and career, in general, and how does Upwork support them?

FREELANCER 2: Well, actually my goal is to be able to become as independent of that platform as possible. Because, in many ways, it is . . . If I think about it as a channel for generating leads, its future is really uncertain on a personal level, since you will never know if you get a bit of an asshole client and how . . . If they give you a negative assessment and your assessment score drops all of a sudden, by a lot, and then you cannot get basically any clients through that platform for the next six months, because your score there is so poor, on average, that you never get picked. [. . .] An average client there is a business that has just started or something, and they don't always scale their pricing that well, so you will always have limits to how much you can charge from them, and they just don't have the budget to pay as much as those companies that come from outside Upwork would have. So, the reputation of the entire platform is like that, like it's meant for small businesses that want to get their work done pretty cheaply.

The most important mediator in the client-freelancer relationship is the project, which in activity theory terms, may form a temporal and a partially common object between the client and freelancer. Upwork does not influence the objects or outcomes of projects, but its mechanisms such as categorization, communication, and rating systems greatly affect what kind of projects are successful.

What Are the Upwork Platform's Characteristics in Terms of Activity Concepts?

The concept of market is strong within Upwork as a marketplace, which aims at doing business by matching demand and supply of work tasks.

Upwork responds to a market need of clients by offering them a solution in which instead of building capacity into their organization, they can be more flexible by buying projects from Upwork. The client creates project specifications typical to the market concept (Figure 9.1).

With its rules and means for achieving stability and control in a highly diverse and global ecosystem, the Upwork platform obviously has hierarchical elements. For instance, the rating system described earlier represents a hierarchy because it is standardized, internally created in Upwork, and implies a (semi-) institutionalized order and control for freelancers. Freelancers may respond to only a limited number of client offers (30 per month) without payment. Hierarchy is also visible in the way Upwork accepts or ends freelancers' memberships.

According to the so called "network effect" (Parker et al., 2016), the more participants Upwork attracts to build a larger ecosystem of clients and freelancers, the more profitable the platform becomes. This means that Upwork tries to balance the needs of both clients and freelancers, and here, the network characteristics are needed. Besides being flat, Upwork represents the network concept in at least three ways.

First, Upwork's diminishing provision system encourages freelancers to establish long-term relationships. It may be possible, although not probable, that long-term relationships enable "tacit terms of exchange" typical of networks so that a freelancer can do a favor in exchange for an undefined favor from the client in the future (Adler et al., 2008). Second, the rating system is reciprocal, so both clients and freelancers give scores for each other. If a freelancer does not rate his or her client, s/he cannot receive the client's rating, either. This system enhances a sense of fairness. Third, Upwork functions in a social media format and is mainly based on online, social relations between clients and freelancers. This manifests relationality that has an informal and horizontal appearance, which is also typical of networks (see Figure 9.1). The network concept assumes that actors join in voluntarily, and this seems mostly to be the case with Upwork.[1]

These characteristics are likely to build transparency for trust, horizontality, and fairness, contributing to a sense of equity. However, they do not necessarily support community-building or launching projects with complex, open-ended, and emerging objects that need many kinds of expertise. We will come back to these in the following section.

How Do Finnish Upworkers Enact Activity Concepts in Their Platform Work?

The interviewees hardly express any sign of the clan concept in their Upwork activities. They do not strive for collective identities, nor do they express a need for belonging in their platform work. Features of clans are, however, present outside Upwork in interviewees' activities with colleagues, local partners, work-related friends, or spouses. Freelancers encounter aspects of the hierarchy concept in the platform's authoritative rules described previously, but the status and discretion they themselves can enact can better be understood through market or network concepts, not hierarchy. Therefore, in this section we concentrate mainly on the market and network concepts.

Market Concept

All interviewed freelancers entered the Upwork platform to market their skilled work to attract clients and receive projects and income. As stated in the section "Clan, Hierarchy, Market, and Network as Activity Concepts", an object embeds the motive and purpose of an activity, and acquiring clients and carrying out projects for income as an object represents the market concept. Aside from income, freelancers working on Upwork mostly learn to transform and polish another object, their reputation, visible on the platform for potential clients. It seems that for success, freelancers need to place effort not only on doing good work on client relations and projects, but on continuously paying attention to how they are represented by Upwork. The importance of the rating system is illustrated in Excerpts 2 and 3. The latter also shows the uncertainty of reputation building of Upwork due to differences in client behavior.

However, not all Upworkers share this reputation object. One of our interviewees, Number 1 in Table 9.1, was apparently an experienced graphic designer who carefully acknowledged potential clients' needs as expressed in their offers, put effort into accomplishing those needs, and assumedly responded to offers with good quality bids. However, he did not consider his reputation and visibility on the platform site. As he had had no projects for a long time, both his income earned and job success rate were most probably very low, or non-existent, on the platform site. Despite appealing bids, it may be difficult for a client to trust a freelancer with little or no reputation. The freelancer in question stayed on Upwork anyway because as he was unemployed and receiving unemployment benefits, he had plenty of time available. His attitude can even be interpreted as resistance to the market concept of the platform.

Skilled and entrepreneurial Upworkers may have developed more advanced marketing means to attract clients, such as YouTube channels, careful design of cover letters for clients' offers, short consultative telephone conversations free of charge, and even using a client position in Upwork to discover competitors' applications. Sometimes speed, research, and early response to offers can be key in securing projects.

Competition among freelancers is another market concept feature on Upwork. A recent survey revealed that Finnish Upworkers experienced the competition among Upwork freelancers as relatively intense (71 on a scale of 0–100; Pajarinen et al., 2018). It seems that competition differs according to project domain. Many Finnish Upworkers do translation projects. As Finnish is a rare language, those who translate to or from Finnish have an advantage in this market. Translators working as freelancers on Upwork do not dislike competition between professionals, and a clan concept, formed outside the platform, may help them tolerate the competition among professional translators. However, they shun the amateurs (e.g., students) who translate with minimal prices, thus making themselves more competitive with professionals. They also dislike clients who concentrate on price and do not have expertise to identify quality translation.

The global nature of Upwork naturally increases competition with price. When starting on Upwork, it is wise for freelancers to accept cheap, routine projects from trusted clients just to obtain a successful rating in their Upwork profile. Some years ago, many Finnish Upworkers made small projects for Google by translating or pronouncing words or sentences in Finnish, even in regional dialects. Google rated them well, which helped them get subsequent projects.

Obtaining more status through the rating system gives freelancers better discretion in setting their own prices. When they gain expertise and entrepreneurial insight, they may start outsourcing parts of their projects through Upwork and be simultaneously both clients and freelancers. Upwork consists of multilayered markets because both skilled expertise and cheap routine work can be bought through the platform. Upwork thus encourages freelancers' entrepreneurial orientation.

Network Concept

The network concept is not as present in freelancers' Upwork activities, but there are some potential elements, namely in freelancers receiving support, the potential for exchange between freelancers, and how Upwork enables freelancers to expand their networks.

Upwork assists freelancers both in technical issues and in clarifying the platform's mechanisms. For instance, one of our interviewees received information about the factors for losing and regaining Top Rated status after he suddenly had lost it from his profile. There is a separate help channel dedicated for the Top Rated freelancers, and sometimes even the clients help freelancers in carrying out the projects.

According to interviews, Upwork does provide a channel for exchange between freelancers. One of the interviewees had read freelancer experiences, while others either did not mention it or claimed that such forums do not exist. This means that many freelancers do not experience Upwork's support for their social relationships or community formation within the platform, nor do freelancers expect or express any need for community or alliances within Upwork (Excerpt 4).

Excerpt 4

INTERVIEWER: Yes, right. You mentioned networking, so do you think that it would be possible to build your own professional network through Upwork?

FREELANCER 3: Well, not really, everyone here, like freelancers, work pretty separately from each other, so there is no system where you could recommend someone or something like that. So, I think that it would be better to find contacts outside the platform, in your own field, so that you could get work through others.

However, Upwork does help freelancers build and expand their network contacts with clients. These are market relationships. After building trust, it is possible that freelancer-client relationships may develop network features. The freelancer-client relationship may also continue after they have finished working through Upwork. Of course, this is forbidden on Upwork. According to our interviewees, if this happens twice, the freelancer loses their profile and is no longer eligible for projects on the platform.

Although freelancers' projects are mainly well defined as objects in the market concept, they also may deal with more open-ended or complex objects, which carry network features. As an example, a Finnish student freelancer guided and coached a person in the United States in using a programming software in an Upwork project. It was about finding solutions to the client's evolving questions and needs and thus was relatively open-ended. The project took 4–6 hours per week for the freelancer and lasted six months, which enabled a long-term, informal, and relaxed exchange between the two individuals. The project proceeded through questions posed by the client—the freelancer could use his discretion in suggesting ways to proceed with programming, but he had to leave the decision to the client. Here, we see the freelancer's discretion as a characteristic of the network concept but still bound by the paid client-freelancer relationship, in line with the market concept.

As noted previously, the contracts for Upwork projects can be either hourly or fixed-price. Such a condition makes the formulation of open-ended, complex projects difficult. This implies that a fixed-price project mechanism may not be suitable for network concepts dealing with tacit or emerging objects. For freelancers, it is important that a project is defined well, so that they can assess the amount of work and the criteria by which the project is seen as successful. Excerpt 5 is an example of this. Freelancers cannot know in advance how skilled clients are in their domain and in elaborating clear offers, so they need to be critical.

Excerpt 5

FREELANCER 4: I actually did apply for one of those contract work projects. I think the payment was 500 dollars. It was a statistical analysis project, but the reason why I did not take that project in the end was that even though they were interested in hiring me, they did not define clearly enough what the conditions were for completing that project. And then, they did not have any previous offers there, so it seemed a bit vague, and I didn't think I would even get any money from them in the end, so it was a bit of a challenging situation. And even when you really want to do the job or make a lot of money, you always have to think about or stay tough that you will not work at any price and, on the other hand, you have to be sure that you will receive your payment.

The programming software coaching project was paid at an hourly rate, and the client was able to control the freelancer's work through screenshots received during the freelancer's working hours. Complex projects with open-ended, emerging objects are easier to handle in hourly contracts than through fixed-price ones, but even then it may not be easy. A client can be a beginner in purchasing a novel skill with a strange vocabulary, and s/he needs to control the freelancer in cases of information asymmetry. In Excerpt 6 we see that part of the open-endedness is that a freelancer must balance between the skill that is expected from him or her at the start and the work done during paid hours of the client.

Excerpt 6

INTERVIEWER: Do you feel that you were able to note down all the work you did for Matt, or was there some. . .?

FREELANCER 4: Well, it was a bit . . . Sometimes I thought that, okay, I should probably know this thing, so I did not always charge for all the research work or similar that I did. But anything that had directly to do with the code, those I usually charged for, and Matt was pretty relaxed about that. That's a bit challenging; it depends on what kind of client you have, whether they understand the nature of coding. How sometimes you write the actual lines for an hour a day and the other seven hours you just spend on researching or clarifying something, like what lines of code you need to write or how the current system even works.

Discussion and Conclusion

By using the four activity concepts as depicted by Spinuzzi (2015), this study examined the logics and practice of expert online platform work in light of the characteristics and ideas of the sharing economy. Despite the early rhetoric of the sharing and trust-based community of platform organizing (Sundararajan, 2016) and the idea of social cues and motivations replacing price as means to motivate action (Benkler, 2004), the network features of freelancers' platform work remain rather limited. This may be due to a general difference or gap between written rhetoric and practical action, or it may be because the sharing or platform economy, still in its development, has diverged from its early aspirations.

Sundararajan (2016, p. 34) argues that the distinction between the two economies—commercial and sharing—will become increasingly blurred. Our findings do show that market and network concepts overlap in platform work, but in freelancers' concrete activities, the few characteristics of the network concept seem to be subordinated to the confines of the client and freelancer roles of the market concept. The platform for online labor has a social character which is part of the trust building in this activity. The object and motive of freelancers is money, and social relationships are there to help support them in earning income.

Related to social relations is the question of community. Adler et al. (2008) see trust-based collaborative community, crossing organizational boundaries, as an ascending trend in professional work. "In the emerging collaborative model, collaboration demanded from professionals increasingly embraces relations with other occupations, clients, administrators, regulators, and with other organized stakeholders, and it seems to manifest an outward-looking, civic kind of professionalism" (Adler et al., 2008, p. 366). Spinuzzi (2015) emphasizes similar features in adhocratic networks.

Freelancers do expand their client networks, but the functioning mechanism of the platform, as represented in our data, leads them to more bilateral relations rather than building interorganizational and interprofessional partnerships, or a sense of communal belonging. As said by one Upworker (Number 1, Table 9.1): "Now, I have the whole planet as my clientele," expressing that platform work is market with expanded scale.

Claussen et al. (2018) recently studied success factors in Upwork projects. They found that on average, simple projects are executed better than more complex ones. The pricing mechanism is central in constructing the concept of platform activity, and price setting, together with trust building, seems to require that projects are well defined. Platforms like Upwork support their clients well in defining projects, but a question remains: If Upwork profiles itself as a mediator of high-skilled work, how complex and many-sided can projects be?

The network concept is particularly strong when innovations are sought. The theoretical perspective of activity concepts tells us that the dynamics or potential contradiction between market and network concepts can be interesting for platforms like Upwork. Theoretically, we can conclude that activity concepts have potential for examining new forms of work such as platform work. This potential is especially due to their explanatory power in highlighting cultural changes. Practically, our study suggests that developing a platform to actively embrace open-ended innovation possibilities would probably benefit all parties. It is possible that Upwork may already have the means for this, but it is not reflected in our data.

Discretion in terms of freedom and flexibility that platform work offers is valued by Upworkers. The conceptual framework in Figure 9.1 shows how emerging, open-ended objects of activities can offer more discretion on work than markets, where objects are defined very explicitly. Although the platform mechanism tends to guide projects towards well-defined objects, platform workers always do have agency in carrying out their projects. Nevertheless, we argue that platform workers enforce or learn the most discretion through using the rating system, interacting with customers, and learning how to price their work. Generally, tensions in how freelancers negotiate the many dynamic dimensions of their work in the platform market/network clearly call for more empirical research.

To conclude, this study suggests that this expert type of knowledge work, mediated by an online freelancer platform such as Upwork, strongly enacts and enhances the market concept. While the findings are preliminary due to the small sample and the heterogeneity of freelancers, the study suggests interesting avenues for further study. The network concept has potential for enhancing both freelancers' proactiveness and collective innovations, but the network concept and its benefits seem marginal in the Upwork activity. We argue that the boundary between market and network concepts needs to be considered in further developing the online labor markets for expert knowledge work.

Note

1 Upwork, or any other voluntary platform work, is not considered voluntary when other alternatives for income do not exist. All our interviewees were voluntarily on Upwork, even those who were unemployed.

References

Adler, P., Kwon, S. W. and Heckscher, C. (2008). Professional Work: The Emergence of Collaborative Community. *Organization Science*, 19(2), pp. 359–376.

Anderson, L. and Westberg, C. (eds.) (2016). *Voices of Workable Futures: People Transforming Work in the Platform Economy*. Palo Alto: The Institute for the Future.

Benkler, Y. (2004). Sharing Nicely: On Shareable Goods and the Emergence of Sharing as a Modality of Economic Production. *Yale Law Journal*, 114(2004), pp. 273–358.

Boisot, M. H., MacMillan, I. C. and Han, K. H. (2001). *Explorations in Information Space: Knowledge, Agents and Organization*. Oxford: Oxford University Press.

Cameron, K. S. and Quinn, R. E. (2006). *Diagnosing and Changing Organizational Culture: Based on the Competing Values Framework*. San Francisco: The Jossey-Bass Business & Management Series.

Claussen, J., Khashabi, P., Kretschmer, T. and Siefried, M. (2018). Knowledge Work in the Sharing Economy: What Drives Project Success in Online Labor Markets? Available at: https://ssrn.com/abstract=3102865 or http://dx.doi.org/10.2139/ssrn.3102865 [Accessed 18 April 2019].

de Stefano, V. (2016). *The Rise of the "Just-in-Time Workforce": On-Demand Work, Crowdwork and Labour Protection in the "Gig-Economy." Conditions of Work and Employment Series No. 71*. Geneva: International Labour Organization.

Engeström, Y. (2008). *From Teams to Knots: Activity-Theoretical Studies of Collaboration and Learning at Work*. New York: Cambridge University Press.

Engeström, Y., Puonti, A. and Seppänen, L. (2003). Spatial and Temporal Expansion of the Object as a Challenge for Reorganizing Work. In: D. Nicolini, S. Gherardi and D. Yanow, eds., *Knowing in Organizations: A Practice-Based Approach*. Armonk: M. E. Sharpe, pp. 151–186.

Engeström, Y. and Sannino, A. (2012). Whatever Happened to Process Theories of Learning? *Learning, Culture and Social Interaction*, 1(1), pp. 45–56.

Eurofound. (2018). *Employment and Working Conditions of Selected Types of Platform Work*. Luxembourg: Publications Office of the European Union. Available at: www.eurofound.europa.eu/publications/report/2018/employment-and-working-conditions-of-selected-types-of-platform-work [Accessed 1 May 2019].

Fabo, B., Beblavy, M., Kilhoffer, Z. and Lenaerts, K. (2017). *An Overview of European Platforms: Scope and Business Models*. JRC Science for Policy Report. Luxembourg: Publications Office of the European Union.

Heusinkveld, S., Benders, J. and Hillebrand, B. (2013). Stretching Concepts: The Role of Competing Pressures and Decoupling in the Evolution of Organization Concepts. *Organization Studies*, 34(1), pp. 7–32.

Launis, K. and Pihlaja, J. (2007). Changes in Production Concepts Emphasize Problems in Work-Related Well-Being. *Safety Science*, 45, pp. 603–619.

Leont'ev, A. N. (1978). *Activity, Consciousness, and Personality*. Englewood Cliffs: Prentice-Hall.

Mintzberg, H. and McHugh, A. (1985). Strategy Formation in an Adhocracy. *Administrative Science Quarterly*, 30(2), pp. 160–197.

Pajarinen, M., Rouvinen, P., Claussen, J., Hakanen, J., Kovalainen, A., Kretschmer, T., Poutanen, S., Seifried, M. and Seppänen, L. (2018). *Upworkers in Finland: Survey Results*. ETLA Report 85. Available at: www.etla.fi/wp-content/uploads/ETLA-Raportit-Reports-85.pdf [Accessed 3 May 2019].

Parker, G. G., Van Alstyne, M. W. and Sangeet, P. C. (2016). *Platform Revolution: How Networked Markets Are Transforming the Economy and How to Make Them Work for You*. New York: W. W. Norton & Company, Inc.

Pihlaja, J. (2005). *Learning in and for Production: An Activity-Theoretical Study of the Historical Development of Distributed Systems of Generalizing*. Helsinki: Helsinki University Press.

Ruusuvuori, J., Nikander, P. and Hyvärinen, M. (2010). Haastattelun analyysin vaiheet. In: J. Ruusuvuori, P. Nikander and M. Hyvärinen, eds., *Haastattelun analyysi*. Tampere: Vastapaino, pp. 9–36.

Seppänen, L. (2014). Examining Ingredients for Business Models in Public Service Networks. *Paper Presented at the 24th Annual RESER Conference*, September 11–13, Helsinki, Finland.

Seppänen, L. (2017). Learning Challenges and Sustainable Development: A Methodological Perspective. *Work: A Journal for Prevention, Assessment and Rehabilitation*, 57(3), pp. 315–332.

Spinuzzi, C. (2015). *All Edge: Inside the New Workplace Networks*. Chicago: University of Chicago Press.

Sundararajan, A. (2016). *The Sharing Economy: The End of Employment and the Rise of Crowd-Based Capitalism*. Cambridge, MA: The MIT Press.

Thornton, P. H., Ocasio, W. and Lounsbury, M. (2012). *The Institutional Logics Perspective: A New Approach to Culture, Structure and Process*. Oxford: Oxford University Press.

Upwork.com. (2019). How It Works. Available at: www.upwork.com/ [Accessed 10 May 2019].

van Doorn, N. (2017). Platform Labor: On the Gendered and Racialized Exploitation of Low-Income Service Work in the 'On-Demand' Economy. *Information, Communication and Society*, 20(6), pp. 898–914.

Virkkunen, J. (2007). Collaborative Development of a New Concept for an Activity. *@ctivités revue éléctronique*, 4(2), pp. 158–164.

Virkkunen, J. and Ristimäki, P. (2012). Double Stimulation in Strategic Concept Formation: An Activity-Theoretical Analysis of Business Planning in a Small Technology Firm. *Mind, Culture, and Activity*, 19(3), pp. 273–286.

Vygotsky, L. S. (1978). *Mind in Society: The Psychology of Higher Mental Functions*. Cambridge, MA: Harvard University Press.

Weick, K. E. and Sutcliffe, K. (2007). *Managing the Unexpected: Resilient Performance in an Age of Uncertainty*. San Francisco: John Wiley & Sons, Inc.

10 Ontologically Sound Basis for Analyzing Academia, Digitalization, and Entrepreneurship Together

A Solution to the Sociomaterialistic Puzzle of "Strong Relationality"

Seppo Poutanen

Introduction

How should research on academia and digitalization, in relation to entrepreneurship, be undertaken? This question is both banal and intriguing. If one does indeed need models for such a study, one can be referred to rapidly growing research libraries, collections of journal articles, etc., in which these three concepts are theorized and defined in numerous ways, as well as variously combined for the needs of versatile analyses of related empirical phenomena.

Intrigue can come into play when the question is taken as an invitation to consider the matter more generally and in certain holistic ways. This entails taking as a starting point the view that digitalization and entrepreneurship (mainly in the sense of an "entrepreneurial university": see, e.g., Slaughter and Leslie, 1997; Etzkowitz and Zhou, 2017) are not just happening in and to academia, but that the relationship of the three is becoming mutually constitutive in ways qualitatively different from previously. To define this starting point more precisely, a holistic basis requires the presumption that when academia, digitalization, and entrepreneurship converge, they cannot do so without changing themselves in some important respects. I conceptualize and analyze these relationships between the three in terms of what I call *strong relationality*.

New emerging formations also essentially concern, of course, "the outside" of academia, a fact that can be readily illustrated by the somewhat novel phenomenon of massive open online courses (MOOCs) (e.g., Iniesto et al., 2016; McGrath et al., 2017). Former spatio-temporal certainties and boundaries of academia are clearly being eroded: universities, with varying innovative spirit and entrepreneurial goals, increasingly use digital technologies to deliver their teaching materials to a population of students that is potentially limitless and free to study whenever and wherever their laptops, tablets, or smartphones can function.

The reader can hold on to his or her possibly precise definitions of "academia", "digitalization", and "entrepreneurship" (they probably do not differ radically from each other), because in this chapter my interest lies in areas other than discrete definitions and related efforts. I am interested in reformulating the key conception of strong relationality in the kind of general *ontological* manner that might create ground for new insights into the relationship between digitalization, academia, and entrepreneurship and enable novel and relevant research questions. The ontological viewpoint concerns how the existence of this strong relationality should be understood, but the analysis is not intended to operate only at some abstract philosophical level. On the contrary, the triad (principally, however, academia and digitalization) is analyzed in its particularity and concreteness to make space for creative changes of perspective concerning these matters.

My starting point is to see academia, digitalization, and entrepreneurship as various modes for organizing all kinds of matters and things. Their analysis can therefore be naturally positioned in the field of organization studies. With my holistic interest in what may be termed concrete particulars, I base the discussion on *sociomateriality*, which, as a theoretically vibrant if complex approach, has aroused growing interest among scholars of science and technology studies, information systems, and organization studies in the last decade or so. In a manifesto for sociomateriality, Wanda J. Orlikowski specifies the need for a new viewpoint by claiming that "these insights (of organization studies—SP) are limited in large part because the field has traditionally overlooked the ways in which organizing is bound up with the material forms and spaces through which humans act and interact" (Orlikowski, 2007, p. 1435; Orlikowski, 2010; Orlikowski and Scott, 2015).

In the light of sociomateriality, the human and material components of organizing in the modes of entrepreneurship, digitalization, and academia, for example, should be ontologically understood as converging in a kind of strong relationality. Orlikowski's "material forms and spaces," which usually consist chiefly of various and multiple technological artefacts, must not be seen merely as giving humans a footing or toolbox to operate on and with. Instead, there is an ontologically deeper co-construction or co-creation at play between the human and non-human elements (ibid.).

Although I accept sociomateriality's basic angle for the study of the things that interest me here, I think Orlikowski's formulation of sociomateriality fails to fulfill its true radical potential. This is mainly because Orlikowski adopts her idea of relationality from a rather sketchy source—Karen Barad's "agential realism" (Barad, 2003, 2007). I will argue that the reconceptualization of "sociomateriality," with the help of A. N. Whitehead's processual ontology (Whitehead, 1964, 1967, 1978), can better accomplish the goals of the approach, while avoiding certain criticisms typically aimed at the Orlikowski-Barad view (Faulkner and Runde, 2012; Leonardi, 2013; Mutch, 2013).

Because academia provides the main empirical frame for this analysis, I will next introduce and examine Mathias Decuypere and Maarten Simons's important empirical studies, which focus precisely on this subject. They apply the broadly Orlikowskian sociomaterial approach and detail, and interpret the kinds of practice and modes of organization of which contemporary academic life essentially consists (Decuypere and Simons, 2014a, 2014b, 2016). I will also address the attention (or lack thereof) they pay to digitalization and entrepreneurship. The chapter then proceeds to outline a broadly Whiteheadian alternative conceptualization for sociomateriality. I close by recommending a notable change in how such organizational research is undertaken, the need for which digitalization itself bolsters.

Into the Sociomaterial Texture of Professors' Life— Decuypere and Simons's Research

Across several articles, Mathias Decuypere and Maarten Simons have developed a distinctive sociomaterialist "third way" for studying the remarkable challenges and changes through which universities are going today (Decuypere and Simons, 2014a, 2014b, 2016). They analyze academic practices and the minute composition of academic work in contrast to approaches that, on the one hand, survey individual academics' opinions concerning the changes and, on the other, theorize how such societal processes as neo-liberalization, globalization, marketization, and digitalization impact universities and research in general (Decuypere and Simons, 2014a, p. 117).

Decuypere and Simons base their research on the actor-network theory (ANT), which has provided an important analytical approach especially in science and technology studies (STS) in recent decades (e.g., Law, 2004; Latour, 2005). More precisely, they adopt three "sensibilities" from ANT, which they call "heterogeneity," "relationality," and "enactments" (Decuypere and Simons, 2014b, pp. 90–92). First, the heterogenic sensibility aims to take as little as possible for granted before any conduct of a study. This means, for example, that human actors are not prioritized over non-human ones, and that universities are not, as is usual, presupposed to consist of research, education, and the third mission to engage with society. According to ANT, anything that can make a difference to a course of events is an actor, and the research goal is to obtain a detailed grasp of all the different actors and the ways in which they converge, interact, and form new actors (ibid.).

Second, ANT carries a strong conception of relationality in the sense that actors are understood to be what they are and do what they do only in their relation to other actors. Decuypere and Simons illustrate this idea with a common printer: a printer is an actor, but its agency is realized and can be comprehended only in its relations with electricity, paper, the technician, the computer network, files, etc. (Decuypere and Simons, 2014b, p. 91). Actors and their webs of relations with other actors, that is, certain kinds of network, are considered inseparable, which means that transformations in actors are always seen as transformations in certain networks and vice versa (ibid.).

Third, concerning the sensibility of enactments, Decuypere and Simons do not conceptualize academic practices as "made things," or as things that have stabilized in time and space with clear boundaries. Instead, they emphasize that the "term 'practice' refers to things that happen and that are made to be happening by several people and by lots of things" (Decuypere and Simons, 2014b, p. 91). The key challenge for ANT research now is to capture academic reality in its dynamic processes of becoming and emerging, where various kinds of actor and network are momentarily enacted before they give way to new assemblages (ibid.).

For the two articles most relevant here, "An Atlas of Academic Practice in Digital Times" (2014a) and "On the Composition of Academic Work in Digital Times" (2014b), Decuypere and Simons interviewed six professors from different countries, universities, and fields of research. The professors' outwardly simple task was to explain what they had done during the previous working day. However, Decuypere and Simons were not interested in the actual content of the interviewees' work or their interpretations, feelings, etc., concerning it. Instead, the goal was to obtain as concrete and detailed a picture as possible of all the different actors (in the ANT sense) and interactions a professor was involved in from the moment he or she woke up until going to bed after a busy day. If an interviewee said that he or she had used a computer to do something, this was not considered a sufficient description. He or she was further asked about the program (e.g., Microsoft Word)—and even its repertoire (e.g., sending or receiving an email using Microsoft Outlook)—that he or she had in fact used (Decuypere and Simons, 2014b, p. 94). From the descriptions, Decuypere and Simons could also infer the ways in which different software programs synchronized as actors, for instance (Decuypere and Simons, 2014a, p. 118).

No professor's workday appeared as a haphazard chain of interactions, but several subnetworks emerged in which actors closely interacted with each other. This sometimes meant that certain actors in subnetwork *a* had practically nothing to do with some actors who operated intensively in subnetwork *b*. A professor, say "Sandra," was the key actor who connected certain subnetworks as a group, which Decuypere and Simons in their map-like visualization call a "region." In the course of the analyzed working day, Sandra was involved in six different regions, two of which took place in her private sphere. A strict dependence of the analysis results on what interviewees actually talked about is revealed, because Sandra's waking up (in cooperation with actors like a battery, wake alarm, and snooze alarm functions) appears as separate from her interaction with her family (in a region populated by actors like daughter, husband, microwave, Skype-enabled tablet, search engine, schoolbook, and chocolate paste) (Decuypere and Simons, 2014a, pp. 118–128, 2014b, pp. 92–97).

One distinct academic practice—a region that involved all six professors—entailed preparation for many kinds of things. Sandra thus spent time preparing educational courses in a region that included, for example, Microsoft Word, notes, paper, printer, and colleague (course designer) as actors; "Eugene" prepared for project management with, for example, two colleagues, desk, coffee, and Mindmap program (tablet); "Patricia" prepared for a conference presentation in interaction with, for example, beamer, Microsoft PowerPoint, slides, postdoctoral student, PhD student, and conference speakers. Human (colleagues, postdoc, PhD student, conference speakers) and analog (paper, notes, desk, coffee) actors participated in the preparation practices. The most noteworthy fact yet is that digital (Microsoft Word, Mindmap program, Microsoft PowerPoint) and digital/analog (printer, computer screen) actors contributed essentially to all preparation work (Decuypere and Simons, 2014a, pp. 122–136).

Although the professors were from different countries, universities, and fields of research, Decuypere and Simons's analysis shows that digital actors operate not only inside most of the regions that constitute workday maps (the number of regions per professor varies between five and seven). Digital actors also connect with different regions in necessary and more or less overlapping ways. For example, Sandra's map includes two regions that can be called "email in/email out" and "webinar implementation." Enactment of the first region was realized by such actors as tree structure, email headings, delete button, newsgroups, colleague, student, and head of department; enactment of the second by those including software, microphone, camera, technician, broadcast, and Microsoft PowerPoint (Decuypere and Simons, 2014a, pp. 122–136, 2014b, pp. 96–98).

However, at the same time, the email in/email out functions of the first region contributed to the planning, actualization, and assessment of the second region, namely the webinar (all this happened over a period longer than one day). Furthermore, Sandra sent and received work emails, which also interacted with regions other than the webinar, in her private sphere at home. There she consulted the same web browser she had utilized in communication with her ex-promoters (a distinct region in Sandra's day), while physically staying at her workplace. By turns, the different digital software interacted with the variable analog properties of PC, laptop, tablet, and mobile phone (ibid.).

Decuypere and Simons describe how various co-acted operations (e.g., numerification, delegation, gradation) in different regions (e.g., processing of students) produce multiple operational effects (e.g., value to students) in professors' working days (Decuypere and Simons, 2014b, pp. 99–100). The key point from my perspective is their observation that all kinds of digital actor "form a cloud or a swarm that is spread all over the network and are in that sense *inciting* the network" (ibid., p. 101). Digital actors, for their part, not only constitute different operations but participate in delimiting regions and shaping operational effects.

In addition, there are certain digital "super actors" like email and the web browser that in general might be considered even more reliable than human actors, but whose collapse would paralyze a great deal of every region's operations. It is the professor who holds his or her whole day together, but participation in the essentially digitalized actor-networks entails the two-sided freedom/obligation to do one's work at (almost) any time in (almost) any kind of space. Unsurprisingly, constant haste and being at least in "standby mode" characterize the professors' days (Decuypere and Simons, 2014a, pp. 122–140).

Decuypere and Simons conclude that digital actors have become "immanently present in academic work" (Decuypere and Simons, 2014b, p. 103) in ways that make commonplace talk about the digitization of academic professions obsolete (ibid.). Significantly for my aims, they adopt a strong relational view concerning the ontological status of the networks' actors, although they do not elaborate on this view in detail. They only state that "it seems not to make much sense anymore to talk about academic practice in terms of humans or non-humans, material or digital etc. It perhaps makes more sense to speak of each actor in the network as being *humandigital*" (Decuypere and Simons, 2014b, p. 103). The pointed co-construction of human and non-human elements thus elaborates the Orlikowskian sociomateriality (although "digital" seems to hover somewhere between "material" and "immaterial"). Yet, there emerges the implicit question of the kind of concepts that should grasp the subject in the first place. In the section "From Orlikowski and Barad's Strong Relationality Toward Whiteheadian Rethinking of the Matter," I introduce ingredients for answering this question by applying the conceptual tools A. N. Whitehead developed in his processual ontology.

The Complex Question of "Entrepreneurship" in Decuypere and Simons's Analysis and Other Problems

Although Decuypere and Simons's "purposefully sampled group" (Decuypere and Simons, 2014a, p. 118) is small, and they give little detail of how they ended up interviewing just these six professors, the case they make for the absorption of contemporary academic work in digitalized systems, practices, and tools looks plausible. One point that supports their results is the fact that contemporary science is a fundamentally collective effort. Breakthroughs in cutting-edge research are almost always achieved by huge research groups, whose members often come from various specialties and many universities all around the world. Concrete face-to-face interaction in conferences, etc., is still considered fairly significant (otherwise, the global business of organizing scientific conferences would no longer exist), but the necessary day-to-day communication and cooperation within research groups has become unthinkable without digital infrastructure.

In the introduction, I delimited the starting point of this chapter to analyzing academia and digitalization as modes of organizing all kinds of matter with entrepreneurship. The delimitation derives from my interest in the perceived and extensive rise of the "entrepreneurial university" in academia (Ferreira et al., 2018). In light of this, it is striking that Decuypere and Simons do not use "entrepreneurship" or related terms ("enterprise," "entrepreneur," "entrepreneurial," etc.) *once* in their study of the professors' working days. No literally entrepreneurship-related terms or concepts belong to Decuypere and Simons's tools of analysis, as they do not conceptualize co-acted operations such as "entrepreneuring," for example. Furthermore, the empirical materials they present indicate that no professor referred to "entrepreneurship," being "entrepreneurial," etc., in any way in the interviews, either. A clear problem for elucidating the tripartite relationship with Decuypere and Simons's sociomaterialist studies seems to arise here.

It must be noted that the surmised problem that entrepreneurship has been neglected may mean different things, not all of which appear relevant to my effort to understand academia, digitalization, and entrepreneurship through a strong ontological relationality. Starting with the obvious, there are numerous professors and other academics around the world who practice "entre-speak"—especially in business schools—and entrepreneurship as meaningfully defined activity in close association with digital things. For some reason, such professors simply did not seem to be included in Decuypere and Simons's "purposeful sample" (Decuypere and Simons, 2014a, p. 118)! This can indeed be considered somewhat peculiar, because the concepts and practices of the so-called entrepreneurial university have spread globally in academia in recent decades (Foss and Gibson, 2015; Etzkowitz and Zhou, 2017; Ferreira et al., 2018).

However, solving my theoretical question is not actually hampered by the absence of literally entrepreneurship-related terms and references in Decuypere and Simons's studies and materials. This is because, in addition to the distinctive illustrative benefits of their focus on digitalization in academia, the key point of departure they offer is their sociomaterialist, ANT-inspired mode of analysis. From the inherent logic of this mode, it is possible to extrapolate how entrepreneurship might emerge in its involvement with digitalization and academia for a sociomaterialist analysis of the kind described.

For most people, "entrepreneurship" and its cognates do not appear very concrete, but they are taken to refer generally to businesses taking risks in commercial markets or, where people are concerned, being innovative and having initiative, for example.[1] Decuypere and Simons attempted to get the professors to describe their working days in as concrete and detailed a manner as possible, so it might be the case that the interviewees willfully avoided the kind of abstract accounts to which entrepreneurship-related terms could have contributed. This is clearly possible, although the matter cannot really be solved in either case. Yet, Decuypere and Simons emphasize that "every-thing and every-one might possibly be an actor" (Decuypere and Simons, 2014b, p. 94), and indeed, how the professors elaborated their workdays was their own choice.

Decuypere and Simons group the revealed actors into human (e.g., colleagues, technicians, postdocs), analog (e.g., table, pen, paper, whiteboard), digital (e.g., email, web browser, Microsoft PowerPoint) and digital/analog actors (e.g., printer, computer screen) (Decuypere and Simons, 2014a, pp. 122–136, 2016, pp. 146–149). Nevertheless, when the maps that illustrate each professor's day are examined more closely, actors occur who fit awkwardly into Decuypere and Simons's grouping. For example, in Max's map, an actor operates that he has named "Theories," and this actor intensively cooperates with "Enzyme," "Lab Assistant," "Slides," and several "MSc Students" and "PhD Students" (ibid.). From the relational perspective, it is through such interactions and their effects that the nature of theories can be understood, but it should be equally clear that not everything about theories can be reasonably categorized as "human," "digital," or "analogical."

As processes and results of abstract thinking for various purposes, theories obviously cannot emerge, exist, or affect without relationships to wetware/software/hardware, but this does not mean that theories can simply be reduced to the last of these. Furthermore, it seems quite evident that "entrepreneurship," at least in its conventional meanings, resembles "theory" in the sense that there is more to entrepreneurship than merely human, digital, or analog actors cooperating in certain ways. Formal models for assessing acceptable risks in launching a new product to market are themselves explicit theories of a certain kind, for example, and constitute a necessary part of many entrepreneurial activities.

On the basis of my observations, a couple of points can be made. First, as potential "abstract" actors (at least partly) in the mode of theories, things referred to with entrepreneurship-related terms can evidently participate in such academic actor-networks in which various kinds of digital actor govern. However, because the authority concerning what "entrepreneurship" means and how its referents contribute to actor-networks now belongs to the articulate human participants of those networks, an

ANT-inspired researcher can give no decisive external definition of how the entrepreneurship-related terms/concepts should be understood in such contexts. For example, professor Mary's map shows connections between actors named "Patent," "Conference Session company X" and "Gmail 2 (Startup company)," but, following their methodological ANT principle, Decuypere and Simons refrain from proposing that "entrepreneuring" or "commercializing" is occurring here. Mary herself does not conceptualize the interactions in this way (Decuypere and Simons, 2014a, pp. 131–135, 2014b, pp. 96–100).

Second, while Decuypere and Simons's methodological approach liberally guarantees the status of actor for practically anything, it remains unclear how the guiding ontological principle of strong relationality should actually be understood. What are its differences compared with some possible weaker forms of relationality, for example? The picture Decuypere and Simons paint of contemporary academic work's immersion in digital infrastructure and tools indeed looks plausible, but what insight is added by claiming that certain actors in the referenced networks are, in fact, *humandigital* (Decuypere and Simons, 2014b, p. 103)?

For comparison, an academic might claim that it is necessary for him or her to go hiking regularly in the woods to relieve work stress, and so, following the implied logic, a *humanwooded* actor would emerge in specific actor-networks. Indeed, Decuypere and Simons seem to tie *ontological* relationality (as "strong" but otherwise unclear) too tightly to *empirical* relationality (people can be seen to interact with computers and woods with varying intensity). The significance of Decuypere and Simons's empirical results is not contradicted by their vague ontological position, but explicit coherence between ontological and empirical starting points looks preferable.

Although Decuypere and Simons's division of actors into human, digital, analog, and digital/analog may look crude, from the ANT perspective the division is competently derived from the professors' own conceptualizations, and it usefully maps their workday networks. However, it must be stressed that there is no point in ANT where relationality might cease to exist. A pencil seems a plain analog actor, for example, but from a fine-grained perspective it reveals itself as a network to which certain raw materials, design work, and industrial processes have contributed as actors and enabled it to act as a pencil. The ANT standpoint maintains that the suitable level of particularity in detailing networks is determined by the research questions an analyst has, but the potential number and quality of different actors-as-networks looks limitless (Latour, 2005, pp. 27–42).

Because of ANT's liberalism toward actors' nature and number, the original ontological question about strong relationality is specified further: how is it possible that all those apparently *different kinds* of actor can *converge* and perform various strongly relational networks?

A professor and email can do things together they cannot do separately, but is it unnatural to call this relationality weak: do not a professor and email hold on to their very different "essential" selves before, during, and after the interaction, meaning all talk about "humandigitals," etc., is metaphorical at best? The sociomaterial approach that is tied up with the Orlikowski-Barad conception of strong ontological relationality (see the Introduction) cannot, in my view, answer such questions coherently.

From Orlikowski and Barad's Strong Relationality Toward a Whiteheadian Rethinking of the Matter

Orlikowski's conception of strong relationality originates from the philosopher-theoretical physicist Karen Barad's "agential realism" (e.g., Orlikowski, 2007, p. 1438, 2016, pp. 88–96). There is insufficient space here to elaborate upon Barad's complex epistemological/ontological theory, but she essentially gives an original philosophical reading of certain core results of modern quantum physics. It is quite easy to grasp what strong relationality is intended to mean when we realize that, at the ultimate level of matter, the seemingly self-evident distinction between the *observer* and the *subject of observing* collapses. The observation of electrons, for example, can materialize only via scientific technological apparatuses built for the specific purpose of this observing, but, depending on how an apparatus has been constructed, the same subject of observation in fact behaves differently, either like a wave or as a particle. Accordingly, there is no single answer to the question "What is matter fundamentally like in itself?" This is because matter emerges in varying ways in its strongly relational "intra-actions" with different but equally competent apparatuses of observation (Barad, 2003, pp. 801–820, 2007, pp. 97–185).

Orlikowski, both alone and with colleagues, has produced innovative empirical studies to show how various "social" and "material" elements in organizations/organizing are entangled with each other and can be understood only via the kind of strong relationality that denies entities "inherent" properties (cf. Jones, 2014, p. 897). For instance, with Susan V. Scott, she elaborates how the purported anonymity of hotel reviews becomes different things, depending on the material practices involved in producing them. Hence, the Automobile Association's sending of "mystery" guests to inspect hotel rooms produces a disparate anonymity compared with TripAdvisor, which collects and publishes nameless reviews of presumably genuine hotel guests online (Scott and Orlikowski, 2014). Although Orlikowski and Scott do not lean on human actors' own concepts in the same way as Decuypere and Simons (yet they, too, utilize rich interviews), a strong identical view on ontological relationality as well as ANT-inspired insights are shared by all the authors (Decuypere and Simons, 2014b, pp. 90–103; Orlikowski, 2007, pp. 1437–1439; Scott and Orlikowski, 2014, pp. 877–879).

However, no obvious valid method exists for understanding the entanglements of academics with digital infrastructure or entrepreneurial precepts by reducing them to the level of elementary particles/waves. Furthermore, the strong Orlikowski-Barad relationality has not received unanimous support from organizational researchers. Many promote a more "moderate" understanding of relationality. Thus, although a professor's transition from digitalization-immersed work (humandigital) to a refreshing hike in the woods (humanwooded) might raise interesting research questions, the claim that the professor herself essentially changes from one context to another stretches credibility too far for many researchers. Relationships of the aforementioned kind, when they concern the question of who the professor really *is*, should arguably be considered relatively external and weak when compared with her individual genetic code and upbringing (Faulkner and Runde, 2012, pp. 52–54; Leonardi, 2013, pp. 65–74; Mutch, 2013, pp. 30–37; Cecez-Kecmanovic et al., 2014, pp. 809–810).

Scott and Orlikowski have explicitly replied to the kind of critique outlined above (2013). However, they do not exactly argue for the preferability of their own stance but appeal for tolerance of different theoretical approaches in the field, summarizing that "the challenge and opportunity is to turn unsettled and unsettling ideas into inspiration, and differences into analytic edge for deepening understanding so that we might understand the world anew" (Scott and Orlikowski, 2013, p. 80). By the end of this chapter, I will reformulate, in an unavoidably schematic way, Scott and Orlikowski's explicit challenge from the ontological perspective of A. N. Whitehead's process philosophy.

When assessed critically, a certain awkwardness emerges at the heart of Decuypere/Simons/Orlikowski/Scott's conceptualization of their sociomaterial approach. In my view, this is explained by their underdeveloped ontological framework for understanding reality and its analysis. To begin with, Decuypere and Simons's goal of getting at the most concrete details of a professor's working day is more ambiguous than they seem to acknowledge. Their strict dependence on the professors' own terms makes, for example, "Software Webinar" and "Conference Session company x" appear as unproblematically homogeneous or discrete actors (Decuypere and Simons, 2014a, pp. 128–132). Such a result blurs the manifest differences more than it clarifies them.

On the other hand, Decuypere and Simons's implied "scale," which presumes a kind of smooth shifting from abstract things to concrete things and back, is itself profoundly misleading. Not only are all *concepts*, whether we think about "persons," "emails," "startups," "chairs," or "quarks" abstractions, but—and this is a crucial Whiteheadian move—we must also think about *reality itself* as consisting of abstractions (Whitehead, 1978, pp. 7–21; Stengers, 2011, pp. 73–100; Halewood, 2011, pp. 147–149). This is not a theoretical physicist's or other scientist's claim in her field, but a key step in Whitehead's effort to lay a sound philosophical foundation for general ontological thinking.

Figuratively speaking, reality consists of abstractions in the same sense as wine is a result of abstraction from grapes and the fermentation process. This is to say that becoming a distinct entity consists of "pushing" or processing innumerable things to the outside of an entity's relative and transient boundaries. At the same time, to highlight the abstract nature of both terms/concepts and their assumed referents means subscribing to the view that reality is ontologically indivisible. Concepts and material things (as well as emotions, greenness of trees, digital software, etc.) accordingly all belong to the equal "plane" of reality in the sense that no such ontologically dissimilar entities exist in between which there would be "gaps" in need of some kind of special "bridging" (Whitehead, 1964, pp. 30–31, 1978, pp. 18–20).

There is a notable coherence between a certain flatness of the Whiteheadian ontology with ANT-inspired efforts to analyze "social" and "material" elements together as equal parts of networks and to displace humans as the only real actors in the world. Nevertheless, and concerning the ANT part of this equation, the striking theoretical distance of Barad's insights into the behavior of elementary particles/waves from the analyses of sociomaterial/technological organizations is detrimentally reflected in Orlikowski and Scott's approach. To put it bluntly, Orlikowski and Scott provide no detailed elaboration of what the strong relationality in the inseparable entanglements of social and material elements is supposed to mean beyond claiming that the elements are always strongly related in this manner (Scott and Orlikowski, 2013).

Orlikowski and Scott then stamp an ontological dogma without arguments on their empirical analyses, a move whose apparent problems are highlighted by Paul Leonardi among others. Leonardi observes that (human) actors typically do not perceive their world as inseparable entanglements, but "they can relatively easily point to a hammer or piece of software and say 'this is material' but they would likely have a hard time fathoming that a hammer was in any way social" (Leonardi, 2013, p. 66).

Nevertheless, the introduced empirical analyses and others of their kind can be accepted as innovative and illuminating, while the need for a novel ontological strategy in tackling the constitutive theoretical problem of strong relationality is simultaneously acknowledged. This strategy entails a painstaking effort to distance us from the way things "self-evidently" look (in the way they very much look in Leonardi's example), or, as Michael Halewood puts it, an aspiration to reject our deeply ingrained "culture of thought" (Halewood, 2011, pp. 1–23).

Neither digitalization nor entrepreneurialism belonged to A. N. Whitehead's (1861–1947) conundrums, but he wanted to replace the classical and still pervasive substance-centered metaphysics with a new processualist ontology (simply put, a move from an ontology of being to an ontology of becoming). Whitehead sees classical metaphysics as the root cause of what he considers the central malaise in modern thinking, that is "the bifurcation of nature" (Whitehead, 1964, pp. 30–31):

> What I am essentially protesting against is the bifurcation of nature into two systems of reality, which in so far as they are real, are real in different senses. One reality would be the entities such as electrons which are the study of speculative physics. This would be the reality which is there for knowledge; although on this theory it is never known. For what is known is the other sort of reality, which is the byplay of mind. Thus there would be two natures, one is the conjecture and the other is the dream. [. . .] Another way of phrasing this theory which I am arguing against is to bifurcate nature into two divisions, namely into the nature apprehended in awareness and the nature which is the cause of awareness.

There are ever-growing volumes of research in, for example, the philosophy of the mind and cognitive science that analyze how (human) consciousness is related to material reality, but Whitehead's aim is not to contribute to such studies. Instead, he rejects the *framing of the question*, which leads us to analyze, among numerous other ontologically related things, what the necessary or sufficient elements for (human) consciousness to emerge into being are—or, to use an adjacent conceptualization, to ponder the kind of strong (intrinsic), in contrast with weak (extrinsic), relationality in between elements that causes (human) consciousness to come into existence. Whitehead disarms the *general question* of bifurcation (that is, the general bifurcation problem also spreads to the ostensible puzzle of fitting "the social" and "the material" together) by radically reconceptualizing the basis of ontological thinking. With this approach, he goes against our most deep-rooted ideas and intuitions of how reality is put together. In the place of conventionally defined "subjects" (e.g., social actors) and "objects" (e.g., material technology), and "primary" and "secondary" qualities, for example, Whitehead sets *experiences* as the fundamental building material for everything there is (Whitehead, 1978, pp. 160–167).

"Experience" clearly expresses a dynamic relationality, but in Whitehead's treatise, experiences are not limited to the human or even the organic world. A piece of stone or digital software both literally experiences its surroundings and has become a provisional subject ("superject" in Whitehead's original terminology) in a process of numerous experiences becoming together. It is obvious that Whitehead is not confined by what our intuitions or psychological research might say about experiences, because he aims to capture the most general ontological nature of reality. To express this concisely, to Whitehead, reality is an unceasing process of becoming through time, and to ask what a thing in reality *is*—for clearly the world is structured and not merely a formless flow—is to ask *how* that thing came into its fleeting existence (Whitehead, 1978, pp. 23–29, pp. 160–167; Halewood, 2011, pp. 23–32).

A detailed exposition of Whitehead's complex thinking is impossible here, but Table 10.1 briefly introduces certain key concepts of his theorization. Of particular importance is the second column, created not by

Table 10.1 Methodological Implications of Whitehead's Key Concepts

Concept	Meaning	Methodological relevance
Abstraction	Reality is thoroughly constructed; that is, quarks, tables, selves, social systems, digital infrastructures, etc., are abstractions in the sense of being achievements that always leave something out of themselves.	No ontologically primary dimensions of, for example, "social," "material" or "digital" exist for study, but the goal is to analyze the processes that bring about such various fleeting abstractions.
Experience	Process whereby abstraction takes place; experiences constitute both "subjects" (i.e., those who know) and "objects" (i.e., what is known), and are thus primarily compared with them.	Human subject and his or her social environment/ technological tools cannot be starting points for social scientific explanation, because they are achieved unities of experiences in need of explanation.
Actual Entity	Reality does not consist of formless flux and motion, but relatively stubborn facts exist that are actual entities in the sense of being particular processes of becoming.	Research subjects are typically societies or occasions of actual entities, which deny conventional ontological boundaries between, for example, subject and object, psychological and social, agency and structure.
Prehension	An actual entity perishes when its process of becoming ceases, and it turns into prehension, that is a piece of "material" of which new actual entities will be constituted.	It is possible to distinguish beginnings and terminations in research subjects and to examine the closing and opening of the "stubborn facts."
Creativity	Links "the completed actual entities [i.e. prehensions] which act as data for the concrescences or experiences which constitute novel subjects."[1]	The world can potentially turn in almost infinite ways and is ever-changing, but creativity explains the actual processualist structuration of the world.

Source: Materials of the first column come from Whitehead (1964, pp. 1–48; 1967, pp. 35–150; 1978, pp. 18–344).

[1] Halewood and Michael, 2008, p. 42.

Whitehead but by the author, which outlines methodological starting points for rethinking "sociomateriality" and "strong relationality" in organization studies.

Conclusion

In this chapter I have argued that, although the sociomaterialist approach has achieved important empirical results in studying academia, certain shortcomings in its ontological basis expose sociomaterialism to pertinent criticism. I have introduced some tools from A. N. Whitehead's processualist ontology for dismantling the criticism and laying sociomaterialist studies of academia, among other things, on a coherent ontological basis.

What advantages might there be in taking Whiteheadian processualism as the general ontological framework? With a theoretical interest in ontological relationships between academia, digitalization, and entrepreneurship, I have elaborated the concept of strong relationality. Orlikowskian sociomateriality defines an influential version of the concept, but I argue that Orlikowski's tying of her sociomateriality to Barad's interpretation of quantum physics is not the best available approach. The problems can be summarized in two statements:

1. The ontological implications of the strong relationality concerning substantial theory and empirical analysis are left without specification.
2. To derive one's ontological outlook from the particular scientific conception entails a complex question of levels: how are the particles/ waves related to the more familiar things analyzed in organization studies? Are we talking about kinds of reductive or emergent relationships? Orlikowski does not address such questions (Scott and Orlikowski, 2013).

Whiteheadian processualism actually makes the question of strong relationality a quasi-problem. The reality is not bifurcated into strong and weak relationalities, intrinsic and extrinsic properties, or substances and non-substances. What may appear as strong relationalities or essences are comparably enduring societies of actual entities (i.e., "stubborn facts," see Table 10.1). The pivotal research interest therefore concerns the ways in which such societies have become relatively stubborn. When and how did these societies begin to make themselves distinguishable from other societies? How are the "stubborn facts" inexorably changing? For example, a surgeon performing an operation with an algorithm-steered medical robot represents a rather new kind of society. When and how did such a society begin to emerge as distinctive? Evidently, the standardization of surgical practices met the advancement of certain technological artefacts, but how, exactly? What actors/experiences contribute to the relative stubbornness of this society, and what kind of creativity is simultaneously metamorphosing it? Is something involved that should be defined as entrepreneuring?

As for social and organizational research, the symmetry and relationality promoted by the ANT match well with Whiteheadian precepts, although another kind of social research might also be Whiteheadian. Nonetheless, the ANT focus on actors and their assemblages may distract from the crucial question of how such actors come into being, and where the relative openings and closures of their tracks or careers should be pinpointed. For example, concerning the case of Mary in her interactions with "Patent," "Conference Session company X," and "Gmail 2 (Startup company)"—see the previous section "The Complex Question of 'Entrepreneurship' in Decuypere and Simons's Analyses and Other Problems"—attention must be paid to the specific processes of, for example, digitalizing, innovating, and entrepreneuring, which together make the particular actors fleetingly emerge and are already turning them into something else.

The Whiteheadian ontological framework does not, by itself, bring novel "empirical" methods of analyzing interrelationships between digitalization, academia, and entrepreneurship. Whitehead's (possibly factitious) technical concepts are not intended to replace useful analytical tools of research. Yet, as a strategy to contest the prevailing "culture of thought" (Halewood, 2011), the "free and wild creation of concepts" (Stengers, 2011) is a reflection of one great promise of Whitehead's philosophy. Inventing audacious concepts to capture new emerging phenomena and reassess old ones is, of course, a part and parcel of all innovative research. The Whiteheadian framework encourages boldness and open-mindedness in constructing research designs and can make conventional boundaries between theory, methods, and empirical materials disappear, for instance (for fascinating examples of broadly processualist entrepreneurship research, see Gartner, 2011; Steyaert, 2012; Hjorth, 2015).

Decuypere and Simons's studies show how digitalization has become deeply woven into the kudos of academics' daily life. It compresses and stretches academic space and time; enables, realizes, and shuts down complex networks; and problematizes how a (human) academic actor exists and operates. The emergence and rapid advance of "intelligent" digital infrastructure, commercial algorithms, etc., as new actors further complicates the picture. At the same time, concepts like "academia" and "entrepreneurship" are becoming radically ambiguous and difficult to pin down (e.g., Poutanen, 2018). From the Whiteheadian perspective, it seems that digitalization in its manifold dimensions (concerning not just academia and academics, of course) has come to vividly demonstrate the general principles of reality's processualist structuration. This demonstration expands in intensity practically every day and is quite easy to perceive, meaning the accomplishment of a fundamental change in our ontological framework has begun to look increasingly welcome.

Note

1 See Poutanen (2018) for more reflection on the matter.

References

Barad, K. (2003). Posthumanist Performativity: How Matter Comes to Matter. *Signs: Journal of Women in Culture and Society*, 28(3), pp. 801–833.

Barad, K. (2007). *Meeting the Universe Halfway: Quantum Physics and the Entanglement of Matter and Meaning*. Durham and London: Duke University Press.

Cecez-Kecmanovic, D., Galliers, R. D., Henfridsson, O., Newell, S. and Vidgen, R. (2014). The Sociomateriality of Information Systems: Current Status, Future Directions. *MIS Quarterly*, 38(3), pp. 809–830.

Decuypere, M. and Simons, M. (2014a). An Atlas of Academic Practice in Digital Times. *Open Review of Educational Research*, 1(1), pp. 116–143.

Decuypere, M. and Simons, M. (2014b). On the Composition of Academic Work in Digital Times. *European Educational Research Journal*, 13(1), pp. 89–106.

Decuypere, M. and Simons, M. (2016). What Screens Do: The Role(s) of the Screen in Academic Work. *European Educational Research Journal*, 15(1), pp. 132–151.

Etzkowitz, H. and Zhou, C. (2017). *The Triple Helix: University-Industry-Government Innovation and Entrepreneurship*. London: Routledge.

Faulkner, P. and Runde, J. (2012). On Sociomateriality. In: P. M. Leonardi, B. A. Nardi and J. Kallinikos, eds., *Materiality and Organizing: Social Interaction in a Technological World*. Oxford: Oxford University Press, pp. 49–66.

Ferreira, J. J., Fayolle, A., Ratten, V. and Raposo, M. (eds.) (2018). *Entrepreneurial Universities: Collaboration, Education and Policies*. Cheltenham and Northampton: Edward Elgar.

Foss, L. and Gibson, D. V. (eds.) (2015). *The Entrepreneurial University: Context and Institutional Change*. London and New York: Routledge.

Gartner, W. B. (2011). When Words Fail: An Entrepreneurship Glossolalia. *Entrepreneurship and Regional Development*, 23(1–2), pp. 9–21.

Halewood, M. (2011). *A. N. Whitehead and Social Theory—Tracing a Culture of Thought*. London and New York and Delhi: Anthem Press.

Halewood, M. and Michael, M. (2008). Being a Sociologist and Becoming a Whiteheadian: Toward a Concrescent Methodology. *Theory, Culture and Society*, 25(4), pp. 31–56.

Hjorth, D. (2015). Sketching a Philosophy of Entrepreneurship. In: T. Baker and F. Welter, eds., *The Routledge Companion to Entrepreneurship*. New York: Routledge, pp. 41–58.

Iniesto, F., McAndrew, P., Minocha, S. and Coughlan, T. (2016). Accessibility of MOOCs: Understanding the Provider Perspective. *Journal of Interactive Media in Education*, 20(1), pp. 1–10.

Jones, M. (2014). A Matter of Life and Death: Exploring Conceptualizations of Sociomateriality in the Context of Critical Care. *MIS Quarterly*, 38(3), pp. 895–925.

Latour, B. (2005). *Reassembling the Social*. Oxford: Oxford University Press.

Law, J. (2004). *After Method: Mess in Social Science Research*. London and New York: Routledge.

Leonardi, P. M. (2013). Theoretical Foundations for the Study of Sociomateriality. *Information and Organization*, 23(2), pp. 59–76.

McGrath, C., Stenfors-Hayes, T., Roxå, T. and Bolander Laksov, K. (2017). Exploring Dimensions of Change: The Case of MOOC Conceptions. *International Journal for Academic Development*, 22(3), pp. 257–269.

Mutch, A. (2013). Sociomateriality—Taking the Wrong Turning? *Information and Organization*, 23(2), pp. 28–40.

Orlikowski, W. J. (2007). Sociomaterial Practices: Exploring Technology at Work. *Organization Studies*, 28(9), pp. 1435–1448.

Orlikowski, W. J. (2010). The Sociomateriality of Organizational Life: Considering Technology in Management Research. *Cambridge Journal of Economics*, 34(1), pp. 125–141.

Orlikowski, W. J. and Scott, S. V. (2015). The Algorithm and the Crowd: Considering the Materiality of Service Innovation. *MIS Quarterly*, 39(1), pp. 201–216.

Poutanen, S. (2018). Critical Perspectives in Entrepreneurship Research. In: D. De Clercq, J. Heinonen and R. Blackburn, eds., *The SAGE Handbook of Small Business and Entrepreneurship*. London, Thousand Oaks, and New Delhi: Sage Publications, pp. 594–613.

Scott, S. V. and Orlikowski, W. J. (2013). Sociomateriality—Taking the Wrong Turning? A Response to Mutch. *Information and Organization*, 23(2), pp. 77–80.

Scott, S. V. and Orlikowski, W. J. (2014). Entanglements in Practice: Performing Anonymity Through Social Media. *MIS Quarterly*, 38(3), pp. 873–893.

Slaughter, S. and Leslie, L. L. (1997). *Academic Capitalism: Politics, Policies and the Entrepreneurial University*. Baltimore: The Johns Hopkins University Press.

Stengers, I. (2011). *Thinking with Whitehead—A Free and Wild Creation of Concepts*. Translated by M. Chase. Cambridge, MA, and London: Harvard University Press.

Steyaert, C. (2012). Making the Multiple: Theorising Processes of Entrepreneurship and Organisation. In: D. Hjorth, ed., *Handbook on Organisational Entrepreneurship*. Cheltenham: Edward Elgar, pp. 151–168.

Whitehead, A. N. (1964). *The Concept of Nature, The Tarner Lectures Delivered in Trinity College November 1919*. Cambridge: Cambridge University Press.

Whitehead, A. N. (1967). *Science and the Modern World, Lowell Lectures, 1925*. New York: The Free Press.

Whitehead, A. N. (1978). *Process and Reality: An Essay in Cosmology, Gifford Lectures of 1927–1928*. Edited by D. R. Griffin and D. W. Sherburne. New York: The Free Press.

Index

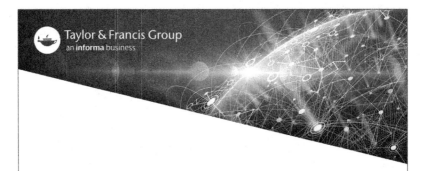